Combat and Consensus: The 1940's and 1950's

Inquiries into American History

Our Colonial Heritage: Plymouth and Jamestown
by William Gee White

The Middle Colonies: New York, New Jersey, Pennsylvania
by James I. Clark

The American Revolution
by D. Duane Cummins and William Gee White

The Federal Period: 1790–1800
by Lloyd K. Musselman

Andrew Jackson's America
by Thomas Koberna and Stanley Garfinkel

The American Frontier
by D. Duane Cummins and William Gee White

The Origins of the Civil War
by D. Duane Cummins and William Gee White

Reconstruction: 1865–1877
by James I. Clark

Industrialism: The American Experience
by James E. Bruner, Jr.

American Foreign Policy: 1789–1980
by Thomas A. Fitzgerald, Jr.

Contrasting Decades: The 1920's and 1930's
by D. Duane Cummins and William Gee White

Combat and Consensus: The 1940's and 1950's
by D. Duane Cummins and William Gee White

Conflict and Compromise: The 1960's and 1970's
by D. Duane Cummins

America at War: World War I and World War II
by Douglas Waitley

America at War: Korea and Vietnam
by Douglas Waitley

Women in American History
by William Jay Jacobs

Combat and Consensus: The 1940's and 1950's

D. Duane Cummins
William Gee White

Glencoe Publishing Co., Inc.
Encino, California

Contributing Editor:

Dr. James I. Clark

Portions of this book appeared originally, in somewhat different form, in *Consensus and Turmoil: The 1950's and 1960's* by D. Duane Cummins, copyright © 1972 by Benziger, Inc.

Glencoe Publishing Co., Inc.
17337 Ventura Boulevard
Encino, California 91316

Collier Macmillan Canada, Ltd.

Library of Congress Catalog Card Number: 79-54224

Printed in the United States of America

ISBN 0-02-652940-8

1 2 3 4 5   84 83 82 81 80

ACKNOWLEDGMENTS

Acknowledgments are due to the authors and publishers who kindly granted us permission to reprint excerpts from the following copyrighted works:

From news stories in *The New York Times*, 1 January 1940, 6 June 1943, 24 September 1957, and 1 January 1960. © 1940/43/57/60 by The New York Times Company. Reprinted by permission.

From news stories in *The Chicago Tribune*, 1 and 2 January 1940. Reprinted, courtesy of The Chicago Tribune.

From *The 1940s: Decade of Triumph and Trouble* by Cabell Phillips, Macmillan Publishing Co., Inc. Copyright © 1975 by The New York Times.

From *Time Capsule: History of the War Years, 1939-1945,* Bonanza Books. Reprinted, courtesy Time-Life Books Inc.

From *The Social History of a War-Boom Community* by Robert J. Havighurst and H. Gerthron Morgan, copyright 1951. Published by David McKay Co., Inc. Reprinted with permission.

From "Detroit Auto Worker." Reprinted from the August 1946 issue of *Fortune* Magazine by special permission; © 1946 Time Inc.

From *The Best Years: 1945-1950* by Joseph C. Goulden. Copyright © 1976 by Joseph C. Goulden. Reprinted by permission of Atheneum Publishers.

From *A Generation on Trial: USA versus Alger Hiss* by Alistair Cooke. Copyright 1950, 1952 by Alistair Cooke. Reprinted by permission of Alfred A. Knopf, Inc.

From *Cold-War America: From Hiroshima to Watergate,* Expanded Edition, by Lawrence S. Wittner. Copyright © 1978 by Holt, Rinehart and Winston. Copyright © 1974 by Praeger Publishers, Inc. Reprinted by permission of Holt, Rinehart and Winston.

From *The Crucial Decade—and After: America, 1945-1960* by Eric F. Goldman. © Eric F. Goldman, 1960. Reprinted by permission of Alfred A. Knopf, Inc.

From *The American Heritage Dictionary of the English Language.* © 1978 by Houghton Mifflin Company. Reprinted by permission.

From *Days of Shame* by Charles E. Potter. Copyright © 1965 by Senator Charles Potter. Reprinted by permission of Coward, McCann & Geoghegan, Inc.

From *McCarthyism: The Fight for America* by Joseph R. McCarthy. Copyright © 1952 by Joseph R. McCarthy. Reprinted by permission of The Devin-Adair Company, Old Greenwich, Conn. 06870.

CONTENTS

In the early 1940's, most Americans—like these in Grundy Center, Iowa—were peacefully preoccupied with their own lives. "Let Europe stew in its own juices," many people were saying, but soon the whole world was involved in war.

INTRODUCTION

The dawn of the year 1940 brought an end to the depression that had plagued the United States for a decade. It was true that the country's renewed prosperity was anchored in war in Europe, where England and France were engaged in combat with Germany , and in the Far East, where Japan had over-run much of China. But on the whole Americans felt safe, with oceans separating them from the conflict. (The intercontinental ballistics missile was then a thing of the far future.) For millions, the fact that the nation's industries were gearing up for war production was important primarily because it meant that they would once again have jobs.

Viewed from today, the 1940's seem a world away. More people then than now entertained themselves with radio programs and movies. In a small town, one could enjoy a motion picture for as little as a dime. There was no television. There were fewer cars, but gasoline was cheap. There were roadside stands offering food for those who stopped, but few of the fast-food chain outlets that dot the country now. TV dinners were unknown. Frozen food was around, but most people had to store it in "locker plants" where they rented freezer space. The home freezer, on a large scale, was yet to come. Secretaries made carbon copies of letters they typed; there were no copying machines and, consequently, less waste paper in the land. One could travel coast to coast by air, but it took longer then, for there were no jet airplanes. The moon still suggested only romance, not exploration, and what most people knew about space they learned from science fiction. Few computers existed; certainly the general public was not familiar with these electronic devices. Although many people had charge accounts with local merchants, credit cards were rare. Synthetic fibers were in their infancy, nylon having been patented only in 1937. Phonographs played heavy, breakable 78-rpm records; the modern long-playing $33^1/3$-record was not introduced until 1948, and stereophonic equipment lay still further in the future.

During the depression decade of the thirties, government had grown much bigger. Decisions made in Washington now affected the daily lives of Americans as never before. But, except for the rich, who objected to higher taxes and greater regulation of business and financial transactions, most people did not perceive this growth as threatening. On the contrary, for those with low to middle incomes, bigger government had resulted in real benefits—Social Security, unemployment insurance, protection against bank failures and mortgage foreclosures, and sometimes even jobs on public works projects. The majority of Americans trusted their government and its leaders—in fact, in 1940 they broke precedent and elected a president to a third term.

It was a slower and more quiet time, but it was not to last. Germany conquered France in the spring of 1940, and suddenly war seemed closer. It came a year and a half later, after the Japanese bombed Pearl Harbor in Hawaii. Young men could now look forward to being drafted, if they did not volunteer, and for many the prospect of an easy summer's transition between high school and college went by the board. Young women would have their opportunity to volunteer for the armed services, too.

The history of the 1940's splits into two parts. The story of battles on land and sea, and war production on the home front, forms one. The other concerns the shift from wartime to peacetime, which began in earnest in the fall of 1945, following the defeat of Japan. For many people, the second part marked a tumultuous time of finding new jobs and new homes, coping with shortages of consumer goods, and watching prices rise.

There would be, though, no going back to the quieter, more inward-looking existence that had characterized the beginning of the 1940's. The United States had demonstrated that it was the most powerful nation in the world. While Americans had once believed it possible to stay free of foreign entanglements, the view—and the responsibility —now was global. There was a rival power, Soviet Russia, which established control of Eastern Europe and sought influence throughout the world. And there was more war, beginning in 1950—a conflict in Korea in which more than fifty thousand Americans died.

The history of the 1950's is one of the two fronts—the home front which in the main exuded prosperity and conservative allegiance to the status quo, and the various areas of the Cold War, in which the United States and the Soviet Union contested for influence while former British, French, and other colonies struggled toward independence and nationhood. The two intertwined as fear of the spread of communism produced at home a "red scare" similar to that of 1919–1920, following the Russian Revolution. And there were some challenges to the status quo, particularly from blacks. In 1954 the Supreme Court of the United States declared segregated schools unconstitutional. Efforts to desegregate schools in the 1950's laid the groundwork for the abolition of all segregation and the black push to achieve equal rights in the 1960's.

It is as yet too early for anyone to sum up precisely what the 1950's meant with respect to the overall development of the nation. Some observers see it as a benchmark by which to judge the neo-conservatism of the 1970's, placing the radicalism and turmoil of the 1960's as a break in between. Generally speaking, it is true that youth of the 1970's, like its counterpart of the 1950's, avoided crusades and displayed a primary interest in obtaining good marks in school, viewing education mainly as preparation for a particular job. And it is true that many people in the 1970's viewed the efficacy of government-promoted social programs of the 1960's with skepticism similar to that which people in the 1950's displayed toward governmental programs of the 1930's. But the historical pendulum never swings all the way back. Each era contributes, but each is also unique in itself. The 1940's and 1950's must be viewed as decades in their own right. The nation waged a successful war, went on to greater peacetime prosperity than ever before, and at the end of the 1950's stood poised on the edge of a different era. Old problems continued, to be sure, but the way in which they were perceived and dealt with would not be the same.

This picture, which won a photography contest in 1944, was entitled "She'll Be Nice to Come Home To." The star in the window signifies a member of the family—in this case probably a son—in the armed forces. Similar pictures appeared often in newspapers and magazines and helped to keep homefront morale high.

UPI

1

WARTIME YEARS

AT HOME

To the Chinese, New Year's is a time for reflection on the past, for honoring ancestors, and for reaffirming family solidarity. They celebrate the occasion chiefly at home. Americans are different. Looking backward and inward does not characterize them on the eve of the New Year. Americans symbolize the year about to end as a bearded, soon-to-fade old man and the new year as a smiling baby, the future. They view the new year as a clean tablet, another chance, and most prefer to welcome it in crowds—at parties, in nightclubs, or on the street.

On New Year's Eve, 1939, Americans looked forward not only to a new year, but to a new decade as well. Economic depression had marked the preceding ten years, changing millions of lives and scarring many. Now there were signs that the economy was improving. Even better times, everyone hoped, lay ahead. The *New York Times* reported:

> Nineteen forty arrived frostily last night, welcomed
> by an estimated 1,250,000 New Yorkers between
> Times and Duffy Squares with a raucous
> demonstration that combined the original Armistice
> Day [ending World War I in 1918], any Fourth of
> July, and a pre-depression ticker tape parade.[1]

New York nightclubs did twenty million dollars' worth of business that night. Chicagoans wishing to celebrate in New

[1] *New York Times*, 1 January 1940, p. 1.

York could get there fairly quickly on one of three daily United Airlines flights for a one-way fare of $44.95. The journey in a twin-engined DC-3, with several stops, took three and a half hours.

The people who remained in Chicago shivered in the same New Year's Eve temperature as did New Yorkers—twenty-two degrees Fahrenheit. And, according to the *Chicago Tribune:*

> With traditional gaiety, Chicago roared a happy and hearty welcome to the New Year and the new decade last night and early today. In the Loop and other parts of the city, hundreds of thousands of celebrators concentrated on noisy fun and revelry. From all outward signs the celebration was the largest and gayest since 1929.[2]

On New Year's Day, those Americans who were sufficiently rested from the night of merrymaking could attend one of the five football games scheduled across the country, or could listen on the radio. The University of Southern California battled Tennessee in the Rose Bowl, Missouri opposed Georgia Tech in the Orange Bowl, Texas A. and M. stood against Tulane in the Sugar Bowl, Clemson faced Boston College in the Cotton Bowl, and Catholic University met Arizona Teachers in the Sun Bowl. Those who did not care for football could attend a matinee showing of *Gone with the Wind,* which had begun its record-breaking run only a few weeks before, or *The Hunchback of Notre Dame* with Charles Laughton, or *The Thin Man* with William Powell and Myrna Loy.

The *Chicago Tribune* was equally optimistic about the economic indicators:

> Steel set the pace for the big 1939 recovery. As 1940 opens, it promises to hold its place far out in front of the industrial procession. All business and industry looks to steel—the nation's No. 1 heavy industry—for signs of what's ahead.[3]

[2]*Chicago Tribune,* 1 January 1940, p. 1.
[3]Ibid.

Automobile manufacturers looked forward to selling more than three million cars in 1940. A new Hudson Six could be bought in the Midwest for $789, and a Ford or Plymouth for slightly less. On the used-car market, 1939 four-door Plymouths and Fords were priced at $395 and $445 respectively, a Nash and a De Soto at $595, and a La Salle at $775.

In the January post-Christmas sales, Bond's in Chicago offered men's two-trouser suits at prices ranging from $22.50 to $27.50, and overcoats at $19.95. At another store were women's coats of squirrel, Persian lamb, Hudson seal, muskrat, and mink for prices ranging from $145 to $295.

American women in 1940 eagerly awaited the appearance of stockings made from a new chemical material called nylon. Silk had been scarce because of the war in the Far East. New York's allotment of six thousand pairs of nylons, priced at $1.19 a pair and up, was placed on the market in March, 1940. It quickly sold out, as did allotments in other cities.

In the Midwest, eggs cost twenty-five cents a dozen, butter thirty cents a pound. A shopper could buy a pound of spaghetti for five cents, three cans of green beans for eighteen cents, two pounds of coffee for thirty-three cents, and a dozen rolls of toilet tissue for $1.19. Bacon or pork roast cost twenty-three cents a pound, a rib roast was twenty-five cents a pound, and turkey was priced from nineteen to twenty-three cents a pound. Milk was eight cents a quart. A comfortable, five-room apartment in a city could be rented for about a hundred dollars a month. A person living in a small town could rent a house for fifteen dollars a month.

Wages, like the prices of consumer goods, reflected economic depression. Five thousand dollars a year was a very handsome income. Only 2.3 percent of a population of 131.6 million lived in families whose incomes were $5,000 or more a year. The median income for urban families was $1,463 a year, while that of farm families was much lower. The average factory worker took home about twenty-five dollars a week. Skilled workers were better off. In the building trades, wages averaged $1.65 an hour in Chicago, $1.31 in San Francisco and Atlanta, $1.35 in Detroit, and $1.76 in New York. The average federal tax on personal incomes was about four percent.

A demonstration of the rugged qualities of the miracle fiber, nylon. Soon after Pearl Harbor, the new synthetic was diverted to the manufacture of parachutes, and women had to resort to leg make-up—"bottled stockings"—which with luck (and no baths) could last up to three days.

During the 1930's, the federal government had spent
billions of dollars for subsidies, direct relief, and public
works programs to put people to work and stimulate the
economy. But as 1940 opened, 8 million of the 42.7 million
non-agricultural labor force could find no employment. This
figure compared favorably, however, with the 12 million
unemployed in 1932.

In most capitals of Europe, a continent at war, people
celebrated New Year's Eve in much the same fashion as
Americans did. London was blacked out against air raids,
but according to the *New York Times:*

> London hotels were thronged with merrymakers
> and in the English spirit of "carry on" civilians
> wore evening dress while men in the forces appeared in
> uniforms to dine and dance with women friends.
> The streets were thronged as midnight approached.[4]

Across the continent, said the *Times,* "Red Moscow is
celebrating the advent of the New Year with a Christmas
card atmosphere in its snow-covered streets." But Parisians,
like Londoners, celebrated under threat of air attack:

> The new year is beginning with a sure confidence
> that if it does not bring victory it will be the beginning
> of victory and the establishment of the new order in
> Europe. It is not going to be easy.[5]

However, a reporter from another newspaper noted a more
somber mood among the French:

> One would have to go back to the last war to see
> France begin a new year as it did today. The year 1940
> was ushered in with less celebration, fanfare and
> hornblowing and happy predictions for the future than
> at any time since 1918.[6]

[4] *New York Times,* 1 January 1940, p. 1.
[5] Ibid.
[6] *Chicago Tribune,* 2 January 1940, p. 1.

UPI

UPI

UPI

Benito Mussolini, a great manipulator of crowds, was described by Adolf Hitler in 1937 as the very embodiment of the Fascist "superman."

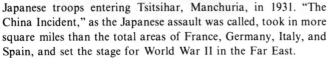

Japanese troops entering Tsitsihar, Manchuria, in 1931. "The China Incident," as the Japanese assault was called, took in more square miles than the total areas of France, Germany, Italy, and Spain, and set the stage for World War II in the Far East.

Background to War

The 1930's had been a decade of armed conflicts in many parts of the world. Japan, whose government had fallen under military control, invaded the Chinese province of Manchuria in 1931. The following year Japan annexed that province. Then, in 1937, Japan invaded China itself. Italy had come under the dictatorial rule of the creator of fascism, Benito Mussolini, in 1922. Mussolini, styling himself *Il Duce* ("the leader"), dreamed of restoring to Italy the power and glory of ancient Rome. In 1935, he sent troops to invade and conquer Ethiopia, an independent country in northeast Africa. The next year civil war began in Spain, where Fascist rebels sought to overthrow the democratically elected government.

Germany received its dictator in 1933, in the person of Adolf Hitler. Hitler headed the National Socialist German Workers' party, whose members became known as Nazis.

Adolf Hitler modeled himself after Mussolini during his early career, but he added to German Fascism an ingredient which had not been part of *Il Duce's* program. That ingredient was racial hatred, and it led eventually to the ruthless murder of millions of Jews.

U.S. Army

A column of Hitler's tanks entering Poland, quickly and without warning, on September 1, 1939. The attack made two German words familiar throughout the world. The first was *blitzkrieg* ("lightning war"); the second was *panzer* ("armor"), the name given to the tanks and motorized forces that combined with dive bombers to wage this new kind of warfare.

He promised to restore Germany to the rank it had enjoyed among the nations of Europe prior to its defeat in World War I. Like Mussolini, he called himself "the leader"—*Der Fuehrer* in German. And under his leadership Germany began to rearm and then to expand. In 1936 German troops entered the Rhineland, which by treaty was supposed to be a permanently demilitarized zone between Germany and France. In 1938 Germany annexed Austria. That same year Germany took over a portion of Czechoslovakia, swallowing up the remainder in the spring of 1939. Wishing to avoid war, Great Britain and France did not oppose the German conquests—all of them, so far, relatively bloodless.

Hitler now turned his attention to Poland, making territorial demands. Poland refused to be bullied. Late in August, 1939, Hitler made a non-aggression pact with his Russian counterpart, Joseph Stalin. Then, on September 1,

German armies and aircraft moved against Poland. Two days later, Britain and France declared war on Germany. Poland fell before the month was out, and Germany and Russia divided that hapless country between them. Russia then made territorial demands on Finland. When the Finns stood firm, Russia invaded.

During the months that followed the conquest of Poland, the war in Western Europe turned peculiar. The attack and defeat of Poland had been *blitzkrieg*—"lightning war." Now the conflict, as comedians put it, was "sitzkrieg." German and French soldiers manned pillboxes along the heavily fortified Siegfried and Maginot lines near the border between the two countries, but few shots were fired. Aircraft appeared over the cities, but mainly to drop propaganda leaflets. The whole thing, said Senator William E. Borah of Idaho, was a "phony war."

Joseph Stalin, a former seminary student from the province of Georgia, made himself absolute dictator of Russia in 1928. Born Joseph Djugashvili, he chose to be known by his *nom de guerre*, which meant "man of steel."

UPI

No Involvement

Meanwhile, the Finns resisted bitterly and for a time successfully fought back against the Russians. Americans sympathized with the Finns, partly because they traditionally favored the underdog and partly because Finland was one of the few European nations to have made payments on its World War I debt to the United States. Americans also sympathized with the Poles, who had been independent only since 1919, after a hundred years of foreign domination, and whose freedom was once again lost as German troops overran their country. Americans sympathized with the Chinese, who had been at war with Japan since 1937. And they sympathized with the Ethiopians, the proud black Africans who had resisted European colonization until Mussolini's bombs and tanks had overwhelmed their brave but ill-equipped armies.

But only a small minority of Americans favored aid to the Allies, Britain and France. Even fewer people wanted the United States directly involved in either the European or the Far Eastern conflict. A great many people firmly believed that American involvement in World War I had been a dreadful mistake. They wanted no part of Europe and its troubles, or of troubles in any other part of the world. As one writer observed:

The country was predominantly isolationist as 1940 began, reflecting a cynical reappraisal of the motives and strategems that had led us into the First World War, and disillusionment over its political consequences. For a decade there had grown up a hardening attitude toward Europe's endemic power struggles, its chronic inability to put its house in order, which was sharpened by resentment of the failure of most of those nations to repay their war debts. Many Americans, moreover, had started out in life with an ingrained suspicion of most foreigners, Europeans especially—of their morals, their ideologies, their "stuck-up" ways—and a belief that they were ready to outsmart us at every turn. For all such reasons (and many more) there was a popular consensus in the land, that, at all costs, we should avoid involvement in the quarrels and intrigues of other nations. We had burned our fingers once, trying to pull Europe's chestnuts out of the fire: Never again. Furthermore, the United States was big enough to go its own way and could best stay out of trouble by strictly minding its own business.[7]

Still, in a New Year's Eve statement, Secretary of State Cordell Hull was prompted to say, "The outlook for 1940 is one of fear that war clouds may grow blacker mingled with hope for peace." The report of Hull's speech continued:

In his cautious prophecy of what the next twelve months may bring, the secretary did not promise that America would not be at war except by indirection. He said it would be "a rash man, indeed, who would undertake to forecast the course of international developments during the coming year."[8]

Congressional legislation reflected the strong American sentiment for neutrality. In 1935 Congress passed and President Franklin D. Roosevelt signed the Neutrality Act, which

[7] Cabell Phillips, *The 1940s: Decade of Triumph and Trouble* (New York: Macmillan, 1975), pp. 5–6.

[8] *Chicago Tribune,* 1 January 1940, p. 1.

forbade U.S. aid to any belligerent nation—that is, to any nation at war. Two years later Congress amended the act to allow belligerents to purchase non-military goods from the United States, but only on a "cash and carry" basis. There would be no credit, and buyers would have to transport goods in their own ships.

At the time the Neutrality Act was amended, in 1937, Italy had invaded Ethiopia and Japan had invaded China. Fascist rebels in Spain were in their second year of war against the government. Germany, rapidly rearming, had moved troops into the Rhineland. These events led President Roosevelt, on October 5, 1937, to deliver what has been called his "Quarantine the Aggressor" speech. In it, he said that "innocent peoples [and] innocent nations are being cruelly sacrificed to a greed for power and supremacy. . . . If those things come to pass in other parts of the world, let no one imagine that America will escape." Roosevelt seemed to be suggesting concerted action by peace-loving nations to "quarantine" aggressors, although he remained vague about just how this might be accomplished.

The speech attracted overwhelming criticism. Seventy percent of the Americans polled in 1937 rejected the notion that the United States ought to do something about aggression. Nor would they approve of aid to Britain or France if those nations became involved in war.

Quarantine speech or not, Germany under Hitler remained threateningly expansionist. Roosevelt, and some other observers as well, feared for the security of the United States should Europe be united under German rule.

The War Heats Up

Following the conquest of Poland in 1939, President Roosevelt called Congress into emergency session to amend the Neutrality Act once again. After six weeks he did obtain an end to the embargo on arms sales, but this change was saddled with the same "cash and carry" stipulation that had been affixed to non-military goods in 1937. Congress again reflected the mood of the nation.

American neutrality did not hurt Germany and had little effect on Britain and France until the spring of 1940, when the war's "phony" stage came to an abrupt end. In April,

Library of Congress

German soldiers parading in Paris in June, 1940, after occupying the city.

Germany invaded and conquered Denmark and Norway. During the following month, German divisions, with overwhelming air cover, smashed into Belgium and the Netherlands, quickly subduing those two nations. France was the next to fall, the country and its armies being split in two parts by swift-moving armored columns—the dreaded German Panzers—which penetrated all the way to the English Channel within a matter of days. Italian troops also invaded across France's southern border, but German mastery of the situation was so complete that this action was important only because it marked Mussolini's formal entry into the war. On June 22, the French accepted Hitler's peace terms.

Germany now turned its attention to Great Britain. Beginning in July, 1940, Britain underwent almost nightly bombing raids by the Luftwaffe, Germany's air force. Thousands of people, mostly civilians, were killed. At the same time, German submarines in the Atlantic were sinking thousands of tons of British shipping, including merchant vessels that were transporting goods from the United States on a "cash and carry" basis.

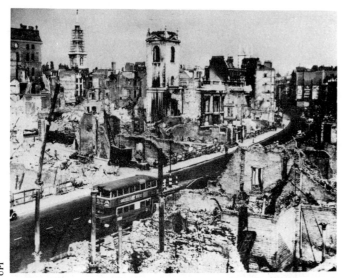

UPI

In September, 1941, four months after the heavy bombing attacks on London finally ceased, the cleaning up process was just beginning. Hundreds of thousands of tons of precious iron and other materials would eventually be salvaged from the ruins and recycled for the war. Shown is Victoria Street, which received extensive damage in two of the heavy fire raids.

The war now seemed much closer to America. And with the Battle of Britain, American feelings about aid to the British began to change. In May, 1940, one-third of the people polled had favored all aid "short of war." More and more people would join this aid-to-Britain group as the year wore on.

Rearmament

America was beginning to stir in other ways, too. The nation had a standing army of 275,000 men, ranking it seventeenth in military strength among nations. It had been eighteenth before the Netherlands' defeat. But in less than a year, as the country began to rearm, there would be 1,500,000 men in military service.

This rapid rise in the number of men at arms resulted from the first peacetime conscription law ever passed in the United States. Proposed in June, 1940, the draft bill quickly

On October 29, 1940, blindfolded Secretary of War Henry Stimson drew the first number from a glass container to determine the order in which men would be called to service under the new Burke-Wadsworth Selective Service Act.

came under attack from isolationists in and out of Congress. These people maintained that the bill was not only unprecedented but unconstitutional—a step toward dictatorship at home and involvement in war abroad. However, at a time when pictures of bombed and burning London were appearing daily in newspapers and newsreels, the isolationists found themselves outnumbered. The bill became law in September. Opinion polls indicated that seventy-one percent of the population approved it.

All men between the ages of twenty-one and thirty-five were required to register with their local draft boards, which were made up of volunteers from the community. Each man was assigned a number and, if physically and mentally fit, was called up when his number appeared in a lottery. By the middle of October, seventeen million men had registered. Stories about the draftees, like this one, made the rounds:

> "Don't scribble!" a draft register in Chicago begged. "I can't read your first name."
> "Can't help it," the registrant mumbled. "First name's Ignatius. Never could spell it."[9]

Jewelry stores experienced a run on wedding rings, many young men believing that marriage would save them from the draft. It did not.

That summer the National Defense Advisory Board, which eventually became the War Production Board, had been established to oversee defense production. By October, when draftees began to report for induction, the board had awarded more than seven billion dollars in war contracts. Of this amount, the lion's share went for aircraft—a total of ten thousand planes. But, despite the profits to be made, many manufacturers were reluctant to switch over to defense work. Believing the buildup would be only temporary, they preferred to continue producing for the civilian market.

Although money poured into war production, for months output lagged far behind military needs. Recruits drilled with broomsticks instead of rifles, and went on maneuvers with pieces of stovepipe for cannons and trucks labeled "TANK."

[9] *Time Capsule: History of the War Years, 1939-1945* (New York: Bonanza Books, 1972), p. 1940/42.

UPI

Members of the 12th Infantry, Michigan National Guard, training with a log representing a trench mortar.

Aid to Britain

In addition to producing arms and other necessities for sale to Britain, the United States extended aid in other forms to that embattled country. By executive order, President Roosevelt exchanged leases on British air and naval bases in Newfoundland, the Caribbean, and South America—the bases deemed important to American defense—for fifty old but still serviceable U.S. destroyers. Although isolationists regarded the exchange as another example of Rooseveltian "warmongering," the public in general approved.

In 1940 Congress appropriated $50 million for British relief, and considerable aid was also flowing to Britain through non-governmental channels. In the public mind, all such assistance was lumped together under the slogan "Bundles for Britain." The Red Cross, in June, 1940, raised $14 million for relief work in England. American women knitted socks and sweaters, made clothes, and collected non-perishable food to be sent in actual bundles for distribution to the thousands of people evacuated from their homes in London and other heavily bombed cities. Many American organizations held benefit dances, sales, concerts, and contests to raise funds. Much of the money went for medical supplies and equipment, and for direct relief. It has been

UPI

A child weeps in the ruins of his house after a German bombing raid on London. Pictures like this were turned into war posters in the United States and aided in the program for British relief.

estimated that approximately $100 million was raised for the British by private groups and charitable organizations in the United States.

The Presidential Election

Although the war was uppermost in people's minds, in 1940 Americans also had a presidential election to think about. Since George Washington set the precedent, no president had ever sought a third term in office. So firm was this tradition that some people erroneously believed a third term to be forbidden by the Constitution. On the other hand, the question of a third term had never arisen at a time when the future seemed so uncertain. Would FDR seek a third term? No one knew, and for weeks Roosevelt kept silent.

Expressing no desire for the nomination, Roosevelt left matters in the hands of party chieftains. They did their jobs well. In July, at the Democratic convention in Chicago, they whipped up a "spontaneous" demonstration that gave Roosevelt his renomination on the first ballot. Later, at the White House, FDR made his acceptance speech:

> When, in 1936, I was chosen by the voters for a second time as President, it was my firm intention to turn over the responsibilities of government to other hands at the end of my term. That conviction remained with me . . . . When the conflict first broke out last September it was still my intention to announce clearly and simply that under no circumstances would I accept re-election.
>
> It soon became evident, however, that such a public statement on my part would be unwise from the point of view of sheer public interest. It was also my obvious duty to maintain to the utmost the influence of this mighty nation in our effort to prevent the spread of war. The normal conditions under which I would have made public declaration of my personal desires were gone.[10]

Wendell Willkie speaking in front of a "No Third Term" banner. His campaign was energetic—he traveled 30,000 miles and made 540 speeches—but poorly organized. Still, he came closer to defeating Roosevelt than the president's two previous challengers, winning 22 million popular votes to FDR's 27 million.

In Philadelphia that summer, the Republicans nominated Wendell L. Willkie as their candidate for the presidency. This came as something of a surprise. Willkie had campaigned hard for the nomination, but few people had expected him to win it. He was not a politician, but rather a Wall Street lawyer who had been president of the Commonwealth and Southern Utilities Corporation. He was not even particularly well known in Republican party circles, having voted Democratic as recently as 1938. However, like other successful "dark-horse" candidates, Willkie had organized his drive for the nomination well—far better than his opponents, who included Robert A. Taft of Ohio and Thomas E. Dewey of New York, had suspected. As part of their efforts, Willkie aides planted a claque in the convention gallery, and at every opportunity its members created bedlam with

[10]Quoted in ibid., p. 1940/15.

UPI

shouts of "We want Willkie!" More important, however, was Willkie's efficient team of floor and caucus managers. By the sixth ballot they had persuaded a sufficient number of delegates to change their minds, and the nomination of their candidate was secured.

Willkie conducted a vigorous election campaign, scouring the country for votes. He averaged ten speeches a day, many without the aid of a public address system, and occasionally lost his voice. He agreed in the main with Roosevelt's foreign policy, but disagreed on domestic policy. He tried to lure the president into debate on such issues as economic recovery, "the suppression of free enterprise by big government," and the propriety of seeking a third term. But Roosevelt refused to be drawn. He presented himself as a busy leader concerned with the national welfare, not with running for re-election. He left responses to such aides as Secretary of the Interior Harold Ickes, known as "Old Curmudgeon." To emphasize the fact that he had come from humble beginnings, Willkie spoke of himself as "the barefoot boy from Indiana"—his native state. Ickes skewered that with "Willkie, the rich man's Roosevelt; Willkie, the simple, barefoot Wall Street lawyer." These few words painted Willkie as a friend of the rich only, while enhancing the image of Roosevelt (a wealthy man himself) as a friend of the people.

Roosevelt's strategy paid off. He won re-election with 27 million popular votes to Willkie's 22 million, 449 electoral college votes to Willkie's 82. George Washington's precedent had been broken.

More Aid to Britain

The election over, the war once again received undivided attention. Under the Neutrality Act's "cash and carry" provision, the British had spent about $4.5 billion buying arms from the United States. Their treasury was running dry, down to only $2 billion as 1940 drew to a close. Winston Churchill, Britain's prime minister, wrote to Roosevelt inquiring if some other form of aid might be arranged. At a news conference on December 16, Roosevelt responded with a new concept, to which the label "lend-lease" became attached. The United States would supply war matériel to

English servicewomen unpacking American-made .38 revolvers, part of a lend-lease shipment of arms and ammunition.

National Archives

Imperial War Museum, London

A British ship lays mines at sea as part of an intensive effort initiated early in the war to protect Atlantic sea lanes from attack by German U-boats.

Great Britain with the understanding that Britain would return the matériel "in kind" once the war was over. It was an imaginative idea, and it pulled the props from under the Neutrality Act.

Congress debated the Lend-Lease Act for weeks, finally passing it in March, 1941. The act made an initial grant of $9 billion for aid to Britain.

Lend-lease, which in President Roosevelt's phrase made the United States "the arsenal of democracy," effectively removed any lingering question of American neutrality. It was a definite commitment to the Allied side, a decisive step toward active involvement in the conflict. To prevent lend-lease aid from falling victim to German submarines (known as U-boats), American warships were soon assigned to convoy merchant vessels across the Atlantic. At first, the U.S. ships were permitted only to track the U-boats, leaving actual attack to British ships. Following submarine attacks on American destroyers, however, Roosevelt gave the order to "shoot on sight." In July, 1941, the United States began to use Iceland as a major base from which to patrol shipping lanes.

In the meantime, the European war had expanded. Late in

1940, Rumania, Bulgaria, and Hungary joined the German side. Yugoslavia refused to do so, and was brutally conquered by Hitler's troops in April, 1941. Moving south, the Germans quickly subdued Greece, against which Italy had launched an unsuccessful invasion. Then came Hitler's most fateful move of all. Ignoring his treaty with Russia, Hitler attacked that nation on June 22, 1941. German troops advanced rapidly toward Moscow and Leningrad.

To Pearl Harbor

Events in Europe had preoccupied President Roosevelt and his advisers. They had given relatively little attention to affairs in Asia. But in 1941 their attention began to shift.

The fall of France in 1940 prompted Japan to move toward Indochina, then a French colony. The United States protested, and backed up its words with an oil embargo against Japan, which depended almost entirely on imports for petroleum. Some observers predicted that the embargo would not halt Japanese expansion, as Roosevelt's advisers hoped, but instead would cause Japan to drive on British and Dutch possessions, rich in minerals, in Southeast Asia.

In July, 1941, Japan moved fifty thousand troops into Indochina. The American government responded by freezing all Japanese assets in the United States—about $130 million. It offered to lift the oil embargo and the assets freeze only if Japan withdrew from Indochina and from China.

From the Japanese point of view, the United States had become a menace to their plans to dominate Asia and become industrially self-sufficient. Some members of the Japanese government argued for a swift strike at the U.S. Pacific fleet to immobilize it and remove the threat of American power. And early in November, plans for such an attack were put into motion. On November 26, a huge fleet of aircraft carriers and escort ships sailed from a northern Japanese island. Its destination was the U.S. naval base at Pearl Harbor, Hawaii. Warplanes and small submarines attacked on a Sunday morning, December 7. The American forces were totally unprepared. Airplanes, parked in neat rows, were easily destroyed. Battleships, berthed side by side in the harbor, were sitting ducks.

Since the United States had broken a Japanese code some months before, American military leaders knew that Japan

U.S. Navy

"Pearl Harbor was still asleep in the morning mist," recalled a Japanese commander. Minutes later, smoke rose from the wreckage of the naval air station, where planes parked in rows made an easy target. Roosevelt, stunned and angry on hearing the news, pounded the table and repeated, "Our planes were destroyed on the ground, *on the ground!*"

was planning a major move. But no one knew where Japan would strike, nor when. No one, it appears, dreamed that it would be Pearl Harbor, even though commanders there were alerted. The Philippines, then a U.S. colony, seemed more likely.

The surprise attack on Pearl Harbor killed more than two thousand Americans. A number of battleships were sunk, and others were severely damaged. Land-based American air power there was all but wiped out. But the American aircraft carriers, at sea when the Japanese hit, escaped harm.

News of the disaster reached Washington early that Sunday afternoon. Presidential press secretary Steven Early released the information to the newspaper wire services at 2:25 P.M., Washington time. As the announcement interrupted radio programs, football games, and other public events, Americans reacted first with disbelief, then shock, then anger. The attack accomplished something no government could do: in an instant, it unified the nation. Americans were no longer isolationists or interventionists. They were simply Americans, determined to defeat Japan.

After receiving the news of Pearl Harbor, President Roosevelt spent the remainder of that day meeting with the secretaries of war, army, navy, and state, with legislative leaders, and with his full cabinet. On December 8, a cold and blustery day in Washington, Roosevelt appeared before Congress to speak over a nationwide radio hookup. The president began: "Yesterday, December 7, 1941—a date which will live in infamy—the United States of America was suddenly and deliberately attacked by naval and air forces of the Empire of Japan." Reviewing the damage at Pearl Harbor and the lives lost, Roosevelt went on to underscore subsequent Japanese attacks on Hong Kong, Guam, the Philippines, and Wake and Midway islands. He concluded: "I ask that the Congress declare that since the unprovoked and dastardly attack by Japan on Sunday, December 7, a state of war has existed between the United States and the Japanese Empire."

Italy and Germany, complying with a treaty they had made with Japan, declared war on the United States a few days later.

Although Americans were united in their determination to win the war, once the initial shock of Pearl Harbor had worn off there was a good deal of debate over just how the United States had become involved in the war. The argument usually centered on President Roosevelt. Had he deliberately led the nation into war? Those who believed so cited the record of the quarantine speech, the ever-increasing aid to Britain, convoys in the Atlantic, and the "hard line" toward the Japanese. American policy toward Japan, they said, had been unnecessarily severe. It had placed that nation in a position of having to attack the United States or else losing face and abandoning its plans for a more powerful role among the world's nations.

On the other hand, some observers asked, could the United States really have stayed out? It seemed certain that

UPI

President Roosevelt asks Congress for a declaration of war against Japan on December 8, 1941. In less than an hour, both houses approved the declaration. Sixty million Americans listened to the speech on the radio.

Hitler planned to dominate Europe and Russian Asia, and that Japan planned to take over the remainder of the Far East. So far only Britain had effectively resisted those plans. If Britain fell, and if Europe were united under the Germans and the Pacific under the Japanese, the United States would have faced an exceedingly hostile world. Could the United States have "done business" with a world controlled by powerful dictatorships? Would not Latin America, or Canada, have been next on the list for conquest? And then the United States itself?

Commentators friendly to FDR have concluded that he viewed first German expansion, and later Japanese expansion, as threats to the freedom and interests of the United States. While he did not wish to see the United States at war, he did believe that the defeat of Britain would be disastrous and that all possible steps should be taken to prevent it. In the Far East, his administration followed a long-established U.S. policy of friendship and support for the Chinese, as well as support of Western colonialism in Asia. The Japanese threatened both China and Western colonies.

Whether the United States was deliberately and unnecessarily led into war, or whether it was drawn into the conflict through a necessary defense of its own interests, is a question that has not been answered to everyone's satisfaction. There is no doubt, however, that by the middle of 1941 most Americans believed that Britain must be saved and approved of the administration's aid programs. Most believed, too, that Japanese expansionism was dangerous and that the United States was right in taking a firm stand against it. So, while it may be true that Roosevelt's policies precipitated the United States into war at the end of 1941, it is true also that those policies were supported by the majority of the American people.

The Draft and Civil Defense

Pearl Harbor was of particular concern to those who had been drafted into the armed services and to those of draft age generally. The original conscription law of 1940 called on draftees to serve only one year. Much of 1941 was spent arguing about whether this term should be extended by an additional eighteen months. Many soldiers, paid thirty dollars a month while their acquaintances on defense jobs were earning several times that, were anxious to return to civilian life. And when the president asked Congress to extend the draft, the acronym OHIO—"Over the Hill in October"—appeared in army camps on the walls of buildings and in latrines. Soldiers would depart the army without leave, if necessary.

Draft extension came up for a vote in Congress in August, 1941, less than four months before the Pearl Harbor attack. As one reporter noted:

> The eyes of the world were on the House as the
> draft bill came finally to a vote. The 20 other
> American republics watched; the President watched
> from his sea conference with Winston Churchill [the
> two leaders were meeting on warships off the coast of
> Newfoundland, Canada]; Adolf Hitler's representatives

UPI

Sir Winston Churchill, responding to Roosevelt's remark that he would like to meet Churchill "in some lonely bay or another," chose Placentia Bay in southeast Newfoundland. With Roosevelt traveling on the U.S. cruiser *Augusta* and Churchill on the British battleship *Prince of Wales,* the two men met there on August 9, 1941, to confer and to draw up the Atlantic Charter. The charter, which curiously was not issued in written form, endorsed the rights of free people to choose their leaders, trade freely, and enjoy freedom—from want, from fear, and of the seas.

and Emperor Hirohito's observers waited. If the draft extension bill failed to pass, most of the half-trained U.S. Army would slowly dissolve as draftees and guardsmen went home. The nation would have to start again building and training another army.

The roll call began; 45 minutes of grinding suspense as the clerk growled out the 432 names, listened for an answer, repeated the vote. The jammed galleries seemed hung over the rails. The little tally meter of Tally Clerk Hans Jorgensen registered 204 aye votes, 201 nay votes. (Twenty-seven were not voting.) Hubbub boiled around the rostrum. Lean, dyspeptic Democrat Andrew L. Somers of New York, hoping to defeat the bill, changed his vote from Aye to No. The Chair took hold. Whacking the gavel block like a

Air raid wardens in New York City point to outside building lights that must be put out in the event of a blackout. All over the country, Americans tacked up blackout curtains and manned searchlights and gun emplacements in fear of enemy attack.

"He also serves who sits and waits." An air raid warden perches atop a World War I tank in hopes of catching a glimpse of an enemy plane.

smith at the forge, Speaker Sam Rayburn announced the vote: 203-to-202.[11]

There was a good deal of grumbling, but very few soldiers carried out their threat to go "Over the Hill in October."

The Battle of Britain in 1940–1941 had made Americans air-raid conscious. Pearl Harbor made them more so. Early in 1941, under government auspices, local volunteer civil defense forces had begun to form. New York, for example, had registered more than sixty thousand air-raid wardens in a few months. Volunteer fire brigades were also organized. People kept buckets of sand for fire-extinguishing purposes around the house and in public places. There were practice blackouts in cities, during which wardens patrolled streets to see that lights were out or their glare shielded. Hundreds of thousands of people took first-aid courses and courses in air-raid survival techniques. In addition, a nation-wide network of aircraft spotters was set up.

These precautions may not have been necessary. Apart from its U-boats, which were limited in range, Germany had relatively little seapower. Japan was fully occupied in taking over chunks of Southeast Asia, including Malaya, Burma, the Philippines, and the Dutch East Indies (now Indonesia). Still, many Americans foresaw the possibility of hostile aircraft overhead and enemy invasion forces on the beaches. They were jumpy, and they soon learned that their civil defense system left something to be desired.

San Francisco, Seattle, Los Angeles, and New York all underwent false alarms that caused considerable confusion. In San Francisco, sirens shrilled three times one night just after Pearl Harbor, and a radio station went dead. The sirens actually were on fire engines racing to a fire, but they thoroughly frightened the public. The city government swung into action, ordering wardens to patrol the streets to get lights out, finally ordering the power company to close its master switch. Police ordered motorists to use only parking lights. Buses and streetcars did the same. Panic grew—and so did the noise level—as enormous traffic jams

[11] Ibid., p. 1941/40.

developed and the accident rate soared. General John L. De Witt, head of the Fourth Army and the Western Defense Command, insisted that Japanese carrier-based planes were over the city. But there were no planes. The only casualties of that sleepless night resulted from traffic accidents and panicky stumbling in darkened buildings.

The Seattle experience was similar. Following an alert, as the city became increasingly blacked out, a thousand or more people gathered in the downtown area to enforce the lights-out order. By about midnight, all lights were out except one blue neon sign. The crowd, turning into a mob, began hurling objects at it. Soon the mob was breaking shop windows and looting. By the time the police stepped in, a six-block business area was mostly shattered glass.

Internment

Panic expressed itself in yet another way. The surprise attack on Pearl Harbor quickly ignited a long-smoldering anti-Japanese feeling among white Americans, especially on the West Coast. Although Americans condemned the dictatorships in Germany and Italy, they were not particularly anti-German or anti-Italian. But after Pearl Harbor, Caucasians turned on the Japanese in America, whether citizens or not, as a class and with a vengeance.

In 1940, Congress had passed the Alien Registration Act. This law required all aliens—that is, citizens of foreign countries who were living in the United States—to register, be fingerprinted, and carry identification cards. The outbreak of war in December, 1941, made nearly one million Germans, Italians, and Japanese "enemy aliens."

Before Pearl Harbor Day ended, the Federal Bureau of Investigation began rounding up some ten thousand aliens considered dangerous to the nation's security. The aliens were placed in army stockades. About half were Italian and German, the remainder Japanese. Most of the Italians and Germans were released within a year. The Japanese who were interned, along with those who were still free early in 1942, fared worse.

Air-raid alarms, false or not, reminded white Americans on the West Coast of the thousands of Japanese in their midst. Among them were Issei, those born abroad and not citizens, and Nisei, citizens of the United States by right of birth. Most Issei kept traditional ways. Nisei, on the other hand, often were thoroughly Americanized. But whether Japanese were citizens or not, or whether they were assimilated into the culture or not, made little difference to most whites. And neither did the fact that there had been no Japanese sabotage or subversive activity of any kind. The Japanese—all Japanese—were perceived as potentially dangerous, as enemies within the country who might be waiting for just the right moment to strike.

This climate of suspicion was heightened by certain government officials who greatly exaggerated the Japanese "menace." General De Witt, for example, reported seizing "many guns and 60,000 rounds of ammunition" during a raid on a Japanese establishment in California. Only later, after the panic created by the report had hardened into prejudice, was it revealed that the raid had been on a Japanese-owned sporting goods store.

General De Witt favored removing all Japanese from the coast and interning them in camps in the interior. So did California's attorney-general, Earl Warren, who later became governor of the state and still later chief justice of the United States Supreme Court. Appearing before a congressional committee early in 1942, Warren said:

> A wave of organized sabotage in California accompanied by an actual air raid or even by a prolonged blackout could not only be more destructive to life and property but could result in retarding the entire war effort of this Nation far more than the treacherous bombing of Pearl Harbor.
>
> I hesitate to think what the result would be of the destruction of any of our big airplane factories in this State. It will interest you to know that some of our airplane factories in this State are entirely surrounded by Japanese land ownership or occupancy. It is a situation that is fraught with the greatest danger and under no circumstances should it ever be permitted to exist. . . .

To assume that the enemy has not planned fifth column activities for us in a wave of sabotage is simply to live in a fool's paradise. These activities, whether you call them "fifth column activities" or "sabotage" or "war behind the lines upon civilians," or whatever you may call it, are just as much an integral part of Axis warfare as any of their military and naval operations. When I say that I refer to all of the Axis powers with which we are at war.[12]

In discussing the problem with the president, U.S. Attorney-General Francis Biddle argued that to intern the Nisei, who were citizens, would violate constitutional guarantees of due process of law. J. Edgar Hoover, the director of the FBI, also opposed the idea. His bureau had turned up no evidence of Japanese subversion. On the other hand, Secretary of War Henry L. Stimson argued in favor of removal and internment. He, like Warren and others in California, had public opinion solidly on his side.

Attorney General Francis Biddle.

Finally, on February 19, 1942, President Roosevelt issued Executive Order No. 9066 calling for the internment of all Japanese in camps to be constructed in Arizona, California, Idaho, Utah, Wyoming, Colorado, and Arkansas. Eventually there were ten camps in all, each at its peak holding about ten thousand persons.

The Japanese could take only a few personal belongings with them, which meant that many possessions as well as homes and businesses were lost. The internees were taken first to assembly centers—tent colonies in stadiums, race tracks, and fairgrounds—and then transported by bus and rail to the camps. A U.S. government report, oddly sympathetic given the circumstances, described the process:

Then in June, with gathering momentum, the next phase of the forced migration got underway. At the former migratory labor camp doing duty near Sacramento as an assembly center, trains were loaded

[12] From House Committee Hearings, 1942. Quoted in Richard Polenberg, ed., *America at War: The Home Front, 1941-1945* (Englewood Cliffs, N.J.: Prentice-Hall, 1968), p. 99.

Library of Congress

Armed soldiers stand guard as Japanese-American evacuees wait to register at an assembly center set up at Santa Anita race track in California.

with men, women, children and babies and moved northward to unload their cargo near the little town of Tule Lake, California. Here the rough barracks of one of the first relocation centers were still under construction. Farmers from the rich Salinas Valley were transported to the Arizona desert. San Francisco businessmen were sent from the Tanforan race track to the bare, intermountain valleys of central Utah. From the fertile central valley of California to the sandy flats of eastern Colorado, from southern California to the plains of Wyoming, from the moist coastland of the Northwest to the sagebrush plains of southern Idaho, from the San Joaquin Valley to the woodlands of Arkansas, the trains moved during the spring, early summer, and fall.

For the involuntary travelers, the break with the accustomed and usual was now complete. In the assembly centers behind fences and under guard by military police, the evacuees had suddenly found themselves, although looking out at familiar hills and highways, in a strange new world of social relationships. They were outcast but still in their own country. Now the world of human relations was matched by an equally strange physical world. It was clear, as the trains moved over the wastelands of the mountain states, that they were to be exiled in desert and wilderness.[13]

According to an anthropologist who visited some of the camps, "A three-year-old child, who had lived among Caucasians, mistook the meaning of the strange faces around him and asked his mother why they had come to Japan."

For the exiles, even memories of home were soured by anxiety. What was happening to their property during their absence? If and when they were released, would they have a house, or farm, or business to return to?

This child, tagged like a piece of luggage, awaits relocation with his family as Japanese-Americans were rounded up and sent to internment camps at the outbreak of the war.

Woodrow Wilson Higashi, a Nisei, owned a small but prosperous drugstore in Los Angeles. He was unable to dispose of his stock and fixtures before being taken to the holding center at the Santa Anita race track, preliminary to internment. He was visited there by one "Edwards," a white acquaintance, who said he could dispose of the store's fixtures and Mr. Higashi's seven-year-old automobile for approximately $500, and he also offered to store his friend's household goods and personal possessions. The offer was gratefully accepted, and "Edwards" requested and was given a power of attorney to handle Higashi's affairs. That was the last Higashi saw of "Edwards."

After a few weeks at Santa Anita, Higashi was transferred to the Granada relocation center in Colorado. In October 1943, after he had been interned for more than a year, he persuaded the WRA [War Relocation Authority] authorities to demand from "Edwards" an accounting of his stewardship. Months later, WRA reported that all of the property, including household and personal possessions, which had been placed in "Edwards'" care had simply vanished; that "Edwards" had no assets which could be attached to recover the value of the store fixtures and automobile, and that, furthermore, the Los Angeles district

[13] Quoted in Phillips, *The Nineteen Forties*, p. 111.

attorney was not inclined to bring any charges against "Edwards."[14]

Higashi's loss was typical. The total monetary loss to Japanese-Americans has been estimated at $400 million. Some years after the war, Congress passed a law making it possible for the Japanese to recover some of what they had lost. Under this legislation, about thirty thousand persons received about ten cents for every dollar lost, a total of some $30 million.

Camp life was bleak. Bulldozers had scraped the areas bare of vegetation in preparation for building. Housing consisted of army-style barracks, constructed of wood and tar paper. Some were open barracks affording no privacy. Others were partitioned. Two couples or a family of four were allotted a twenty-by-twenty-foot room. The daily menu was standard army fare, making no allowance for dietary preferences. But, despite the hardships, in each camp the interned Japanese managed to create an orderly, peaceful community. They elected leaders, formed work details (in which a person could earn a maximum of nineteen dollars a month), and established recreational facilities and programs. At most camps there were no fences, only military patrols. But few internees were tempted to try escape. An unfriendly world lay outside, and a Japanese face would be easily recognizable.

Late in 1943, with the Allies taking the offensive in the war and the fear of invasion past, internees were permitted to leave the camps. About thirty thousand did, finding homes mainly in the Midwest. Several thousand Nisei youth accepted an opportunity to join the army. Many served in a regimental combat team in Italy and posted a spectacular record for bravery.

Near the end of 1944, a Supreme Court decision validated Attorney-General Biddle's contention concerning due process. The Court found that it had been unconstitutional to intern Nisei. The remaining internees were freed, dispersing about the country to start life all over again. So ended what

[14]Quoted in ibid., pp. 112–113.

most historians consider one of the darker, more shameful episodes in American history.

Conscientious Objectors

Expansion of the armed services accelerated rapidly following Pearl Harbor, with the number of men in uniform eventually reaching about twelve million. The draft law had already been amended to lengthen the term of service required of draftees. After the United States entered the war, the law was further amended to make men between the ages of eighteen and forty-five eligible for the draft. (The original ages were twenty-one and thirty-five.) In addition, men between the ages of forty-five and sixty-four were required to register with their draft boards so that the country's total manpower reserves could be assessed. Of course, there were thousands who did not wait to be drafted. The rush to enlist remained strong for many weeks after the Japanese attack.

The vast majority of those called up for induction appeared on schedule, ready to accept whatever came. There were some, however, who objected to the war on grounds of conscience. Among these were Mennonites, Plymouth Brethren, Quakers, Jehovah's Witnesses, and members of other religious groups. There were also individuals who opposed war on purely philosophic grounds.

More than twenty-five thousand objectors accepted assignments in the armed forces as non-combatants. Many served, for example, in the medical corps. About twelve thousand chose to live in Civilian Public Service camps. There, receiving food, clothing, and shelter but no pay, these men worked on conservation projects, fought forest fires, offered themselves for medical experiments, and worked on public health projects. Another five thousand men chose prison, refusing to lend support to war in any way. Fully three-quarters of this group were Jehovah's Witnesses.

Women in Uniform

Women were not subject to the draft, but nonetheless thousands served in the newly established women's auxiliary service groups. There was the Women's Army Corps (WAC), the Women's Naval Reserve (known as the

Posters such as these were used to recruit women into service. It was an advertising campaign that hardly seemed necessary since so many women eagerly sought to join up.

WAVES), the Women's Air Force Service Pilots (WASP), the Coast Guard auxiliary (SPAR), and the Women's Reserve, U.S. Marine Corps (which, unlike the others, had no acronym attached to it). A few hundred women with commercial pilot's licenses joined the Women's Auxiliary Ferrying Squadron (WAFS) as civil service employees, not as members of the air force.

To have women in the armed forces was something new in the United States, and some people feared that life in the army (or any other branch of the military) would have a harmful effect on female morality. But whether this occurred or not, no one could be sure. There were also many jokes—about women inductees and medical exams, about whether the army should issue girdles (it did), and about the attitudes of male officers. One marine officer, told that women would be assigned to his base soon after guard dogs had arrived, snorted: "First they send us dogs. Now it's women!" A news magazine reported:

> Essential difference between G.I. Joe and G.I. Jane was pointed out by a Fort Des Moines recruit who was being loaded into an already jampacked Army truck. "Hey sergeant," she protested, "have a heart, this bus is full." Said the tough male sergeant: "Lady, I been getting 18 men into these trucks and I sure as hell can get 18 WACS in." Wailed the squeezed WAC: "But men are broad in the shoulders."[15]

Organized in the spring of 1942, the women's auxiliaries contained more than a hundred thousand volunteers by December of that year. Another two hundred thousand enlisted before the war's end. Women pilots ferried aircraft from points of manufacture to air force bases. WACS, WAVES, SPARS, and women marines served on bases in the United States and abroad as clerks, medics, drivers, mechanics, and in many other jobs. The main purpose behind the auxiliaries was to release men for combat duty.

Of all the women in uniform, those in the armed forces

[15] *Time Capsule*, p. 1944/204.

UPI

"Rosie the Riveter," the famous industrial symbol of the 1940's, takes form in these aircraft assembly workers. Suspicious of women workers at first, by 1944 managers in heavy industry had 3.5 million women employees.

nursing corps had perhaps the most dangerous assignments. As in World War I, the service nurses often worked incredible hours under the most difficult conditions, attempting to save lives in primitive field hospitals at or near the front lines of the fighting.

Women in Industry

Women contributed to the war effort in other ways. Unemployment disappeared, and the need for workers stimulated a dramatic change in the ratio of women to men in the labor force. Between the spring of 1940 and the summer of 1943, nearly four and a half million women entered the labor force. More than a million women were in agriculture, many taking over the family farm while their husbands were off at war or at work in a nearby defense plant. Slightly more than half the new female workers were married. They took jobs because their husbands were away in the armed forces, or because they wanted to help in the war effort, or because jobs that normally would have been closed to them were now open. For the first time, women found employment as riveters ("Rosie the Riveter" was a popular song), welders, hydraulic crane operators, aircraft mechanics, railroad engineers and brakemen, taxi drivers, bellhops, barbers, and even lumberjacks.

For industrial jobs, the government decreed that women should be paid equally with men for equal work. Many large companies followed this practice. Many smaller ones did not. On the average, women took home from ten to twenty dollars a week less than men doing the same jobs.

Of course, many women worked at more conventional jobs as clerks, typists, and secretaries. The big change here was that such jobs were more numerous than ever before. Thousands more women than formerly—particularly young, single women—left farms and small towns for the city. They found jobs readily enough, but many also discovered how lonely city life can be. For them, as for young servicemen far from home, the centers operated by the United Service Organization (USO) filled an important need. This organization, sponsored by the government but staffed largely by volunteers, provided places where young people could meet. They offered food, entertainment, dancing, and other recreational activities. Many wartime romances, leading often to marriage, began at USO centers. The USO also organized tours of singers, dancers, and comedians to entertain on military bases, both at home and overseas.

With mothers at work and fathers at war, families were subjected to strain. Many young children scarcely remembered their fathers. While their mothers were working, they were most often cared for by a grandmother, or some other relative or friend. Day-care centers were established by a few communities and by several industrialists, including Henry J. Kaiser. But most families had to make their own arrangements. In many cases, school-age children were left to shift for themselves after classes and during vacation time. Thousands of teen-agers, both male and female, found it easy to get jobs. This often added a needed supplement to the family income. It also added to family strain, however, because financial independence made young people less responsive to parental control.

As a result of these unsettled conditions, juvenile delinquency rose during the war. In 1943, for example, juvenile arrests nationwide were 17 percent higher than the year before. In San Diego, California, where a large naval base was located, the arrest rate for boys was 55 percent higher in 1943 than in 1942, and the rate for girls was 355 percent higher. Job opportunities and the glamor of associating with servicemen brought many young girls to towns near military bases. Most arrests of girls were for prostitution. Adolescent boys got into trouble for drunk and disorderly conduct, loitering, and petty thievery. On the whole, drugs were not a problem among young people then.

War Production

Women and men alike contributed to an industrial war effort that was remarkable by any standards. Between 1940 and 1945, the output of munitions rose from $341 million to more than $5 billion. A total of $183.1 billion worth of other war goods was produced. These goods included, among other things, nearly 300,000 planes, 72,000 naval ships and 5,000 merchant ships, 86,000 tanks, and 8,500,000 rifles.

For most companies, producing war matériel was highly profitable. Overall corporate profits went from $5 billion in 1939 to $10.8 billion in 1944. This rise would have been even more spectacular if Congress had not imposed, in 1942, an excess profits tax of up to 90 percent on corporate income. Perhaps inevitably, there was some cheating, some cost padding, and some phony bookkeeping. By the end of the war, a total of sixty-five corporations and more than seven hundred individuals had been convicted of fraud in war contracts. Some individuals went to prison. Fines levied in fraud cases amounted to more than a million dollars.

War posters such as this one helped to create a national spirit which resulted in increased production at home to aid the war effort.

On the other side of the table, even though management and organized labor had agreed to a no-strike pledge after Pearl Harbor, there were many work stoppages—nearly 3,000 in 1942, 3,700 in 1943, and nearly 5,000 in 1944. Labor unions were usually blamed, and the patriotism of their leaders was questioned. Bushy-browed John L. Lewis, president of the United Mine Workers, stirred the most governmental and public anger. Lewis always kept the welfare of his miners uppermost in his mind, accepting angry attacks and even outright slanders as part of the job. And he received many, for the coal his men produced was used to heat millions of homes. During one miners' strike over wages and working conditions, the government threatened that the mines would be taken over and operated by the army. "You can't dig coal with bayonets," Lewis retorted, and he won his point. All things considered, however, work stoppages damaged the war effort very little. And on the whole, labor as well as management prospered during the war.

Weekly earnings in manufacturing, which had been about $25.00 in 1940, reached an average of $45.70 in 1944. There was, in addition, plenty of overtime work, paid at time-and-a-half for anything over forty hours a week and at double-time for Sundays and holidays. And, since many items were not being produced—new cars and new homes, to name only two—people tended to save more of the money they earned. By 1944, personal savings across the country were estimated at $49.9 billion.

The Cost of Living and Rationing

Wages frequently were at issue in labor-management disputes. Early in 1942, to hold down inflation, the government established price controls and limited wage increases to no more than 15 percent over 1941 levels. In 1943, however, labor argued that the cost of living had gone up 30 percent, justifying demands for higher wage increases. The government calculated the cost-of-living increase at 19 percent. The consumer price index, which does not include all the goods and services a family buys, rose 24 percent between 1940 and 1943. This variation in figures provided plenty of room for argument. Although organized labor

UPI

Home economics students are led through the complicated shopping procedures that accompanied rationing during the war years.

did not get all it wanted, it did eventually puncture the 15-percent lid on wage hikes. By the end of the war, many workers had nearly doubled their incomes.

During World War I, inflation had driven prices up more than 50 percent. In an attempt to prevent this from happening again, early in 1942 Congress established the Office of Price Administration (OPA). Eventually the agency was empowered to place price ceilings on all goods except fresh fruits and vegetables. It also imposed rent controls and established a system of rationing for many types of food and other goods, including tires and gasoline.

Few Americans who lived through the war on the home front have forgotten rationing—a frustrating, bureaucratic, and time-consuming nuisance. Having enough money to purchase an item was not enough. First, the item had to be in stock—and many items were available only irregularly. Then, the purchaser had to have the proper ration stamps— and the coding of the stamps was changed monthly to discourage hoarding. Local agencies, staffed by volunteers, distributed the stamps to consumers. Consumers exchanged the stamps, along with money, for commodities at retail

A grocer tears out a ration stamp for sugar. The system proved to be a cumbersome operation—for store keepers and customers alike—when every month some three billion stamps, each less than an inch square in size, changed hands.

shops. Retailers had to turn the stamps over to wholesalers in order to replenish their stocks, and wholesalers then passed them on to producers in order to fill *their* shelves once again. The regulations governing all of these transactions were complicated. They were also frequently changed, so that consumers had to watch the newspapers carefully. The following is a typical announcement:

General Provisions—Blue Stamps in War Ration Book No. 2 are to be used for most canned goods and for dried peas, beans, lentils, and frozen commodities like fruit juice. The Red Stamps are used for meats, canned fish, butter, cheese, edible fats, and canned milk. You have to give up more points when buying scarce foods than when buying the same quantity of a more plentiful one. . . .

Red Stamps J, K, and L may be redeemed through June 20. Blue Stamps G, H, and J are valid through June 7, and Blue Stamps K, L, and M are valid through July 7. Ration stamps are not valid if detached from their appropriate books. . . .

Each person has a Red Stamp quota of 16 points a week (meats, cheese, butter, etc.), allowing an average of approximately two pounds per week per person. Each person has 48 points in Blue Stamps (most processed foods) to expend between June 6 and July 2. You may buy most fresh vegetables without ration stamps. . . .

In Ration Book No. 1, Stamp No. 13 is good for five pounds of sugar through August 1; Stamp No. 24 is good for one pound of coffee through June 30; Stamp No. 17 is good for one pair of shoes until June 15. (Dealers may not accept shoe stamps unless detached from ration book in presence of dealer.)

Gasoline and Tires—All pleasure driving is banned for holders of A, B, and C ration books. All A coupons are valued at 3 gallons; B and C coupons are valued at 2½ gallons. Coupon 5 in A book is good for 3 gallons through July 21. Motorists must write license number and state on back of each coupon before offering it to dealer. . . . No coupons for new

UPI

or recapped tires will be issued unless motorist carries inspection card showing that required tire inspections have been made.[16]

Understandably, Americans became very conscious of ration points. A magazine cartoon showed a mother and father seated at the dining room table as their young son tramped upstairs. Said the father: "We saved thirteen points sending Junior to bed without his supper."

Price ceilings were revised from time to time, depending on supply, demand, and the cost of production. Most of the time, for most goods, the prices were revised upward. A black market soon developed for expensive goods, and for goods in short supply. There was hardly anyone who did not claim to know someone from whom he or she could buy extra ration stamps—particularly for gasoline, which was perhaps the most precious commodity. And there were opportunities to purchase goods without using stamps at all. Just how widespread black marketeering was, however, is not known for certain.

Also uncertain is the extent to which price controls and rationing actually held down the cost of living. The question was argued then, frequently with vehemence, and it has been argued with equal vigor since.

Prices on certain commodities afford one measure of inflation. Table 1 shows the fluctuations in price for eight basic commodities in the years from 1940 to 1945. Using the table, one can easily calculate the percentage of increase in these items over the six-year period. Another measure of inflation is the cost of living index, which shows price increases in percentages. In Table 2, the years 1935-1939 represent 100; by 1945, therefore, the cost of food had risen by 39 percent and the overall cost of goods had risen by 28 percent over the prewar base period.

Although admitting that the systems of price controls and rationing were far from perfect, some observers have contended that inflation would have been far worse without them. They frequently offer figures to show what happened in 1946 after controls on many items were removed and

UPI

Gas rationing was extremely unpopular, with the result that cheating was common and by 1942 had become a national scandal. Eventually, tighter restrictions forced most drivers to turn in the extra cards they had acquired and to make do with the legal three gallons a week.

[16] *New York Times*, 6 June 1943, p. 3.

Table 1. Price Index for Selected Commodities, 1940–1945

Year	Round Steak, Cents per Pound	Bacon, Cents per Pound	Ham, Cents per Pound	Eggs, Cents per Dozen	Butter, Cents per Pound	Milk, Cents per Quart	Pota- toes, Cents per Pound	Sugar, Cents per Pound
1940	36.4	27.3	43.6	33.1	36.0	12.8	2.4	5.2
1941	39.1	34.3	49.8	39.7	41.1	13.6	2.3	5.7
1942	43.5	39.4	54.4	48.4	47.3	15.0	3.4	6.8
1943	43.9	43.1	56.2	57.2	52.7	15.5	4.6	6.8
1944	41.4	41.1	50.8	54.2	50.0	15.6	4.7	6.7
1945	40.5	40.9	50.0	60.2	49.8	15.6	4.8	7.5

Table 2. Food and Consumer Price Indexes, 1940–1945

Year	Food	Consumer Price Index
1940	97	100
1941	106	105
1942	124	117
1943	138	124
1944	136	126
1945	139	128

Table 3. Price Index for Selected Commodities, August 1946

Round Steak, Cents per Pound	Bacon, Cents per Pound	Ham, Cents per Pound	Eggs, Cents per Dozen	Butter, Cents per Pound	Milk, Cents per Quart	Pota- toes, Cents per Pound	Sugar, Cents per Pound
63.1	63.1	77.2	60.2	76.4	19.3	4.5	7.5

WARTIME YEARS AT HOME   53

rationing was for the most part a thing of the past. By comparing Table 1 with Table 3, one can see that this argument has some validity, at least with respect to the eight food commodities listed. The general price index tells a similar story in terms of percentage points. In July, 1946, again using 1939 as a base of 100, the food index stood at 166 and the overall consumer price index at 141. Food costs had risen 39 points in six years, 27 points in the first six months of 1946. The overall cost of goods had risen 28 points in six years and another 13 points in less than one year.

An Abundance of Shortages

To most Americans, if the war meant nothing else, it meant shortages. The hardships were not to be compared with the worst years of the Depression, when thousands lacked adequate food, clothing, and shelter. They were not the kind of hardships that breed desperation, but rather the kind that breed irritation. Housing was an example. There was very little residential construction during the war. The new homes that were available were mostly in housing projects, quickly and cheaply built, near war production plants and military bases. And those projects did not begin to meet the needs of the mushrooming populations in and around such communities. Numerous jokes like this went around:

> A man walking along the waterfront saw another
> man struggling in the water and crying for help.
> "What's your name?" the man on shore called out.
> "Joe Smith," the other gasped feebly.
> "Where do you live?"
> "Two-ten Fifth Street," came the weakening reply.
> The shoreside citizen turned and ran as fast as he
> could to 210 Fifth Street and knocked on the door.
> "Joe Smith has just drowned and I want to rent
> his room," he blurted to the woman who answered.
> "You're too late," she replied. "I just rented the
> room to the man who pushed him in."[17]

As a result of the housing shortage, it was not uncommon for several families (or three or four generations of the

[17]Phillips, *The 1940s,* p. 180.

UPI

Students at Good Counsel College in White Plains, New York, breaking ground for a victory vegetable garden on campus. Pictures like this were published frequently, and they had both practical and psychological benefits. They encouraged Americans to grow their own vegetables and thus changed the diet habits of millions. In addition, they gave civilians a sense of meaningful participation in the war effort.

same family) to share the same small house or apartment. For some families, this togetherness may have relieved some of the emotional strains of wartime. For others, however, it added to those strains considerably.

Other shortages were perhaps less serious, but they were still annoying to Americans who had come to regard a large number of items as necessities of life.

Because nylon was needed for the manufacture of parachutes, there were few nylon stockings to be had. Those available were often sold on the black market for as much as five dollars a pair. Rayon stockings, warm but unflattering, were nearly as scarce. Many women simply went without stockings, some painting a narrow brown or black stripe from the back of the knee to the heel to represent a seam. Cloth generally was in short supply, being needed for uniforms, tents, hospital bedding, and other military purposes. To conserve material, hemlines grew shorter. Cuffless trousers became the fashion, and vests as parts of suits disappeared.

Meat was hard to find, even with the proper ration stamps. Families with enough yard space often raised chickens and rabbits for the dinner table. (And for suburban children, accustomed to regarding animals as pets, the appearance of a favorite rabbit at dinner could be a traumatic event.) To cut costs and make sure of some supply of vegetables, thousands of families planted Victory Gardens in their backyards or in vacant lots.

Community groups conducted scrap drives. They collected items made of iron, steel, copper, and other metals. Even tinfoil was carefully stripped from the inside of chewing gum wrappers and other packages, wadded up into a ball, and turned over to the collection center when the ball was about the size of a grapefruit. Fat from cooking was saved in a tin can on the stove, eventually to be turned in for recycling into soap. Newspapers, too, were saved. Children were enthusiastic collectors and could often be seen going from house to house, pulling coaster wagons full of goods for salvage.

New cars were unattainable. Auto manufacturers now turned out tanks and airplanes. The used-car market did a thriving business. Some workers could not avoid commuting to their jobs by car, and so the car pool was born. Because most natural rubber had come from Southeast Asia, that supply was now cut off. Some synthetic rubber was being produced, but most motorists made do with recapped tires, when they were available. Gasoline was rationed to save rubber and to divert more petroleum into the production of synthetic rubber, rubber of some kind being urgently needed for military vehicles. And, as a further conservation measure, motorists were periodically reminded to observe the national speed limit, thirty-five miles an hour.

Vacation trips by car, except for very short distances, were out. Buses were crowded and uncomfortable. Trains were also crowded and tended to be slow, because passenger trains had to give way to troop trains and freight trains moving war goods. Rolling stock and track beds deteriorated from lack of materials and labor for maintenance, so

The Copperman Collection

To aid in supplying blood to the war's casualties, many social organizations and businesses united in blood-donor drives. These salesmen from Calvert Distillers, for example, each gave blood twenty-five times during the war years.

train rides were rough. Passenger cars had no air conditioning, and during the summer months the windows always seemed to stick shut. In the winter, heating systems failed regularly. Air travel, too, had its shortcomings. It was very expensive, for one thing. Also, a person with a reservation might at any time be "bumped"—forced to give up his or her seat to a military officer, government official, or anyone else with a higher priority.

Wartime Entertainment

Hollywood helped the war effort by churning out war movies. These were essentially propaganda films, intended to reinforce Americans' faith in their fighting men and in their country. There were also movies to take minds off the war, such as *Going My Way*, a 1944 film starring singer Bing Crosby as a Catholic priest. That same year, twelve-year-old Elizabeth Taylor established herself as a star in *National Velvet*. In 1943 another young actress, Jennifer Jones, won an Academy Award for her performance in *The Song of Bernadette*.

Movie actors and other entertainers toured the country or

otherwise helped to sell government savings bonds, popularly known as war bonds. Early in 1942, Hollywood's brightest comedienne, Carole Lombard, made an extensive tour, appearing before huge rallies and raising as much as two million dollars in a single day. It was a tour from which she never returned—her plane crashed in the Rocky Mountains and she was killed. On September 21, 1943, in a forerunner of today's telethon, singer Kate Smith spoke and sang on radio at intervals from 8:00 A.M. until 2:00 A.M. the next morning. Twenty million people heard her, and thirty-nine million dollars' worth of war bonds were sold during those eighteen hours.

A skinny and bow-tied Frank Sinatra—known to his fans simply as Frankie—was by far the most popular wartime singer. Girls squealed and swooned at his public appearances, and even at his voice over the radio.

Americans sang and danced to such popular songs as "I'll Get By," "Together," and "As Time Goes By." A warning to girlfriends from their sweethearts in the service was "Don't Sit under the Apple Tree with Anyone Else but Me." There were silly songs. One of the biggest hits of 1944 was "Mairzy Doats," an adaptation of an old nursery rhyme: "Mares eat oats and does eat oats and little lambs eat ivy. A kid'll eat ivy too, wouldn't you?" Another hit, supposedly a Swedish love ditty, was "The Hut Sut Song." There were also the purely patriotic: "There's a Star-Spangled Banner Waving Somewhere," "Coming in on a Wing and a Prayer," and "God Bless America."

A Sleepy Town Awakens

The war affected small towns as well as large ones. Seneca, Illinois, is a good example. In 1940, Seneca was an undistinguished community of 1,250 residents. Located on the Illinois River in the northern part of the state, the town had been a small trading center for farmers of the surrounding area since its founding in 1850. Employment consisted mainly of supplying goods and services to farmers and local people. About a hundred residents worked in a powder plant southeast of the town. Another sixty men were employed at a grain elevator, built in 1938, which processed wheat that was transported in barges along the river.

BUY WAR BONDS

War bond posters such as this one aided in raising money to pay the enormous costs of World War II—more than $330 billion in military expenditures over a four-year period. Americans purchased about $135 billion in bonds during the war.

A young Frank Sinatra is surrounded by admiring fans in the 1940's.

The people of Seneca were homogenous, or very much alike, being mostly third-generation American families. There was a sizable group of Catholics of Irish background, and a smaller group of Norwegian Lutherans. No blacks resided there, and only one or two Jewish families. Everyone knew everyone else—and everyone else's business. Crime was a rarity, and juvenile delinquency was practically unknown. Seneca's police force consisted of a single officer. Commercial recreational facilities consisted of a pool hall with three tables, and five taverns. "We were all like one big family before the boom," said one elderly, long-time Seneca resident.

In 1940 the town could best be described as "sleepy." For years the biggest excitement had been the annual Fourth of July celebration and parade. This quiet atmosphere, however, was soon to be disturbed.

With the country at war late in 1941, the military anticipated the need to invade enemy-held territory (particularly Japanese-held islands in the Pacific) from the sea. A number of invasion craft were designed which could travel hundreds of miles under their own power, carrying troops and equipment for discharge on beaches. One such craft was known as the LST, or landing ship tank. Because coastal shipyards were working at full capacity, the navy looked for inland sites on which to contruct shipyards where the landing craft could be produced.

Seneca was one of the sites selected. In addition to a ready pool of labor in the surrounding area, it had the right sort of geography and geology. Craft built there could easily proceed down the Illinois River to the Mississippi, and from there to the Gulf of Mexico. A solid bed of sandstone lay under the flat bottom land along the river. Stripped of topsoil, this bed of stone would make an excellent foundation for a shipyard. The expense of driving pilings and constructing launching ways could be avoided. The Chicago Bridge and Iron Company, whose works were located in South Chicago, would supply materials for the construction of the yard and the ships. Steel and other materials would be transported on the Rock Island Railroad, which ran through Seneca.

Chicago Bridge and Iron Company

In this overview of Seneca, Illinois, taken in the 1940's, the shipyard in the foreground dwarfs the town behind it. New housing to accommodate the thousands of workers can be seen at right center behind the shipyard.

The navy's plans proceeded smoothly. By December, 1942, the shipyard was in full operation.

Almost overnight, Seneca's population increased by five hundred percent. Would-be workers—some skilled, many unskilled—swarmed in from a two-hundred-mile radius. About fifteen percent of the total came from southern states. The yard offered regular nine-hour days and fifty-four-hour weeks, with overtime pay after forty hours. Pay initially ranged from 83 cents an hour for unskilled labor to $1.20 an hour for welders, electricians, and other skilled workers. Not all the workers in the yard were men. By the summer of 1944, more than a thousand women were employed on construction tasks. At its peak of operation, the shipyard employed a total of 10,600 workers. Thousands of these workers lived outside Seneca; they commuted in cars each day to a parking lot with space for 2,500 vehicles.

The first important need was housing. Seneca residents rented spare rooms, added rooms to houses, and space for trailers in backyards and vacant lots. This was far from sufficient. To help fill the gap, the Federal Public Housing Authority built about fifteen hundred family units, and four dormitories accommodating three hundred men. A two-room apartment in one of the family housing complexes cost an average of $33 a month furnished, $27 a month unfurnished. Dormitory space went for $20 a month. In the apartments, most families cooked on hot plates. One woman, whose family moved into a furnished War Homes apartment after another family had left, described the dwelling:

> Since we have now tried the furniture we can speak with authority regarding its comfort. The two chairs are dining-room chairs with arms. The bed springs are like cot springs and the bed has two extra legs in the center to keep it from swaying. The mattresses are cotton, the bed pads have shrunk so they lack a foot of covering the mattresses each way. The beds are hard and unyielding.
> The electric plate is two-burner and dirty. It must have received very hard use. The former occupant of this apartment told me that she took her own plates with her. I cleaned the icebox today. It is lined with wood, and has wooden shelves. Since we have an apartment that was really planned for a two-room, we have a larger box than the other one-room apartments have. The icebox walls are about an inch thick and sound hollow when tapped. We can't get ice until tomorrow so I don't know its capacity. The icebox is placed in the farthest corner from the door so the iceman has to cross the complete length of the apartment. The cabinet contains four open shelves over the sink and stove; one drawer, two closed shelves and three open shelves, below. Former tenants built two shelves over the icebox. The sink is a deep one and the working surface on the side is already warped and cracked. The floors are stained, but look as if they have been stained over dirt. Neither cupboard nor floor was sanded before finishing. The floor boards are already spreading and quarter-inch cracks before the sink are common.

The clothes closet is merely an alcove with a shelf,
clothes poles, and hooks. The entire front is open
to the living room. We plan a curtain for it. The only
feature that shows any intelligent planning is the
kitchen cabinet. I swept the porch after it stopped
raining. Porch floor is laid with one-half-inch spaces
between the boards. It looked as if water drained
under the porch. One wonders about the mosquitoes
this summer with such a good breeding place close at
hand. Despite the chilly weather the apartment is
warm. The furnace is on and we have plenty of hot
water. Our first night is a quiet one; both neighbors
went to bed early. Now the stillness is almost
unbelievable.[18]

A sociologist who studied the boom in Seneca described
some of the problems that arose when the weather turned
from chilly to really cold:

The weather added to the frustration of the tenants
and to the confusion of management. Fall and
winter were wet at first, then cold. Without paved
streets or sidewalks, the approaches to the dwellings
were stretches of mud and ice. The central heating
plants in War Homes failed during the first cold
spell. Water pipes froze. Stoves had to be secured for
every dwelling unit while the central heating plants
were being reconstructed. Tenants blamed the
management for all these inconveniences.[19]

Even in the best of weather, the flimsy construction of
the War Homes presented problems. It was said, with only
slight exaggeration, that a person could hear a neighbor
brushing his teeth. A researcher reported this conversation
with the mother of a five-year-old:

[18] Quoted in Robert J. Havighurst and H. Gerthron Morgan, *The Social
History of a War-Boom Community* (New York: Longmans, Green, 1951;
reprint ed., Westport, Conn.: Greenwood Press, n.d.), pp. 68–69.
[19] Ibid., p. 71.

"It will be so good to have a yard and trees and privacy once more," she said. "This is no place to bring up a family."

The interviewer heard a child whimpering. "There's your little one calling," she said.

"No," said Mrs. Roberts, "that's next door, though it does sound as if it is in this house. You can hear so plainly, the next-door neighbors and even the ones next to them. And you can see their light at night through the cracks."[20]

Community Services Expand

The Seneca school system was the next to feel the impact of increased population. In September, 1942, the public elementary school had 175 pupils and six teachers. The high school had 131 pupils and six teachers. By January, 1943, owing to expanded enrollments, the school district was out of money and had to await the arrival of federal funds to pay its bills. At the peak, in September, 1944, the elementary school had 700 pupils and twenty-two teachers; the high school had about 250 pupils and twenty-two teachers. By this time a new sixteen-room elementary school had been constructed with federal funds. Later, another six-room building was added. Enrollment in the one Catholic parochial school in Seneca more than doubled, going from 45 to 95 pupils within a year, and from three to four teachers.

Other community services had to expand, too. Formerly Seneca had depended on a volunteer fire department. Now two firemen were employed full time, supplemented by volunteers. An additional well for drinking water had to be drilled. Before the boom, Seneca was a town of septic tanks and outdoor privies, sewage draining eventually into the river. By 1944 the community possessed a municipal sewage system, constructed at a cost of $187,000 to the federal government.

Prewar Seneca had had two small restaurants, serving about sixty meals a day. Now there were eight, serving two thousand meals a day. Seneca had had six food stores

[20] Ibid., p. 113.

before the war. These stores did a huge business during the boom, and they were joined by ten new ones. Thanks to high wartime incomes, people were able to afford better cuts of meat (when rationing made them available) and out-of-season fruits and vegetables (strawberries and tomatoes in January, for example). As for commercial recreational facilities, the boom produced a bowling alley, a movie theater, and an "amusement center" where people could dance to juke-box music and play pinball and slot machines. In addition, the shipyard and the apartment complexes had their own game rooms and other recreational facilities.

The churches in Seneca also felt the impact. Two new churches were built, one attended almost entirely by new-comers to the town.

A Cool Reception

Old-time Seneca residents prospered from the war boom. Yet many remained skeptical of its value and tended to be standoffish toward newcomers, particularly in the beginning. One shipyard worker's wife reported:

> Seneca folks look down on us! Oh yes, they do. I got a washerwoman promised; she lived up there back of Sand's store somewhere. It was all arranged, what day I'd send her the clothes, how much she charged, when I could get them and everything. Finally I remarked how hard it is to get overalls clean when men work so close to dirty machinery. She said, "Oh, I ain't going to work for none of them shipyard riff-raff," and that was the end of it. So I found a woman who lives in War Homes to do it. She does use too much bleach; my pillow cases are all wearing out.
>
> But Seneca people needn't be so snooty; there were only four bathtubs in Seneca before the shipyard came. And look at all the new things they've got since we came. Two new churches, two new school houses, a lot of extra teachers and police, good sidewalks, and a sewer system.[21]

[21] Ibid., p. 103.

Another woman reported that she had not been made welcome in the Lutheran church, and added:

> I took my little boy into the Sweet Shop to buy a paper and git him an ice-cream cone. The clerk, she said to him, "Whaddye want? Well, you don't get no stool if all you want's an ice-cream cone; git right down!" Then she turned to another woman and said, "That damned shipyard trash!" Right in front of my child, too. I went out of there without no ice-cream cone nor paper neither.[22]

A Typical Weekend

The Seneca police force expanded from one man to seven men and a car. Still, contrary to the experiences of some war-boom communities, Seneca remained relatively free from crime, despite the huge population increase. A week-night curfew for those under age eighteen was enforced. Most disturbances were of the "nuisance" variety—public drunkenness, gambling, occasional prostitution, and some window-breaking and other vandalism in apartment buildings. The biggest problem with thievery was pilferage from the Victory Gardens planted by apartment dwellers. Finally, under questioning, a group of children owned up and the looting stopped. More spectacular was the "famous street fight" of October, 1943. A policeman tried to arrest a drunk who was disturbing the peace on a street. The drunk resisted. In the melee that followed, the officer's pistol discharged, wounding two bystanders. Nothing more dramatic occurred during the entire boom, and the general absence of crime in Seneca was credited to "long working hours, recreational provisions for men, women, and children, and the watchfulness of shipyard and housing managements. . . . The town was never 'wide-open.' "[23]

Some old-timers, though, did not agree. "Why it's a wild town," said one elderly man to a postal clerk. "Wild, that's what it is. I was writing to my wife, 'You should come and see, then you'd believe me.' I'd like to have her spend one week-end here, Thursday to Monday."

[22] Ibid.
[23] Ibid., p. 290.

Chicago Bridge and Iron Company

Workers and their families observe the launching of one of the hundreds of LST's constructed at the Illinois shipyard during the war. Sailors claimed the letters LST were an acronym for "Large, Slow Target" because of the ship's large size and limited speed.

But, according to the sociologists who studied Seneca and the boom, a typical weekend progressed like this:

On Friday night the town seemed quite crowded with cars parked on both sides of the street all the way through town. The new bowling alley was jammed with young people, including a number of high school students. They seemed to be amateurs at bowling, but they were enjoying themselves. There was no rough language or anything that might be considered indecent during the evening at the bowling alley. As the evening wore on the bowling group divided into two parts. The younger group went next door for ice cream, and the older group went to the taverns.

There seemed to be more high school boys and girls in Seneca on Friday night than there were on the following Saturday and Sunday nights. On Saturday night between 9:30 and 1:00 o'clock there were distinctly fewer people in town. It was easy to find a parking space and there were approximately half the number of cars lining the streets. The bowling alley was just as crowded, and there were about as many high school boys and girls there as on the night before. It soon became apparent that many of them were simply waiting for the midnight show [movie] to begin. Several boys came in and asked several of the girls if they wanted to go car riding before the midnight show. These offers were all turned down except one. Again the group divided up when they finished bowling and part went to the ice-cream parlor for refreshments and several went to the taverns.

Following the group into a bar, the fieldworker found it filled with patrons, and in a room adjacent to it which had seats and tables, . . . families were eating and having beer and other drinks with their meals. The lateness of the hour did not seem to make any difference in the number of small children accompanying their parents. Slot machines were in evidence and in constant use. The crowd in the tavern seemed orderly on the whole, and were busy with eating, drinking, and general conversation.

The midnight show began not at midnight but at some time after eleven o'clock. There was a long line of people stretching out into the street, most of whom seemed to be high school students. They were a well-ordered crowd and seemed to be having fun.

Sunday night there seemed to be half again as many people as on Saturday night but not as many as there were on Friday night.

As early as twelve o'clock Saturday noon there were men staggering down the main street of Seneca. There were also men in various stages of intoxication on the streets on Sunday morning as early as 9:45. They seemed to be minding their own business and at least progressing toward some known destination. A policeman was in evidence at all times in Seneca on Friday, Saturday, and Sunday nights. . . .

Father Preston told the following story. He spoke to an urchin emerging from the movie house long after the curfew whistle had blown. "My lad, it's time you were home," "Yes, Father Preston, I'll go."

UPI

In August, 1942, U.S. Marines unload from landing craft on Guadalcanal in the Solomon Islands to prepare for an offensive against the Japanese.

But he started into a convenient tavern door. "Here,"
called the priest, "that's not the way home." "No,
Father, but I want to go in and tell my father and
mother I'm going home."[24]

The Course of the War

In March, 1945, at the Seneca shipyard, the hull of the one
hundred fifty-seventh LST was laid. By that time, the war
in Europe was rapidly winding down. Few Americans now
reflected on the dark days of 1942, when the newspapers
and radio carried mostly news of defeat and setback. During
that year, the Japanese overran the Philippines, and
occupied Malaya, Singapore, Burma, and the Dutch East
Indies. They took Wake and Guam islands, both American
possessions. In Africa, from Egyptian bases, the British
barely held their own against German and Italian troops.
Most of the war news from Russia had been grim.

There had been some encouraging events. The American
Pacific fleet defeated the Japanese in the Battle of the
Coral Sea in May, 1942. The following month, American
naval forces successfully defended Midway Island from
Japanese invasion. Then in August, after extensive shelling
from U.S. warships, marine units waded ashore on Guadalcanal, one of the Japanese-held Solomon Islands in the
South Pacific. The Japanese resisted fiercely, and it was
many months before Guadalcanal was securely in American

[24] Ibid., p. 242–244.

National Archives

The Fourth Marine Division moves up the beach at Iwo Jima in the Bonin Islands on February 19, 1945. An LSM (a smaller version of the LST) is seen in the background.

hands. But that invasion marked the beginning of the American "island-hopping" strategy, aimed at the eventual invasion of Japan itself. In November, 1942, American troops landed in Algeria to begin the joint American-British North African campaign.

The year 1943 saw victory in North Africa, the successful invasion of Sicily and the Italian mainland, and Italy's removal from the war. However, German forces invaded Italy from the north, making the Allied advance on Rome and beyond exceedingly costly. In Russia, Soviet troops began to take the offensive. In the Pacific, Americans invaded and secured more islands.

In 1944, American forces took Saipan and retook Guam in the Mariana Islands. Now within fifteen hundred miles of Japan, the United States could initiate regular bombing runs over Japanese cities. In June, 1944, Allied forces from England invaded France, later moving inexorably on Germany itself as the Russians approached that country from the east.

November, 1944, found Americans at the polls once again to elect a president. The Republicans had nominated

Governor Thomas E. Dewey of New York as their candidate. The Democrats stayed with Franklin D. Roosevelt, and there seemed no doubt that Americans would keep their wartime leader in office. Roosevelt won easily, with 25 million popular votes and 432 electoral votes to Dewey's 22 million popular votes and 99 electoral votes. In January, 1945, FDR took the oath of office for the fourth time.

The bombing of Japanese cities continued, and in Europe Allied troops moved ever deeper into Germany. Then on April 12, 1945, came shocking news. At the presidential retreat in Warm Springs, Georgia, President Roosevelt had suffered a cerebral hemorrhage and died. Millions of Americans mourned the man who had led them through twelve extraordinarily difficult years of depression and war—the man who had seemed, to many, more like the nation's father than its elected president. Vice-President Harry S. Truman, a former senator for Missouri, became president. Less than a month later, on May 8, Germany surrendered as Russian troops completed their seizure of Berlin, Germany's capital. Hitler was dead—a suicide—and the war in Europe had ended.

Americans rejoiced, but there was still another war to be won on the other side of the world. Plans proceeded for an invasion of the Japanese homeland, although another factor soon entered the picture. Throughout the war, Allied physicists and other scientists had been working in deepest secrecy on the development of a powerful new weapon, a bomb which would utilize nuclear fission. Early in August, 1945, a nuclear device was exploded on the desert in New Mexico. The bomb worked, and plans were laid to use it against Japan.

On August 6, a lone American bomber appeared in the cloudless sky over the Japanese city of Hiroshima. It dropped a single bomb. Seconds later, as a deadly, radiation-packed cloud mushroomed thousands of feet into the air over the city, a large portion of Hiroshima disintegrated. When conditions permitted some kind of accounting, about 92,000 people were discovered to be dead or missing. Three days later, on August 9, another bomb hit Nagasaki. The Japanese accepted surrender terms on August 14. World War II was over.

UPI

A large flag is displayed on 11th Street in New York City, its forty-six stars representing boys from the street who served in the armed forces.

What of the Future?

Back in June, 1945, the one hundred fifty-seventh LST manufactured at the Seneca shipyard slid into the Illinois River. During thirty months of operation, the yard had produced an average of slightly more than five LST's per month. The one hundred fifty-seventh was the last.

Only about two hundred shipyard families remained in the spring of 1945. The operation had been slowing down for several months. And soon all but five or six of those two hundred families left. The town's population dropped to about two thousand people and stayed there. Seneca's librarian remarked, "Oh, I can't bear all these goodbyes. I'm so blue most of the time. And the Seneca folks who grumbled most at first are all sorry now." Another lady said, "Well, it's getting awfully lonely here! I had the nicest men for roomers; and I always gave them a piece of pie when I baked—things like that. They were so nice it was a pleasure. But now they're gone." In a more practical vein, a businessman observed, "Yes, the boom's been a good thing for business, of course. But we'll get along without it; we did before. We've got to work hard, that's all."[25]

Most of the new businesses in Seneca closed. By November, 1945, there were ten vacant stores on the main street. Most of the new apartment buildings were torn down. Trailers disappeared. School opened in the fall of 1945 with only thirty more students than in 1942. The six-room school building, no longer needed, was demolished. The police force was cut back to two men. The Rock Island Rocket no longer made regular stops at the town's train station to pick up passengers.

Still, Seneca had benefited considerably. The community had a new elementary school, purchased from the federal government for $15,000, a fraction of its original cost. The town now owned a sewage system, acquired from the government for about the same amount. Seneca also had a new bank. It had been without one since 1933, when its only financial institution had failed under the strain of the Depression. The Assembly of God and the Holiness Methodist congregations still had their new churches. Construction of new housing was underway, and numerous older houses had been renovated and painted. "The town," wrote the sociologists who studied it, "had an air of newness it had not possessed for fifty years."[26]

The boom stimulated in Seneca residents a new interest in progress, a fresh feeling of community. One example of this was the formation of the Community Club, which was the primary force behind the establishment of the new bank. The club also pushed for road improvement to make it easier for farmers to get to town, and for the development and lighting of a baseball park. Prewar sleepiness seemed to have disappeared.

On the national scale, during nearly four years of conflict, the war had cost the United States 291,557 persons killed in battle; 113,842 military deaths from other causes; and 670,846 wounded. Compared to the millions of soldiers and civilians who perished in Europe and Japan—twenty million

[25] Ibid., p. 325, 326.
[26] Ibid., p. 330.

National Archives

New York City faced reconversion along with the rest of the country at the end of World War II.

in Russia alone—these figures might be thought to represent a small price for America's victory. But comparative statistics meant nothing to the thousands of American families who had paid that price. Gold-star banners, symbolizing the loss of a husband, son, or other relative, could be seen in the windows of many homes.

It was true, too, that the war had brought little in the way of economic deprivation to the American people. There were frustrating shortages, to be sure, but no destruction of property like that which occurred in Great Britain or other countries subjected to air raids or invasion. Indeed, the war had ended the Depression, literally with a bang. It had fattened savings accounts throughout the country, funds Americans were now eager to spend on consumer goods. Yet, at the same time, there was a feeling of apprehension. Many people had also prospered during World War I. And that war had been followed by severe recession in the early 1920's. As war plants closed and workers were laid off in 1945, the thought of that recession remained in the minds of those who had bitter memories of hardships during the 1920's and the 1930's.

"Reconversion"—the shift back from wartime to peacetime production—was the key word now. How would it work out?

SUGGESTED READINGS

Divine, Robert A. *Roosevelt and World War II*. Penguin Books.

Hosokawa, Bill. *Nisei: The Quiet Americans*. William Morrow.

Jacobs, William Jay. *Mussolini; Hitler; Stalin; Churchill; Roosevelt* and *Truman*. 6 vols. Glencoe, Twentieth-Century Biographies.

Lingeman, Richard. *Don't You Know There's a War On? The American Home Front, 1941-1945*. G.P. Putnam's Sons, Capricorn Books.

Shirer, William. *The Rise and Fall of the Third Reich: A History of Nazi Germany*. Simon & Schuster, Touchstone Books.

Toland, John. *The Rising Sun: The Decline and Fall of the Japanese Empire, 1936-1945*. Bantam Books.

Waitley, Douglas. *America at War: World War I and World War II*. Glencoe.

The *Queen Elizabeth* arriving in New York harbor on June 29, 1945. On board were some 15,000 passengers, most of them servicemen returning from the European Theater of Operations.

2

RECONVERSION

AND THE COLD WAR

When Americans awoke from celebrating their victory over Japan in August, 1945, two questions were uppermost in their minds. First, when would the government bring home the twelve million servicemen and women scattered through-out the United States and abroad? Second, how quickly would reconversion to a peacetime economy be accomplished so that there would be goods on which to spend the billions of dollars accumulated in wartime savings? And from the second question there eventually grew a third concern: What should be done about price controls?

Bringing the Boys Home

Following the end of the war in Europe, nearly a million persons were discharged from military service. The army, estimating that it would need one and a half million men for occupation duty in Germany and Japan, planned to reduce the size of the armed forces gradually through 1946. However, the army was forced to change its plans. Public clamor to "bring the boys home," and discontent within the services themselves, speeded up demobilization. Nearly one and a half million service personnel were released in the single month of December, 1945. The high rate of discharge continued into 1946. And although Congress voted to extend the draft in the spring of that year, it also set a top limit for military manpower at a little over a million personnel. This was a million fewer than President Truman had requested in his message to Congress in January.

Rapid demobilization caused dislocations in the economy and the loss of key personnel to occupation commanders in Germany and Japan. And many observers would denounce it bitterly as tension mounted between the United States and the Soviet Union in the early years of what would come to be called the Cold War. But pressure to get the troops home had been too great for the government to resist.

Most military personnel came home from overseas on troop ships that were crowded beyond belief. Bunks were stacked upon bunks, meals were served to groups almost around the clock, and there was little space for exercise or recreation. Space usually could be found for crap games or poker, however, and thousands of dollars changed hands. Those men shipped across the Atlantic Ocean on vessels such as the *Queen Mary* made it home in five or six days. Those sailing across the Pacific were forced to put up with crowded conditions for a longer period.

There was considerable speculation in the press about how ex-soldiers would adjust to civilian life. In retrospect, it seems that a lot of ink was spilled over very little. Many people feared that men trained to kill would have a hard time breaking the habit once they had shed their uniforms. It was true that a number of the returning veterans had become unhinged, to one extent or another, by combat. And there were some bizarre murder cases involving former GIs. But, on the whole, such fears were unfounded. Very few veterans resorted to killing as a common means of resolving disputes or expressing anger.

How would veterans get along with American girls after being deprived of female company for long periods or—worse, in the opinion of many—after associating with women of other lands? In general, they got along as well as ever. The high divorce rate among veterans caused alarm, but it was a common postwar phenomenon. Young men, stationed at training camps far from home and feeling the fatalism of war, married hastily before going overseas. The long months of loneliness that followed were hard on many young wives, especially those who had scarcely had a chance to get to know their husbands. During 1945, thousands of veterans obtained divorces on grounds of adultery. Many couples who had remained faithful also divorced, finding that the years of forced separation had changed them too

UPI

Like thousands of other veterans, twenty-one-year-old Gino Merli returned to the classroom after the war. Merli attracted more attention from the press, however, because of his war record—he was a winner of the Congressional Medal of Honor.

greatly, so that they were no longer the same persons they had been when they first married.

Would returning veterans be able to find jobs? Many did not want to, at least not right away. To ease the transition, the government provided veterans with twenty dollars a week for a maximum of fifty-two weeks if they were unemployed or earned less than a hundred dollars a month. Relatively few servicemen or women remained members of the "52-20 Club" for a full year.

Ex-soldiers were often treated gingerly at first. But most, left to their own devices, eventually took up life where they had left it some years before, finding employment or returning to school. One great aid to picking up civilian life again was legislation called the "GI Bill of Rights," which Congress had enacted in 1944. The GI Bill guaranteed loans made to veterans for buying houses or starting businesses. Its greatest impact, however, was in the field of education. The GI Bill offered up to $500 a year for tuition and books and $65 a month for living expenses to veterans who wished to go back to school. The stipend was later raised to $75 a month for single veterans, $105 for married veterans, and $120 for married veterans with children. Altogether, nearly eight million people took advantage of the GI Bill's educational benefits. They attended colleges, universities, or trade schools, or received on-the-job training in trades or agriculture. Benefits for World War II veterans ended in 1956. By that time, the total cost of the program had reached $14.5 billion.

The veterans—many of them married, some with children—found living conditions at colleges crowded as enrollments rapidly increased. They attended classes in hastily constructed buildings and lived in one-room apartments, in trailer courts, or in former army barracks. But they put up with inconvenience and discomfort because they were a serious group, determined to obtain degrees as quickly as possible so that they could get into the job market and earn good salaries. No one knows the exact figure, but it is certain that thousands of the young people who received college degrees after the war would not have been able to do so without the GI Bill. Historians have regarded the GI Bill as perhaps the most generous award our nation—or any other—has bestowed upon returning veterans. The legislation had further significance. It put the federal government into the business of subsidizing education to a greater extent than ever before, and it was of considerable benefit to institutions of higher learning as well as to veterans.

Price Controls vs. Inflation

The returning veterans were only one issue for concern. Another issue that generated even more heated discussion—and, in some cases, near hysteria—centered on price controls. Contrary to the World War I experience, no immediate postwar recession materialized. Certainly there were dislocations when the government cancelled billions of dollars' worth of defense contracts within days of the war's end. Millions of people were suddenly unemployed. But, as the economy gradually reconverted to the production of consumer goods, much of this unemployment disappeared. Reconversion was not rapid enough to suit most people, however. At the end of the war, nearly $140 billion had been accumulated in savings accounts across the country. After going without things they wanted or needed—new cars, refrigerators, and so on—for nearly six years, Americans were eager to buy.

Rationing ended. Blue and red stamps became merely souvenirs. But the Truman administration favored keeping price controls in force as a means of controlling inflation. As supply caught up with demand, bringing prices down, then the controls could be gradually lifted. The debate over whether or not to retain price controls raged for many weeks during 1946. The general public was ambivalent about the matter. On the one hand, Americans were weary of controls and shortages, and they had money in their pockets. On the other hand, they feared that if prices were not controlled inflation might run wild, reducing the buying power of their savings.

Special interest groups were clear about what they wanted. Farmers wanted controls lifted from food prices but retained for manufactured goods. Labor wanted all prices controlled but argued that controls on wage increases should be lifted. Manufacturers and businessmen did not make an issue of retaining wage controls. Wages could be dealt with at the bargaining table. But they did make a tremendous effort to persuade the public that it would be folly to continue price controls. Prices, they said, should be determined on the free market, on the basis of supply and demand. The lifting of price controls would spur production, they argued, bringing supply and demand into balance. If price controls were not lifted, manufacturers would have less incentive to gear up for consumer production. To this economic argument they added another, more political argument. They conceded that price controls might have been necessary during wartime, when the national interest demanded sacrifices from all segments of the population, business included. But to continue controls during peacetime, they maintained, would represent unwarranted—even unconstitutional—interference with the American free enterprise system.

In the meantime, as the debate went on, consumers and suppliers found their own ways to establish a free economy. When new cars began to appear on the market, for example,

UPI

As automobile production resumed after the war, thousands of new cars rolled off the lines, including these Lincolns awaiting the addition of bumpers and grilles.

there was a scramble to buy. As consumers competed with one another for the limited supply available, prices were bid upwards. But, to avoid violating price controls, the bidding was seldom direct. Instead, after a prospective customer had indicated a strong desire for a particular model and had agreed that the controlled price was fair, the transaction might go something like this:

Customer: "I'll bet you a hundred dollars you can't tell me on what day Christmas falls."

Dealer: "December twenty-fifth."

Customer: "You win" (handing over a hundred dollars). Or the dealer might add such unusual accessories as a picnic basket for an extra hundred and fifty dollars. Or a customer might buy a used car from a dealer for, say, six hundred dollars. Then he would drive it across the street to the same dealer's new-car lot, where he would trade it in on a new car for three hundred dollars. The effect, of course, was to add three hundred dollars to the price of the new car. Some buyers, disdaining subterfuge, simply handed over extra cash.

Farmers withheld livestock from the market, waiting for an end to controls, or made under-the-counter deals to dispose of it at above-control prices. Manufacturers also found ways around the regulations. Often they produced only items on which controls had been removed, turning out none of the items on which controls still remained. For example, textile manufacturers produced bedspreads but not shirts. Such practices created shortages, which annoyed the public, which in turn blamed the government.

The Office of Price Administration—the agency which established and enforced the controls—was due to go out of business on June 30, 1946, unless Congress passed legislation extending it. And while extension was being debated, there was a flurry of lobbying activity in Washington the like of which the country has seldom seen. Representatives of businesses of all kinds descended on the Capitol to argue for an end to the OPA. Representatives of labor unions, housewives, and other consumer groups arrived to lobby just as vigorously for extension. The OPA itself published material and ran radio commercials warning that serious inflation would follow the lifting of controls. According to one estimate, the agency spent about $250,000 on its own lobbying effort. In the opinion of some congressmen, this was highly improper.

Opinion polls showed that three-quarters of the American people favored keeping controls in force. Congress responded with a bill to do so. But, as the bill worked its way through the legislative process, it became loaded down with amendments making all kinds of exceptions and setting up complicated restrictions. As a law, it would be impossible to enforce. President Truman vetoed it and went on radio to tell the public why: the bill would do nothing to control prices and would merely waste the taxpayers' money by funding a useless bureaucracy. Congress promptly overrode the president's veto.

Meaningful price controls were dead. And the cost of living shot upward. A now-famous *New York Daily News* headline told the story: "PRICES SOAR, BUYERS SORE, STEERS JUMP OVER THE MOON." The last part of the headline referred to beef prices—round steak, for example, jumped nearly twenty-three cents a pound between January and August, 1946. Inflation also hiked the prices of other foods, manufactured goods, and even rent. Having chafed under regulations limiting rent increases, landlords promptly raised rents from fifty to as much as three hundred percent.

Considering itself gouged, the public yelped in protest. Congress quickly backtracked. Late in the summer of 1946, it passed a new law restoring price controls. But again, there were many exceptions. Furthermore, a Price Decontrol Board was created with authority to override the OPA on any item. This time the president signed the bill.

Probably the most dramatic result of the OPA's half-way revival was a nationwide meat shortage. In the fall of 1946, producers refused to ship their livestock to market. And this revolt delivered the final blow to price controls. Raising a ruckus, the public clearly indicated that it preferred high-priced meat to none at all. With this, President Truman gave up. He removed all price controls in the middle of October, 1946.

Prices continued upward in 1947, then backed off somewhat the following year. Table 1 summarizes the fluctuations in price for selected food commodities between 1945 and 1948.

Labor Tries to Catch Up

Months before the debate over price controls became really intense, organized labor had set out to play "catch up."

For the most part the postwar layoffs were temporary, and many workers had sufficient savings to tide them over. Of greater concern was the long-range future. With overtime pay a thing of the past, earnings shrank after the war. There was also the very real danger of inflation. Workers wanted wage increases that would enable them to maintain wartime standards of living, at the very least.

On the other side, industry had done well during the war. A report on profits issued by the United Steel Workers' union showed that the steel companies' after-tax profits had risen more than a hundred percent during the war years. The pent-up demand for consumer goods suggested that profits would remain high. From the labor point of view, industry could well afford to raise wages. The scene was set for some bitter battles.

Table 1. Price Index for Selected Commodities, 1945–1948

Year	Round Steak, Cents per Pound	Bacon, Cents per Pound	Eggs, Cents per Dozen	Butter, Cents per Pound	Milk, Cents per Quart	Potatoes, Cents per Pound	Sugar, Cents per Pound
1945	40.5	40.9	60.2	49.8	15.6	4.8	6.5
August, 1946	63.1	63.1	60.2	76.4	19.3	4.5	7.5
September, 1947	86.7	85.6	81.8	91.6	19.8	4.9	9.8
September, 1948	98.9	79.0	78.4	84.7	22.7	5.0	9.3

A wave of strikes for higher wages began almost as soon as the war ended, but the first big one came late in 1945 when the United Auto Workers struck General Motors. The company was vulnerable. A long strike would delay production, putting its competitors ahead in the race to get new cars on the market. But the strike would not be easy for UAW members, either. The absence of overtime work had cut weekly pay, reducing the amount of money the workers had been able to put aside to see their families through a long strike. In addition, more than a hundred thousand union members at General Motors had been laid off well before the strike, as reconversion to automobile production got underway.

At the time, average hourly pay at General Motors was about $1.10. Through their leader, Walter Reuther, the strikers demanded $1.45 an hour. If granted, this raise would bring average earnings up to nearly $60 a week, which was about the average during the war with overtime included. The company offered $1.20, an increase of only ten cents an hour.

Borrowing an idea from the steel workers' union, UAW economists calculated General Motors' costs and profits and

UPI

Strikers, including ex-servicemen in uniform, picket the General Motors plant in Linden, New Jersey, with placards bearing such slogans as "We Fought the Axis. Now We Fight G.M. for a Living Wage."

concluded that the company could easily pay what the union was asking. The company replied that its costs and profits were its own business and had nothing to do with labor negotiations. Still, publication of the figures was helpful to the UAW from a public relations standpoint. The General Motors strike dragged on through Christmas, with neither side giving ground.

In January, 1946, nearly two million additional workers walked out on strike—in steel, meat-packing, and electrical equipment. All wanted the same thing—higher pay.

The Truman administration expressed concern. Continued strikes in basic industries could seriously delay the shift back to a peacetime economy. The government's concern led to a new development in labor-management relations known as fact-finding. President Truman appointed a panel of experts to study the auto and steel strikes and make recommendations. Noting that the cost of living had increased by about thirty percent over prewar years, the panel suggested a raise of 19½ cents an hour for auto workers and 18½ cents an hour for steel workers. The panel recommended no increase in auto prices, but it did endorse a hike of five dollars a ton in the price of steel. After grumbling that the price increase was not enough, the steel companies accepted the settlement. General Motors refused. The company offered to raise wages by 18½ cents an hour, but no more.

Walter Reuther now took a stand on the penny separating the UAW's demand and the company's offer. Insisting on the full demand seemed obstructionist, however, and Reuther came under pressure from both the government and the public to give in. Finally, after the strike had lasted 113 days, he did. Work resumed at General Motors.

What did all this mean to an auto worker? In August, 1946, *Fortune* magazine published the story of William Nation, a window-molding inspector at General Motors. During the war, with overtime, Nation had averaged about $90 a week. After the strike his pay was set at $1.47½ an hour, or $59 for a forty-hour week. Here is how the Nation family of husband, wife, and five children spent the weekly income:

Walter Reuther, leader of the United Auto Workers, testifying before the Senate Education and Labor Committee on January 26, 1946. He claimed that the strike—then sixty-seven days old—was the result of "arrogance and defiance of G.M. of its legal and moral responsibilities."

Food	$25.00
Home mortgage	8.00
Coal (for heating)	1.49
Electricity	.75
Phone	.75
Gas (for cooking)	.41
Water	.32
Insurance premiums	1.96
Social Security	.62
Group hospitalization	.39
Union dues	.37
Lunch and cigarettes	2.50
Gasoline and oil	3.00
	$45.56

After allowing for these regular expenses, the Nations had $13.44 left each week for medical bills, entertainment, clothing, school supplies, and so on.[1]

Clearly, even after the strike, William Nation's standard of living was not what it had been during the war years. Furthermore, the strike had cost him about a thousand

[1] "Detroit Auto Worker," *Fortune*, August 1946, p. 152.

dollars in lost wages. In an interview with the *Fortune* reporter, he considered his situation:

> Roosevelt had good ideas. He believed that working people ought to have a better break and more security. So does Reuther. Reuther said something once about fighting for a more equitable distribution of wealth, and he went on to say if that was socialistic he was a Socialist. Nation feels the same way. "But it will be a long time before they even things up."
>
> Security is a hard thing to measure. Money is one way and health is another. Bill Nation is not any too sure of either right now. He has got his job, which brings him enough to live on. He has Social Security, of course, and if he works steadily that will mean about $65 or $70 a month after he is sixty-five. He has life insurance, but no pension or annuity to look forward to. He expects to make out all right if he doesn't get sick again. Every so often he has a spell, like the one a year ago when he was out of work three months. The doctors don't seem to know what it is. They give him shots, at $5 a throw, and a lot of expensive pills, and none of them do much good.
>
> The job is O.K.—he's not kicking. But it makes him sore when he reads what people say about the "unreasonable demands of labor." The 18½ cents they got last winter after the strike made it possible for him to feed his kids. Maybe that's unreasonable. "If I had one of the top G.M. guys' salary for just three months I'd be fixed for the rest of my life."[2]

As some strikes were settled, others occurred. In the spring of 1946, the Brotherhood of Railroad Trainmen and the Brotherhood of Locomotive Engineers threatened to walk out. This would tie up the nation's major transportation systems. Although President Truman had found a way to settle the steel and auto strikes, no amount of government pressure—even that applied personally by the president on union leaders—could change the train workers' minds. This angered Truman. With his temper white-hot, he

[2] Ibid., p. 154.

UPI

President Harry Truman (left) and Secretary of the Interior J. A. Krug (center), look on as John L. Lewis, president of the United Mine Workers, signs the agreement settling the coal miners' strike of April, 1946. A few months later, in November, Lewis would again call his union members out on strike after the coal companies refused to meet new demands.

announced that he would go before Congress to request legislation authorizing him to draft railroad workers into the army and force them to remain on the job if they should vote to strike. This was a drastic move, and the railroad union leaders backed down. As Truman began his address to Congress, an aide handed him a message saying that the unions had signed a contract with the railroad companies and would not strike. Although the legislation was no longer necessary, the House passed it anyway. The Senate took no action and the bill died.

Harry S. Truman caught a lot of criticism from organized labor. He had dusted off an old practice which most unionists thought was a thing of the past—the use of governmental power to break a strike.

The president did it again in a coal strike which occurred off and on from April to November, 1946. Here, however, he had strong public support, for the opponent was now United Mine Workers' president John L. Lewis. Few people cared for Lewis—that is, few people who did not mine coal. Over the years, when he appeared to have a choice between making the nation do without coal or calling a strike to benefit his workers, he unhesitatingly chose the latter. The time of year, winter or summer, had no bearing on his decision. Lewis's miners might idolize him—he made them among the highest paid workers in industry—but to the general public he was labor's number-one bogeyman.

It was a time of innovation in labor relations, exemplified by the introduction of fact-finding panels. Lewis came up with a new idea of his own in April, 1946. He demanded a union welfare and pension fund financed by royalties paid by the coal companies on each ton of coal mined. The companies refused to consider the idea, and UMW members walked off the job.

Coal supplies dwindled. Industries went on short shifts. City dwellers experienced "brown-outs"—shortages of electricity. Some trains stopped running. As public and governmental pressure grew intense, Lewis sent his miners back to work. After two weeks, he called them out again. Exasperated, President Truman ordered the Department of the Interior to seize the mines. But when miners still refused to work, the government backed off. The strike ended with coal companies agreeing to pay a royalty of five cents per ton into a union retirement and welfare fund.

That fall, Lewis came back with further demands—an increase in vacation pay and a higher royalty to finance the fund. Again the companies refused to listen. And again Lewis pulled his workers out of the mines.

This time Truman decided to use governmental power in another way. Government officials went to court seeking an injunction against Lewis and the UMW, ordering the miners to cease and desist their strike and return to work. Lewis ignored the injunction and found himself cited for contempt of court. The court fined the union $3,500,000, which was later reduced to $700,000, and levied a $10,000 fine on Lewis himself. After fourteen days on strike, coal miners returned to the pits.

This was one of the few times that John L. Lewis, whose leadership of coal miners went back to World War I, had met defeat. Those who upheld free and open collective bargaining deplored Truman's action. Overwhelmingly, however, the general public believed that Lewis got what he deserved.

Organized labor had come a long way since the 1930's, when the Wagner Act of 1935 granted unions the right to bargain collectively and forbade certain management practices as unfair. It was during the 1930's, too, that the bitter, prolonged, and bloody struggles to organize the auto, steel, and other industries took place. In 1945, union membership stood at fifteen million, three times larger than it had been ten years earlier. Union leaders had grown sophisticated. They dressed as well as their counterparts in management, and they knew how to use the tools of economic analysis and public relations to gain their ends. No longer were heads broken on the picket line. The balance of power between labor and management, which had long been weighted on management's side, seemed to have evened out.

But now, to many unionists, it appeared that government, just as in the past, had come down on management's side. The government had used its vast power to break strikes and had ruptured the process of collective bargaining. To many people outside the union movement, however, such action seemed just. Millions of Americans had concluded that unions had grown too powerful, that they now possessed the ability to injure the country seriously in their pursuit of selfish ends. And this was the opinion of Congress, too, after the wave of strikes in 1945 and 1946.

A Time of Reaction

After ten and a half years of depression and war, of social and economic experimentation, of increased governmental influence on everyday life, the country was in a conservative mood. Most people simply wanted to get back to normal (although their definitions of "normal" might vary). They wanted to experience a period of peace in which they could pursue thier own goals. They were especially weary of labor unrest and the inconveniences it had caused since the war's end.

Harry Truman's popularity, which had been high when he took over the presidency in April, 1945, had dropped considerably. Many factors were involved, not the least of which was his handling of price controls and his action in labor disputes. War, regulation, and strikes became associated with the Democrats. People were ready for a change. "Had Enough? Vote Republican!" was the only campaign slogan that amounted to much in the congressional elections of 1946. And the results showed that when the Eightieth

Congress opened in January, 1947, Republicans would control it. In the House of Representatives, Republicans held a 246-to-188 majority; in the Senate, a 51-to-45 majority.

On the whole, conservative Republicans had opposed such New Deal measures as Social Security, minimum-wage laws, direct subsidies to farmers, and all the increased government regulation that had characterized the Roosevelt era. For years, Republicans had been the minority party. Now, as the majority in Congress, conservatives saw an opportunity, if not to dismantle the New Deal, at least to modify it. And while they realized that it would be politically unwise to tamper with such items as farm subsidies and Social Security, they sensed that the public mood was right for measures to curb labor unions. And that is what Congress did, passing the Taft-Hartley Act.

This bill, a combination of various labor proposals introduced over the years, owed its name to Senator Robert A. Taft of Ohio and Congressman Fred Hartley of New Jersey. The bill aimed to outlaw "unfair labor practices," supposedly to bring labor under rules similar to those the Wagner Act had laid on management. Taft-Hartley made the closed shop illegal. A person no longer had to be a union member to get a job in an organized industry. It did allow the union shop, which meant that a person could be required to join a union after being employed. The bill forbade jurisdictional strikes, which had occurred in the past when two or more unions competed for the right to represent workers in a plant. Taft-Hartley also forbade secondary boycotts. These were strikes called against a company that was doing business with a company already struck. It empowered employers to sue unions for breach of contract. Further, union officials had to swear that they did not belong to the Communist party, and unions could no longer make direct financial contributions to political campaigns. Finally, the bill provided machinery by which the federal government could seek an injunction to hold off a strike for eighty days. During this "cooling-off" period, mediation and other means would be used to try to prevent a walkout.

To unions, Taft-Hartley was a bitter legislative pill. They spent a good deal of money lobbying against its passage. But

Senator Robert A. Taft of Ohio, coauthor of the Taft-Hartley Act, was regarded by many as the voice of conservatism in national politics. Earnest, industrious, and well informed, he was also extremely cautious in his approach to social problems. One liberal critic remarked that Taft had the best mind in Washington—until he made it up.

UPI

the Republican majority in Congress experienced little difficulty in pushing the bill through. When it passed, President Truman vetoed it—partly out of conviction, partly out of desire to rebuild labor support. But Congress overrode the veto by a comfortable majority.

Although unions labeled Taft-Hartley a "slave-labor law" and frequently tried to get it repealed, the law did not prove to be as limiting as it had first appeared. Labor learned to live with it. Ways were found within the law for unions to continue giving financial support to candidates they favored. The union shop did little to diminish union membership. Labor unions struck whenever they considered it necessary or advantageous to do so. And usually they won acceptable settlements.

Taft-Hartley, perhaps, aided Harry Truman more than anyone else. His veto brought him widespread support from labor, and labor's support proved helpful in the 1948 presidential campaign.

Harry Truman at thirteen. By the age of fourteen, he later claimed, he had read all three thousand books in the public library of Independence, Missouri. His favorite subject, then and throughout his life, was history.

A Year of Upset

A bantam-rooster sort of man, born in 1884 and raised in the town of Independence, Missouri, Truman had not gone beyond high school. He had, however, educated himself well, particularly by reading history. After graduating, he worked as a bank teller and construction timekeeper before returning to the family farm at the age of twenty-two. There he stayed until World War I. Volunteering for the army as a member of the Missouri National Guard, Truman ended the war as a captain of artillery. Afterward, with a partner, he established a haberdashery in Kansas City. The shop did well at first, then went bankrupt in the postwar depression that hit the country in 1921.

Turning to politics, Truman won election as a county judge (actually an administrative position in the Missouri system of local government). This job, like the job of presiding judge which followed it, came to him largely through the support of Tom Pendergast, head of Kansas City's Democratic political machine. In 1934, Pendergast selected Truman as a candidate for the U.S. Senate, an election he won with the machine's efficient help. His Senate career was undistinguished except for one thing—he headed

As a young man, Truman joined the Missouri National Guard, paying twenty-five cents a week to attend training sessions at the armory in Kansas City. Later, as a captain of artillery in World War I, he displayed a gift for command that could not have been predicted from his mild appearance, leading his men with distinction through the difficult Meuse-Argonne campaign of 1918.

a committee to police waste and fraud in war contracts, and he made a name for himself as a conscientious and fair investigator. In 1944, conservative Democratic leaders wanted to dump Vice-President Henry A. Wallace, whose liberal and sometimes fuzzy views offended them. They chose Truman as a safe vice-presidential candidate, and Roosevelt went along. On April 12, 1945, upon Roosevelt's death, Truman took over the presidency.

Although he was to gain in stature, few people at the time considered Harry S. Truman capable of handling the office. Unpretentious and folksy—although somewhat colorless and a flat, wooden speaker—Truman at least had a reputation for honesty and plain talk. None of the stigma of machine politics, to which he owed his political career, had rubbed off on him. Mostly, as anyone would, he found Roosevelt a hard act to follow. By his own estimation, he lived in the shadow of Roosevelt until his successful joust with John L. Lewis in the coal miners' strike of 1946 showed his ability to act tough. Now Truman wanted to stand in the limelight of history—as a star in his own right—by winning the presidential election of 1948.

But there were problems. Truman's veto of Taft-Hartley won back some of the labor support he had lost earlier by his handling of the coal and railroad strikes. From the liberal point of view, however, he had not handled the price-control issue well. He also won few friends with his proposal for universal military training; this would have involved reimposing the draft (which expired in 1947) and requiring all youths to serve the nation in some capacity. Mothers in particular disliked the idea, which never got very far. Subversion was a hot issue. Conservatives accused the president of not being sufficiently aware of the danger of Communists operating within the country.

The establishment of a Jewish homeland was another issue that generated political heat. In 1947, the United Nations debated and then approved a plan to partition the British-administered territory of Palestine, creating the independent state of Israel. Many Jewish groups in the United States strongly supported this plan. The Truman administration first endorsed the plan but later hedged, fearful of offending the oil-supplying Arab countries. Finally, Truman came out against the partition of Palestine. His popularity slipped as a result, but he regained much of this lost ground in May, 1948, by officially recognizing Israel as soon as it declared its independence.

On the whole, Truman's position looked weak. He had described himself as a simple man; to some people he seemed simple-minded as well. In March, 1948, only thirty-nine percent of the Americans polled thought that Truman was doing a good job as president.

Nevertheless, it was a job he was determined to keep. Although he made no formal announcement of his candidacy, he kicked off his campaign with his annual message to Congress in January, 1948. He proposed legislation that was essentially the platform on which he would run, a platform that would become known as the Fair Deal. Truman called for the extension of Social Security to millions of people who were not then covered; for increased federal aid to education; for an increase in unemployment insurance; for raising the minimum wage to seventy-five cents an hour; for action to curb further price increases; and for civil rights laws to abolish racial discrimination. Truman had proposed most of this before, in the fall of 1946 and again in his annual message the following year. Congress had not acted.

Truman in the early 1930's, during his second term as presiding judge of Jackson County, Missouri.

As before, most of Truman's proposals fell on deaf congressional ears. The exceptions were his ideas on civil rights —southern congressmen heard those clearly, and reacted with alarm. Truman favored a federal anti-lynching law, which southerners had defeated on numerous past occasions, calling it an encroachment on states' rights. He also favored legislation that would outlaw discriminatory state laws, such as the law requiring voters to pay a poll tax, which had been designed to prevent blacks from exercising the right to vote. He wanted to re-establish the Fair Employment Practices Committee, which had expired after the war, to secure job equality. He also wanted to establish a permanent commission on civil rights. Since 1932, the majority of blacks had supported the Democratic party. By proposing civil rights legislation—to which he had a true and personal commitment—Truman could expect to keep black voters in

Henry A. Wallace
inherited the
editorship of a
successful farm
journal from his
father and
grandfather. He
served as secretary of
agriculture from
1933 to 1940,
becoming vice-
president at the
beginning of
Roosevelt's third
term.

the fold in 1948. But there was a price. Southern Democrats adamantly opposed such laws, and there was talk of bolting the party if it endorsed civil rights.

Truman faced another source of dissension within the party: Henry Wallace. After the 1944 election, Roosevelt had given his former vice-president the job of secretary of commerce. Although the relationship was uncomfortable, Truman had retained him. A liberal—some people said radical—Wallace had become increasingly critical of the administration's policy toward Russia. Russia had expanded its influence in Eastern Europe, often by ruthless methods. From Truman's point of view, Russia was dangerous—an aggressor, and a fomenter of Communist revolution all over the world. Wallace tended to believe that the United States was as much at fault for the Cold War—the increasing tension between East and West—as the Soviet Union. And he said just that in a speech before a political rally in New York. Truman had read the speech earlier, returning it to Wallace without requesting any changes.

The president was roundly censured for allowing a cabinet member to oppose administration policy in public, particularly a cabinet member who seemed to side with the Russians. Truman backtracked, asserting that he had approved Wallace's right to make the speech but not its content. This helped little. Finally, to get himself off the spot, Truman asked for Wallace's resignation.

Henry Wallace went on to form his own party, which became known as the Progressive party, and attracted much support from left-wing political groups. Although he planned to be a candidate, Wallace obviously could not win the election. But he might attract enough liberal Democratic votes to help Truman lose it.

Reflecting on their excellent showing in the 1946 congressional elections, and noting Truman's multiplying troubles, the Republicans looked forward to the 1948 campaign as one they were bound to win. They met in June in Philadelphia, and theirs was the first convention ever televised. A coaxial cable carried the proceedings to about four hundred thousand homes along the East Coast. On the third ballot, the Republicans nominated Thomas E. Dewey, the governor of New York, for the presidency. Governor

UPI

Earl Warren of California became their vice-presidential candidate.

Dewey had made a creditable showing against the unbeatable Roosevelt in 1944. Then, in 1946, he had won reelection to the governorship of New York by the largest majority in that state's history. Furthermore, he had received high marks for his businesslike and efficient administration of the state. The polls showed him far ahead of Truman in national popularity.

Still, Tom Dewey was rather a strange politician. Although he was an affable and friendly person in private, he was quite the opposite in public. There he tended to freeze. His thin, dark mustache gave him a look of primness, which his forced smile and standoffish attitude only reinforced. One observer remarked, "I don't know which is the chillier experience—to have Tom ignore you or shake your hand." No one considered these shortcomings fatal, however, if for no other reason than that it was obviously a Republican year.

The Democrats did not want Truman, but there was no one else they could turn to. They liked General Dwight D. Eisenhower, who had become a national hero as commander of the Allied forces in Europe and was now president of Columbia University. But Eisenhower had never admitted to being either a Democrat or a Republican, denying any interest in politics. He refused to accept the nomination even if drafted. So, since they could find no other candidate who would have a chance against Dewey, Truman it had to be. As the July convention in Philadelphia approached, the Democrats grew increasingly glum.

Truman, ignoring criticism and opinion polls, stuck with the strategy he and his advisers had put together in 1947. Essentially, the plan was to attack, attack, and attack again. Following his message to Congress in January, 1948, Truman bombarded Capitol Hill with special messages, detailing legislation he had requested. This kept his name in the headlines almost daily. In March, he formally announced his candidacy. Early in June, he set out for the West to accept an honorary degree from the University of California and to give the commencement address there. This train trip, billed as a non-political journey and enjoyed

UPI

The Democratic candidates and their families pose for photographers at the convention on July 15, 1948. From left to right: Mrs. Max Truit, Senator Barkley's daughter; Harry Truman; Bess Truman; the Trumans' daughter Margaret; and Alben W. Barkley.

by numerous aides and reporters as well as the Truman family, lasted fifteen days. During that time Truman made several major speeches in such cities as Chicago and Omaha and made innumerable "whistle-stop" appearances on the train's rear platform. Sometimes, late at night, he came out in robe and pajamas to greet crowds. Whenever he could work it in, Truman blamed the nation's troubles—inflation and all the others—on the Republican-dominated Eightieth Congress. The whole trip was a masterful political maneuver and won the president much attention, even though opponents deplored the use of government money for an obviously partisan performance.

Still, the Democrats remained despondent. Their convention in Philadelphia stood in sharp contrast to the jovial and expectant mood that the Republicans had shown there earlier. And the Democrats grew even more morose after a young rebel group rammed through what was at the time an exceedingly tough civil rights plank for the party's platform. The plank had been developed by Americans for

Democratic Action, and Hubert H. Humphrey of Minnesota (soon to make his first bid for the Senate) presented it to the convention. He declared:

> There are those who say to you—we are rushing this issue of civil rights. I say we are a hundred and seventy-two years late. There are those who say—this issue of civil rights is an infringement on states' rights. The time has arrived for the Democratic party to get out of the shadow of states' rights and walk forthrightly into the bright sunshine of human rights.

The plank called for full and equal participation in the political process, equal opportunities for employment, the right of personal security for all citizens, and an end to discrimination in the armed services. It was adopted by the convention.

The South's reaction was predictable. Delegations from the southern states walked out. A group calling itself States' Rights Democrats met in Birmingham, Alabama, on July 17. There they nominated South Carolina's governor, J. Strom Thurmond, for the presidency and Mississippi's governor, Fielding L. Wright, for the vice-presidency.

Back in Philadelphia, the regular Democrats nominated Truman on the first ballot, selecting Senator Alben W. Barkley of Kentucky as his running mate. Accepting, Truman cheered the remaining delegates somewhat with a rousing speech in which he reviewed the last sixteen years of Democratic achievement and flayed the Eightieth Congress. "Senator Barkley and I will win this election and make the Republicans like it—don't you forget!" Truman promised. "We will do that because they are wrong and we are right." The Republicans had also come out for civil rights, public housing, and a minimum-wage increase in their platform. Ending his speech, Truman declared that he would call Congress into a special session that summer to give the Republicans a chance to put legislation where their platform was. He did that, but nothing came of it, which is what the president expected. Two weeks after the convention Truman demonstrated his own commitment to civil rights by issuing an executive order ending segregation in the armed forces.

UPI

J. Strom Thurmond, governor of South Carolina, was the Dixiecrats' candidate in the 1948 election. He carried several states in the lower South, winning 39 electoral votes. Later he represented his state in the Senate, first winning election in 1954 as a write-in candidate. In 1964 he switched parties once again, moving on that occasion to the Republican side of the aisle.

Philadelphia was the scene of still another convention. After the Democrats left, the Progressive party met there to make Henry Wallace's candidacy official. The party chose Senator Glen H. Taylor of Idaho to run for the vice-presidency.

The Democratic party was now split three ways, with the Progressives on the left, the States' Rights group (soon known as the Dixiecrats) on the right, and Truman and the remainder somewhere in the middle. Despite the upbeat note on which he had accepted the nomination, Truman's chances now looked worse than ever.

Confident Tom Dewey ran a cool, low-key campaign. Speaking in generalities—and no more frequently than absolutely necessary—he touched on issues only unintentionally. He behaved rather as if he had already been elected and was merely going through the traditional motions, marking time until inauguration day. Wallace ran a brave campaign, especially when he insisted on going into the South to speak before racially mixed audiences. But Wallace attracted too much support from the far left, particularly the Communists, and from the type of radicals who at a later time would be known as "crazies." His chances of winning many votes grew increasingly slender. The South remained solid behind the Dixiecrats. Truman's strategists wrote off that section of the country.

Governor Thomas E. Dewey.

But no other. Truman repeated and expanded his performance of June. He traveled thousands of miles, criss-crossing the country, delivering 271 speeches, appearing frequently on the back platform of his campaign train, speaking informally to almost anyone willing to listen. Reporters noted that the size and enthusiasm of his audiences seemed to be growing as the campaign progressed, but they attached little significance to this. Truman was putting on a good show, but it was not expected to help him when the votes were counted on November 3.

Over and over, Truman denounced the Eightieth Congress. He called the Republican party "a bunch of old mossbacks . . . all set to do a hatchet job on the New Deal." Said Truman, "If you let the Republicans get control of the government, you will be making America a colony of Wall Street." Truman pointed to the Taft-Hartley Act, with its restrictions on labor, and Congress's new tax bill, which he said favored the rich, as examples of the Republican mentality. He praised the Democratic record—the New Deal—and promised to extend its benefits. The president did not let up until election eve.

The newspapers called Truman's barnstorming a "give 'em hell" campaign. But it did not impress the politically wise, nor did it dampen Republican expectations. In October, public opinion pollsters folded their notebooks and put away their pencils. The figures stood at forty-four percent for Dewey, thirty-one percent for Truman. There seemed no reason to belabor a foregone conclusion.

The conclusion remained foregone until the day after the election, when sufficient votes had been counted to show a winner. And not since 1936, when a poll conducted by *Literary Digest* magazine predicted Roosevelt's defeat, had the pollsters been so wrong. Truman won 303 electoral votes to Dewey's 189. Thurmond had taken only 39, Wallace none. In popular votes, the count was Truman, twenty-four million; Dewey, twenty-one million; Thurmond and Wallace, one million each.

Truman's victory was the upset of the century, but it was not really the fluke that people considered it at the time. The president's strategy had been carefully planned and well executed. Analysis showed that he had held the labor vote. His stand on civil rights had appealed to black voters. He had a good turn-out among Catholics, many of whom were alarmed by Wallace's radical supporters. He won a good share of the farm vote, the farmers evidently fearing that the Republicans meant to dismantle the New Deal's program of farm subsidies. Although Truman carried only Massachusetts and Rhode Island in the Northeast, he ran well in other urban areas. Perhaps as important as any other factor was Truman's role as the underdog. This won him sympathy, while his peppery style, tireless campaigning, and boundless enthusiasm probably persuaded many voters that he deserved a chance to be president in his own right.

The pollsters went wrong because they used sloppy techniques and because they simply quit too soon. Surveys taken later showed that one out of every seven voters had made up his or her mind during the last two weeks of the campaign.

Truman—perhaps inspired by Alben Barkley's urging, "Mow 'em down, Harry!"—traveled twenty-two thousand miles on a whistle-stop campaign. Here in Chillicothe, Ohio, as in numerous other stops along the trail, he lashed out at the "do-nothing, good-for-nothing" Eightieth Congress.

Truman Library

UPI

Truman was delighted with the *Chicago Daily Tribune's* premature and erroneous headline announcing Dewey's victory, especially because the newspaper had always attacked him and his policies. George Gallup, the pollster who had also predicted a Dewey victory, quickly announced that he would conduct a survey to determine "just what happened."

Of these, three-quarters chose Truman. This last-minute support accounted for more than five million votes.

It was a great victory, and Truman savored it. Probably the most frequently reproduced photograph of the campaign shows Truman grinning happily as he holds aloft a copy of the *Chicago Tribune*, whose editors had put the paper to bed on election night with the banner headline "DEWEY DEFEATS TRUMAN."

The Fate of the Fair Deal

The election of 1948 was kind to Democrats in general. They won 263 seats in the House of Representatives, leaving the Republicans only 171. In the Senate, they enjoyed a majority of 54 to 42. As the Eighty-first Congress opened in January, 1949, the prospects looked good—at least superficially—for Truman's Fair Deal program. In his message to the new Congress, the president outlined basically the same legislation he had requested the year before. But a coalition of Republicans and conservative southern Democrats proved too strong for most of the bills Truman proposed. In the end, he found the Democratic Eighty-first Congress nearly as disappointing as the Republican Eightieth Congress he had criticized so bitterly during the campaign.

There was some action. Congress passed a public housing bill, but it turned out to be weak. It called for the construction of 810,000 units of low-income housing within six years, of which only 60,000 were actually built. Estimates at the time placed the need for such housing at 12,000,000 units. Congress also increased and extended Social Security benefits and raised the minimum wage. But Congress turned down the federal health insurance that Truman had asked for. This was partly because the American Medical Association spent about three million dollars for advertising and lobbying efforts to defeat what it called "socialized medicine." Congress did not approve federal aid to education. It did not change the immigration laws, which were then based on a quota system which strictly limited the number of immigrants that the United States would accept from Eastern Europe and most other parts of the world except Western Europe and the Western Hemisphere. And Congress did nothing about civil rights.

The Beginnings of the Cold War

Foreign affairs occupied a great deal of public attention during the second half of the 1940's. Indeed, except in wartime, foreign affairs have seldom affected domestic politics to the extent they did during the Truman administration. Deteriorating relations with the Soviet Union helped arouse a deep fear of internal Communist activity, a fear that would persist well into the 1950's. It is impossible to discuss domestic affairs of the time without first reviewing the foreign picture.

Fear of communism was nothing new in America. It dated from at least the time of labor unrest in the 1890's, and it grew in intensity following the Russian Revolution of 1917.

The United States had joined its World War I allies in sending troops into Russia after the war, hoping that this aid would help the so-called White Russians to overthrow the Communist regime. But the effort was unsuccessful, and the Allies eventually withdrew. After the war, there were many labor strikes in the United States, most of them called to obtain higher wages with which to meet inflation. It was easy for many people, prompted by statements from industrialists, to believe that the strikes had been fomented by "outside agitators"—that is, Communists. There was also, in 1919, a good deal of indiscriminate bomb-throwing and mailing of bombs to public figures. No instigator of these actions was ever caught, but the Communists got the blame. An Italian anarchist was killed by the premature explosion of a bomb he planned to use to blow up the house of U.S. Attorney-General A. Mitchell Palmer. Palmer, who had presidential ambitions, ordered the Justice Department to root out all the left-wing radicals in the country. Early in 1920, he and his agents staged raids in a number of cities, rounding up some anarchists and Communists but also many others—mostly immigrants—who were wholly innocent of political activism, radical or otherwise. Thousands were held without charges, and 556 aliens eventually were deported, most of them to Russia. The "Great Red Scare" finally ran its course. Fear of communism, however, did not. The U.S. government withheld recognition of the Soviet regime until 1933, when Franklin D. Roosevelt became president.

During the 1930's, when millions of Americans suffered from the worst depression in the nation's history, many young artists and intellectuals became disenchanted with capitalism, turning to leftist groups in search of an alternative. Some joined the Communist party. Others fought on the Loyalist side (which the Soviet Union supported) in the Spanish Civil War, which ran from 1936 to 1939. However, most of these people eventually became as disenchanted with communism as they had been with capitalism. Carefully staged purge trials in Moscow, instigated by the Russian dictator Joseph Stalin to eliminate rivals to his power, resulted in the execution or imprisonment of thousands of persons. Seeing in these trials the ruthless realities of the Soviet system, many previously sympathetic Americans turned away from the Communist party. Few Americans remained in the party after Stalin signed a pact of friendship with Adolf Hitler just before the German invasion of Poland

in the summer of 1939. Many men and women, now somewhat older and wiser, changed their political opinions. But
the fact that they had once been members of the Communist
party, or even of some other organization that might later
be called socialist or Communist in sympathy, would return
to haunt them. As early as 1938, the House of Representatives established a committee to investigate "un-American
activities." The term "un-American" was never defined, but
from the beginning the committee focused its search for subversives on the left of the political spectrum.

Because Germany was at war with Russia at the time of
Pearl Harbor, Germany's declaration of war on the United
States made the nation Russia's ally in World War II. Lend-
lease aid flowed to Russia as well as to Britain. Within the
United States, a sympathy developed for the Soviet Union
which was never experienced before or since. The American
Communist party regained strength. At the end of the war it
had about a hundred thousand members.

A falling-out between Russia and the United States began
before the war ended. Its repercussions would be felt, domestically and internationally, for years. It marked the beginning of the Cold War.

Poland was the initial point of dispute. Its future was discussed in a meeting at Yalta, in the Russian province of
Crimea, in February, 1945. Winston Churchill, Franklin
Roosevelt, and Joseph Stalin—representing Britain, the
United States, and Russia—agreed that after the war free
and open elections would be held to choose a Polish government. But the terms of the agreement were fuzzy, open to
interpretation. Both Churchill and Roosevelt supported
members of the Polish government-in-exile, which had existed in Britain throughout the war. Stalin did not.

The Russian army freed Poland from the Nazis and
helped a group of Polish Communists to set up a government there. A few non-Communists were admitted to the
government after the meeting at Yalta, but they were soon
expelled or arrested. The first postwar elections, held in
1947, supported the Communist regime—at least according
to the officially announced results. But the Russian army
was still firmly in control of Poland. From the American

U.S. Army

Churchill, Roosevelt, and Stalin at the Yalta Conference, February, 1945.

The Soviet foreign minister, Vyacheslav M. Molotov, in 1947.

point of view, elections under such conditions could hardly be called free. The United States government denounced the Soviet Union for breaking the Yalta agreement. President Truman personally accused the Soviet foreign minister, V. M. Molotov, of representing a nation that did not keep its word.

Within a few years after the war, Russia had managed either by force or by subversion to establish Communist governments in most of the countries its armies had liberated from the Germans. In addition to Poland, Russia controlled Hungary, Rumania, Bulgaria, and Czechoslovakia. The three formerly independent countries of Latvia, Lithuania, and Estonia were taken over immediately after the war and absorbed directly into the Union of Soviet Socialist Republics (Russia's official name). Native Communists won control of Yugoslavia and Albania on their own. Unlike the others, they refused to accept directions from Moscow. Of the Eastern European countries, Austria fared best. It was occupied jointly by British, American, French, and Russian forces and eventually regained its independence under a democratic government.

UPI

Germany, like Austria, was originally divided into four zones of occupation, with the Russians dominating the eastern sector. The city of Berlin, which lay within the Russian zone, was also divided four ways. From the beginning the Russians refused to cooperate with the western Allies in plans for the reconstruction of Germany, and it soon became clear that nothing short of war could persuade them to accept reunification of that country. Finally, in 1949, the three western zones were combined as the Federal Republic of Germany (usually called West Germany), with a democratic government headquartered at Bonn. In East Germany, the Russians established the German Democratic Republic, which in reality was neither democratic nor republican, being under the tight totalitarian control of the Soviets. Its capital was East Berlin.

To the officials of the Truman administration (and to most other people as well), these events clearly branded Russia as an aggressor. The question was, where would the Soviets stop? After fastening Communist governments on most of Eastern Europe, was it not likely that they would attempt to dominate the entire European continent? Farther east, in Asia, the situation was equally alarming. A Communist government had already been installed in North Korea, and Communist forces were battling with Nationalist forces for control of the vast country of China. Truman and his advisers saw in these developments evidence of a worldwide Communist conspiracy directed by Moscow.

The Policy of Containment

Events in Greece reinforced this idea. British troops had freed that nation from the Germans, reinstalling the monarchy. Britain then aided the Greek government against left-wing rebels, many of them Communists, who accused the king of corruption and oppression and wished to overthrow him. Presumably, Russia was aiding and encouraging the rebels.

Britain, battered by the war and deeply in debt, announced early in 1947 that it could no longer afford to help Greece. Truman's response was immediate. In a message to Congress in March, he said, "It must be the policy of the

General George C. Marshall served as the army's chief of staff during World War II, as U.S. ambassador to China from 1945 to 1947, as secretary of state from 1947 to 1949, and as secretary of defense from 1950 to 1951. The American plan for European recovery, which Truman called the Marshall Plan in his honor, was described by the London *Economist* as "the most straightforwardly generous thing any country has ever done for others." Marshall received the Nobel Peace Prize in 1953.

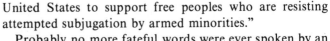

United States to support free peoples who are resisting attempted subjugation by armed minorities."

Probably no more fateful words were ever spoken by an American president. Truman committed the United States to the role of world policeman, ready to support any government, regardless of character, as long as its opponents were Communist. The president himself later called it a turning point in American foreign policy. The Truman Doctrine, as it became known, was a policy of containment. Under it, the United States would apply pressure—financial, diplomatic, and even military—to prevent any more countries from going Communist.

In his message, Truman asked Congress to appropriate $400 million to fight communism in the Mediterranean. The bulk would go to Greece. Some would go to Turkey, which was then under pressure from Russia. The Russians wanted free passage through the Turkish-owned Dardanelles, which would give their ships an avenue from the Black Sea to the Mediterranean Sea and Southern Europe. Congress cooperated with the president. Russian pressure on Turkey ceased. American aid, much of it military, was instrumental in the eventual defeat of rebel forces in Greece.

The same year, carrying containment a step further, the United States established the European Recovery Program. The program was popularly known as the Marshall Plan after Secretary of State George C. Marshall, who first publicly proposed it. Through the Marshall Plan, billions of dollars' worth of goods were poured into the Western European countries to help them rebuild. The Marshall Plan was humanitarian—indeed, Winston Churchill called it "the most unsordid act in history"—but it had underlying political goals. The American government believed that strong European economies would form a bulwark against the expansion of communism. This theory was based on the assumption that poor countries with weak economies were more likely to experience political and social revolution. Twelve billion dollars of Marshall Plan aid was ultimately distributed to sixteen European countries.

West Germany, then still under Allied occupation, received Marshall Plan aid. Economically, it quickly out-

UPI

An American transport plane approaches Templehof Airfield, Berlin, in 1949, bringing supplies of food and coal to the 2.2 million West Berliners blockaded by the Russians in an effort to force the Allies from the city. The blockade, begun on June 19, 1948, lasted 320 days.

stripped Russian-occupied East Germany. Another reason for West Germany's rapid economic recovery was that it possessed most of Germany's industry, while the East was mainly agricultural. Contending that the other Allies had abandoned the idea of a unified Germany, Joseph Stalin demanded that they evacuate Berlin on the grounds that it was no longer useful as a capital. Actually, it was Stalin who opposed reunification. He wanted the Allies out because the prosperity of the western sector of the city provided an embarrassing contrast to the impoverished eastern sector. Berlin lay deep within the Soviet zone, and when France, Britain, and the United States refused to yield, Stalin instituted a blockade. No ground traffic was permitted to enter or leave Berlin. The United States responded with an airlift, which at its peak carried 13,000 tons of food and other supplies into the city each day, at a daily cost of about $400,000

Mao Tse-tung on the Long March, the strategic retreat of his First Front Red Army of 100,000 soldiers from Kiangsi province, which was under heavy attack by Chiang Kai-shek's forces, to Shensi province. The march, which began in 1934, lasted more than a year and covered six thousand miles.

to the U.S. Air Force alone. The airlift continued from June, 1948, until May, 1949, when Stalin, finally convinced of America's determination, lifted the blockade.

In 1949, under American leadership, the North Atlantic Treaty Organization was formed. Consisting of the United States, Canada, and ten Western European nations, this organization was a military alliance designed to resist any armed aggression on the part of Russia. Russia responded by establishing its own alliance of Eastern European nations, an alliance known as the Warsaw Pact.

The year 1949 also witnessed the final collapse of Chiang Kai-shek's regime in China. Communist forces, who had been led to victory by Mao Tse-tung, marched triumphantly into Peking. With the remnants of his Nationalist army, Chiang fled to the offshore island of Taiwan, where he re-established his government. The Communist victory in China dealt a severe blow to containment and to previous policies regarding that country. Over the years, the United States had supported Chiang with billions of dollars' worth of aid. It had all been wasted. Now the United States refused to recognize the new Communist government in Peking. Despite the unreality of the action, and despite Truman's personal contempt for Chiang, the U.S. State Department continued to recognize the Nationalist regime as the only legitimate government of China.

The Cold War at Home

Events in the United States and Canada also tended to reinforce the idea of a Communist conspiracy. Early in 1945 it was discovered that persons involved with *Amerasia*, a journal devoted to Asian affairs and highly critical of Chiang Kai-shek, had access to government documents marked "secret" and "top secret." Several *Amerasia* people were known to associate with Communists, and government officials suspected espionage. The case, however, was never cleared up. Only three of the persons involved, including editor Philip Jaffe, were brought to court. Two pleaded guilty to a charge of illegal possession of documents and were fined. Charges against a third were dismissed. Some newspapers and members of Congress accused the government of covering up, but nothing was ever proved one way or another.

Later in 1945, a Soviet spy ring was uncovered in Canada. Its leader, British scientist Alan Nunn May, an avowed Communist, was tried and sentenced to a term in prison. That one ally (Russia) should spy on another (Canada) was a new wrinkle in diplomacy and to most Americans seemed reprehensible. No similar organization was found in the United States, but not for want of searching by the FBI and the House Un-American Activities Committee (HUAC).

One probable spy was identified, however. The House committee heard testimony from Louis F. Budenz, who had been among the top Communists in the United States before dropping out of the party in 1946. Budenz claimed that a man named Gerhart Eisler was an important Soviet spy in the United States, mainly on the basis of articles Eisler had written for *The Daily Worker*, the newspaper published by the American Communist party. Eisler refused to testify before HUAC and was cited for contempt. He was also held for illegal entry into the country. Before his trial, Eisler escaped to East Germany, where he became an official in the government.

Attention also focused on the entertainment industry, particularly in Hollywood, where there had been in-fighting between Communists and non-Communists in unions connected with the movies. The investigation quickly spread beyond union matters, however, as HUAC moved on the industry as a whole. Many famous stars appeared before the committee with testimony concerning the extent to which Communist propaganda had, or had not, been inserted into movies. But screening motion pictures to single out the "Communist line" proved futile, and to many people HUAC's charges of widespread Communist influence in Hollywood made the committee look ridiculous. One writer has called the evidence of propaganda "laughably thin." He recounted some of the evidence cited by the committee:

—A comedian who carried a party card whistled a few bars of "The Internationale" [the traditional Communist party song] in a scene where he awaited

UPI

Hollywood film stars, including Lauren Bacall, Humphrey Bogart, June Haver, and Danny Kaye, attending a session of the House Un-American Activities Committee in 1947. The stars came to protest the tactics of the committee, which Harry Truman in his memoirs called "the most un-American thing in America in its day."

an elevator. He credited himself with quite a coup. "Even in Brazil they'll know where I stand," he told a colleague. But even the [Communist] party thought he was stupid to expose himself. In any event, the scene was cut, for nonpolitical reasons.

—In a script about a boys' school, Lester Cole used a paraphrase of the old line, "better to die on one's feet than to live on one's knees." A handful of moviegoers perhaps would have recognized the source: the Spanish Communist La Pasionaria [Dolores Ibarruri].

—In rewriting *Sinners in Paradise,* about a group of airline passengers forced to land on a deserted South Seas island, Cole transformed an amusing but harmless U.S. senator into a pompous ass interested in using his government influence in making "private deals" on war supplies ("it's very easy for the government to wink an eye"). A beautiful rich girl became a socially callous heiress "going abroad to absent herself from the growing labor troubles at one

of her great auto plants, which closed on strike."
Some oil men were on the trip to explore munitions
markets ("when these gentlemen dump their munitions
in the Orient, they'll be responsible for . . .
approximately 100,000 lives"). Whatever Cole's
motives, the politicalization did little for the
Communist cause, for the picture flopped.

When pressed by committee critics for chapter and
verse of Communist taints in movies, Parnell Thomas
[HUAC's chairman] fell back upon three wartime films
that were undeniably pro-Russian. *Mission to
Moscow*, about Joseph E. Davies' service as
ambassador to Moscow, was depicted by critic James
Agee in *The Nation* as "almost describable as the first
Soviet production to come from a major American
studio . . . a great, glad two-million-dollar bowl of
canned borscht." Thomas also listed *North Star* and
Song of Russia. The Russian-born novelist Ayn Rand
told HUAC the latter was "terrible propaganda," and
described it as a Potemkin-village USSR with children
in operetta costumes and "manicured starlets driving
tractors." (In the same testimony Miss Rand indicated
she thought the United States had made a mistake
taking on Russia as an ally, and that lend-lease
equipment could have been put to better use by the
American military.) In the end, however, even *Time*,
whose coverage was generally friendly to HUAC,
concluded that the committee "had failed to establish
that any crime had been committed—that any
subversive propaganda had ever reached the screen."[3]

Good or bad, one might expect wartime movies to be favorable to an ally. But by 1947, of course, the political climate
had changed.

After keeping the country in an uproar for several months,
HUAC charged ten movie industry figures—most of them
screenwriters—with contempt for refusing to testify about
their own affiliations or those of their friends. The "Hollywood Ten" served one-year prison sentences at the federal

[3] Joseph C. Goulden, *The Best Years: 1945-1950* (New York: Atheneum,
1976), pp. 303-304.

penitentiary at Danbury, Connecticut. There they were joined by J. Parnell Thomas, the former chairman of the committee that had sent them there. Thomas had been convicted of placing people on his congressional payroll and pocketing their salaries.

Prison was only the first part of the punishment that the Hollywood Ten were to suffer. They, along with hundreds of others, were placed on "blacklists" that were circulated to movie studios, television networks, casting agencies, sponsors of commercials, and other sources of employment in the entertainment industry. Prospective employers were warned that the persons on the list were "politically unreliable" and that hiring them could result in a boycott of the company's programs or products. These blacklists were not government-sponsored, although the idea behind them and some of the names on them derived from HUAC's proceedings. The lists were prepared by private persons and organizations which represented themselves as patriotic but which in fact were often profit-making operations. Some, for a fee, offered to "research" the backgrounds of prospective employees. Others sold newsletters, books, and other materials on the subjects of loyalty and subversion. Because "political unreliability" had no real definition, except that given to it by the blacklister, people could find themselves listed—and suddenly unemployable—without even knowing why. Later investigations showed that some people were listed as "suspect" simply because they had once attended a United Nations fund-raising dinner, or some other such formal occasion, at which a Soviet diplomat happened also to be present.

Like the Red Scare of 1920, the blacklists represent an ugly episode in American history. Unfortunately, unlike Attorney General Palmer's campaign against subversive aliens, the episode was not short-lived. In the entertainment industry, blacklisting was practiced well into the 1960's. During those fifteen or twenty years, careers and sometimes lives were ruined. During that time, too, the practice spread to other industries and professions, including teaching.

Despite the fact that Truman had adopted a popular, "tough" stand against Russia, critics said he was "soft on communism" because he took no action to uncover possible subversives within the U.S. government. In March, 1947, to counter such accusations and shore up his sagging political fortunes, Truman set up the Loyalty Review Board to screen government employees. Because the board was not required to reveal the sources of its information, persons suspected of being security risks were unable to confront the witnesses against them. People were measured not by how well they performed their tasks, not by their present behavior or beliefs, but on the basis of past beliefs and associations. Rumor and doubt, not incontrovertible evidence, became the criteria for judgment. By the end of 1952, more than six million Americans had undergone loyalty checks. Nearly six thousand employees resigned from government jobs and nearly five hundred were dismissed. The resignations and dismissals occurred for a variety of reasons, including alcoholism and other personal problems revealed by the investigation. But the Loyalty Review Board found no spies or subversives.

Communists had been among the leaders in the drive to organize labor in the 1930's, and by the end of the war they could be found in many unions besides those associated with the movie industry. They were prominent in or actually controlled such unions as the longshoremen, office workers, transportation workers, and tobacco workers. Altogether, these unions included about a quarter of the CIO membership. And one result of the concern over internal communism in the 1940's was bitter battles within unions to get rid of Communist influence. By the end of 1947, these efforts, for the most part, had been successful.

The Hiss and Rosenberg Cases

The House Un-American Activities Committee could count few triumphs. Although conservatives praised the committee's work, liberals condemned its proceedings as inquisitorial and accused some of its members of grandstanding to gain publicity and votes. HUAC had named a lot of names but had turned up no conclusive evidence that anyone in public service was actively working to subvert the United States government.

Then, in 1948, came the Hiss case.

Whittaker Chambers, a *Time* magazine editor, opened the curtain on this drama, which would run for months, when he revealed to HUAC that he had been a Communist

Whittaker Chambers.

during the 1930's. Furthermore, he had engaged in passing on government documents. He told the committee that one person with whom he had associated during those years was Alger Hiss. Hiss, Chambers said, had been a member of a top-level group whose "original purpose was Communist infiltration of the American government [and] espionage was certainly one of the eventual outcomes."

Educated at Johns Hopkins University and Harvard Law School, Alger Hiss had been an official in the State Department. He had accompanied President Roosevelt to the Yalta Conference, where Allied leaders had made important decisions about postwar policies. Hiss had also been involved in the San Francisco Conference, where the United Nations was formed. At the time of Chambers's revelation, he was president of the Carnegie Endowment for Peace, an influential private foundation. In his forties, Hiss had enjoyed a bright career in public service, and his future looked even brighter. He was closely connected to the eastern intellectual-financial establishment. He was also well acquainted with numerous government figures, including Dean Acheson (who was to become Truman's secretary of state in 1949) and several Supreme Court justices. Thus, to many people, an attack on Alger Hiss was something more than an attack on an individual man. It was an attack on the New Deal, the United Nations, the State Department —on all that Hiss stood for and on all his associates over the years.

Hiss demanded equal time before the committee, and HUAC granted it without hesitation. Hiss denied that he had been a member of the Communist party or even a Communist sympathizer. Moreover, he denied knowing Chambers. Urbane and self-assured, Hiss made a deep impression on the committee. Most members were willing to let the matter drop.

One member was not—Richard M. Nixon, a freshman congressman from California. Nixon thought he detected evasiveness in Hiss's testimony and urged the committee to look into the matter more closely.

Nixon was persuasive, and HUAC brought Chambers back. In a closed-door session, with Nixon posing most of the questions, the committee learned details of Hiss's life from Chambers that only a close acquaintance might be expected to know. Next, the committee questioned Hiss again, also in a private session. Then it compared answers. Some of them matched, others did not. Nixon had drawn from Chambers the information that Hiss had known him under another name, his Communist party name, "Carl." Hiss conceded that he might have known Chambers under the name "George Crosley," but certainly not as a Communist agent. HUAC later brought the two men face to face in a hotel room in New York. Hiss identified Chambers as the man he had known as Crosley. He then challenged Chambers to repeat his charges outside the committee room so he could be sued for libel. Chambers complied, in a televised interview. He would not say, however, that Hiss had been a Communist party member, or that he had engaged in espionage.

Hiss sued. And in the resulting trial, Chambers for the first time produced a number of confidential State Department documents—some on microfilm, some typed, and some in Hiss's own handwriting—which he said Hiss had passed on to him in 1937 and 1938 as part of the espionage operation. Chambers explained that he had held back the documents before because he had not wished to destroy Hiss but only to disqualify him for any position of public trust. But he was now forced to use them, he said, to clear himself of the libel charge.

With the appearance of the documents, the case against Hiss became blacker. The statute of limitations prevented the government from charging him with espionage. However, a grand jury did indict him on two counts of perjury. He had lied, the jury concluded, when he denied giving Chambers government documents, and he had lied when he said he had not seen Chambers since January 1, 1937.

Much of the government's case hinged on whether some of the documents had been copied on a typewriter Hiss had once owned. Most of the testimony about the typewriter and other matters was contradictory. As a consequence, the trial, which began early in 1949, ended with a hung jury. In November of that year, the government tried Hiss again. This time the jury found him guilty of perjury, and he was sentenced to five years in prison.

The Hiss case aroused bitter controversy. Most liberals supported Hiss, at least up to the second trial. They could

Alger Hiss leaving federal court during his second trial on perjury charges. He was ultimately found guilty and sentenced to prison.

not believe that a man of his stature and credentials could have had anything to do with passing government documents. They considered the case as simply the most glaring example of HUAC witch-hunting. Conservatives, on the other hand, felt vindicated. They had long considered the New Deal, of which Hiss had been an outstanding representative, as socialistic at the very least. The case placed a black mark on the social and economic experiments the New Deal had fostered, and on those involved in them. Battered and bruised, liberalism everywhere was in retreat. The British journalist Alistair Cooke, who attended and reported on both trials, had this to say:

UPI

> Outside on the streets we were caught again in the political reverberations that lapped like waves from this stony center of punishment. If he was indeed innocent, it might never be proved; he had ahead of him only the long trail to the Supreme Court, that grievous distance from the wound to the hospital which makes judicial review so cruel a kindness. If he was guilty, as twenty of the twenty-four "ordinary men looking on" had judged him, then what he owed to the United States and the people who had stood by him was a dreadful debt of honor. For his conviction clinched the popular fear that those who were contriving a "clear and present danger" to the United States were determined it should never be clear and were publicly devoted to showing it was always far from present. The verdict galvanized the country into a bitter realization of the native American types who might well be dedicated to betrayal from within. It gave to ambitious politicians a license to use vigilance as a political weapon merely. It gave the FBI an unparalleled power of inquiry into private lives that in the hands of a less scrupulous man than its present chief could open up for generations of mischief-makers an official wholesale house of blackmail. It tended to make conformity sheepish and to limit by intimidation what no Western society worth the name can safely limit: the curiosity and idealism of its young. It helped therefore to

usher in a period when a high premium would be put on the chameleon and the politically neutral slob.[4]

Alger Hiss never ceased to protest his innocence. And in the mid-1970's he sought to prove it on the basis of thousands of documents and FBI reports he had obtained on the case. However, a scholar who studied the same materials, Allen Weinstein, reached a different conclusion. At first a believer in Hiss's innocence, Weinstein ended up agreeing with the verdict of the second jury. In 1978 he published a book, *Perjury: The Hiss-Chambers Case*, which revived the thirty-year-old debate.

The 1940's ended as one more important spy drama was about to be played out.

In 1949 Russia exploded an atom bomb, ending the American monopoly on that weapon. Early in 1950 a German-born physicist who had worked on the American A-bomb project, Klaus Fuchs, was arrested in Britain. Accused of passing atomic secrets to the Russians, Fuchs confessed. He then named Harry Gold, an American chemist, as the man to whom he had handed information. Gold, in turn, pointed to David Greenglass as his next-in-line contact. Greenglass had also been employed at the Los Alamos laboratory where the bomb was developed. Under questioning, he named his sister Ethel Rosenberg and her husband Julius as members of the group. Rosenberg owned a small machine shop, which he operated with three employees, on New York's Lower East Side. According to testimony, it was the Rosenbergs who had turned over the information to the Soviet Union.

Fuchs, Gold, and Greenglass were all charged with espionage, convicted, and sentenced to prison terms. The Rosenbergs, alleged to have betrayed national secrets directly to a foreign power, were charged with treason. They were convicted on March 29, 1951, and sentenced to death. And, after a great national uproar over the justice of the verdict, they were executed in the electric chair on June 19, 1953.

Like the Hiss case, the Rosenberg case remains controversial. For some people, the question of their guilt or

David Greenglass.

Ethel Rosenberg.

Julius Rosenberg.

[4] Alistair Cooke, *A Generation on Trial: USA versus Alger Hiss* (New York: Alfred A. Knopf, 1950), p. 340.

innocence has never been settled satisfactorily. Nor has the question of how much American atomic secrets helped the Russians. Atomic bombs, as it later turned out, were not terribly difficult to build. And the Russians possessed considerable scientific knowledge and technological ability, as they demonstrated in the 1950's when they placed the first satellite in orbit around the earth.

The Rosenberg case shocked the nation. It first hit the newspapers soon after the Chinese Communists completed their victory over Chiang Kai-shek. Despite billions in American aid, Chiang had gone down. Why? Conservatives found the answer in subversion and sympathy for communism in the government. And to many people, reading about the Hiss and Rosenberg cases almost daily, this answer seemed frighteningly possible.

Legislators shared these fears. In 1950 Congress passed the Subversive Activities Control Act, usually known as the McCarran Act. This law made it illegal to conspire to establish a totalitarian government in the United States, gave the government power to deport certain aliens, and required officers of Communist and Communist-front organizations to register with the U.S. attorney-general. Vetoing the bill as unworkable and contrary to American tradition, President Truman called the registration feature "about as practical as requiring thieves to register with the sheriff." Congress overrode the president's veto. At about the same time, many states passed their own anti-Communist laws as well as legislation requiring loyalty oaths for public employees, including teachers on all levels of schooling.

Other Points of View

American attitudes toward Russia and communism during the 1940's have been discussed and debated ever since. Recently the period has received a good deal of attention from a group of historians known as revisionists because they tend to reinterpret past events, often on the basis of present knowledge.

Some revisionist historians have suggested that the era of the late forties would have been different if those who controlled U.S. foreign policy at the time had had a better understanding of the international situation, and if they

Sovfoto

The city of Kiev, in the Russian Ukraine, as it looked after the occupying German forces were finally driven out in November, 1943. Thousands of other cities and villages across Russia were destroyed during the war, and 25 million Russians were left homeless.

had been more straightforward with the American public in explaining the motives for some of their decisions. Indeed, the more extreme revisionists blame the United States entirely for the tensions that developed after World War II.

Russia's relations with the other Allies were strained from time to time during the war. The most serious dispute arose over the question of when and where Britain and the United States would open a second front in Europe to relieve German pressure on the Soviet Union. As early as 1942, Stalin urged an invasion of France. However, calculating that they did not have enough manpower or equipment to challenge the Germans in Europe, Churchill and Roosevelt opted for the North African invasion. This did little to help Russia. Furthermore, to the Russians, the move seemed to demonstrate Britain's preoccupation with protecting its own interests in the Mediterranean. It had long been British policy to control the Mediterranean in order to safeguard the Suez Canal, Britain's "lifeline" to its Asian colonies. When the United States and Britain established a front in Italy in 1943 and finally in France in 1944, Stalin expressed

UPI

Children on their way to school stop to observe the ruins of St. Maria Church in Warsaw, Poland. Only a cross made of the charred beams indicates that this was once a place of worship.

only grudging gratitude. A really serious strain did not appear, however, until the Polish question arose during the closing weeks of the war.

Russia had suffered more from the war than any other nation—twenty million dead, thousands of towns and villages partially or completely destroyed, thousands of acres of farmland devastated, thousands of miles of roads and rail lines in ruins. Unfortunately, such suffering was nothing new for the Russians. In less than 150 years, Russia had been invaded three times from the west—in 1812 by France under Napoleon, and twice by Germany in the two world wars. In each case the attacks had come through Poland, a table-top land with indefensible borders which for centuries had been hostile to Russia. Revisionists reason that it was only sensible for Russia to insist on a friendly government in Poland following the war. Installing friendly governments in the other Eastern European countries was also a security measure, to insure a buffer zone between Russia and its traditional enemies. No matter what he promised at Yalta (and terms of the agreement were vague), there was no way that Stalin would chance an anti-Communist government in Poland. The establishment of Communist control over Poland was direct and ruthless. Communist domination of the remainder of Eastern Europe was more gradual, and according to the revisionists it was prompted by American actions that Stalin considered threatening.

Immediately after the end of the war in Europe, President Truman halted lend-lease. Ships bound for Britain and Russia were turned back. Truman later reinstated the program for Russia, which had years' worth of rebuilding to do, but the initial act appeared unfriendly and relations were harmed.

In July, 1945, the Allied leaders met at Potsdam, Germany, to tidy up plans for German occupation and to resolve other problems. One intense debate there had to do with Eastern European governments. The United States demanded "free access" to those governments as a price for recognizing them. Late in 1944, Stalin and Churchill had secretly agreed that Britain and Russia would share influence in Eastern Europe, with Russian influence predominating. Stalin considered Truman's demand an intrusion in a Russian sphere of influence. He refused to listen to demands that democratic governments be established. Truman later wrote that his experience at Potsdam left him "determined that I would not allow the Russians any part in the control of Japan. Force is the only thing the Russians understand."

During the Potsdam meeting, Truman informed Stalin that the United States had developed a new and formidable weapon. He did not say what it was, but in August of that year the world found out when an atomic bomb destroyed much of Hiroshima. By that time the Soviets had declared war on Japan, as promised at Yalta, but now their help was neither needed nor wanted. And they were excluded from the occupation of Japan.

The issue of the atomic bomb has remained a troublesome one ever since that fateful August day in 1945. Was its use really necessary? President Truman always maintained that

Library of Congress

The leaders of the three major Allied powers at Potsdam in 1945. From the left are Clement Atlee (who defeated Churchill in a general election in Great Britain), Truman, and Stalin. Truman's attitude at Potsdam was reported to be, "The Russians can either join us or go to hell."

it was, that it saved millions of lives, military and civilian, which otherwise would have been lost in a slow, agonizing island-by-island conquest of the Japanese homeland. But there have been doubters. Rexford Guy Tugwell, an economist and political scientist prominent in the Roosevelt administration, made the following observations:

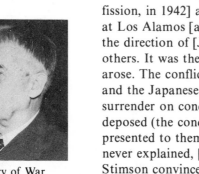

Secretary of War
Henry L. Stimson.

Some time after the Chicago success [with atomic fission, in 1942] an actual weapon was put together at Los Alamos [a laboratory in New Mexico] under the direction of [J. Robert] Oppenheimer and others. It was then that the question of its actual use arose. The conflict with Germany had been concluded, and the Japanese had been trying for months to surrender on condition that the Emperor not be deposed (the condition included actually in the terms presented to them later). Nevertheless, for reasons never explained, [Secretary of War Henry L.] Stimson convinced Truman that use of the bomb to destroy a city or two in Japan would end the war abruptly and would save the lives of a million

UPI

Americans who would die in the invasion being
prepared.

This argument, together with the recommendation
of the scientists' majority, was sufficient. Its use was
ordered; Hiroshima and Nagasaki were pulverized;
and the United States was left with the guilt of an
unnecessary genocidal attack that had overtones of
vast consequences. Was it approved more easily
because the Japanese were not white? Was it done to
forestall the participation of the Russians in the
Japanese defeat? They were getting ready to carry out
the pledge exacted of them at Yalta on the insistence
of General Marshall. After Hiroshima they were not
needed; and the occupation became an exclusive
American affair.

After twenty-five years the answers to these
questions could only be guessed at; but the suspicions
were stronger that issues other than Japanese defeat
had entered into the calculations concerning the
bomb's use. Whatever they were, they cannot have
rested on saving American lives as Truman would
persist in saying to the end of his life.[5]

Revisionists have concluded that President Truman
ordered the bomb dropped as a display to Russia of the
great power the United States possessed. The bomb, from
this point of view, was an important lever in the developing
American plan to prevent the spread of communism.

Revisionists also contend that Truman and his advisers
were mistaken in believing that Communist governments
and Communist parties everywhere were all controlled by
Russia. According to these historians, there was no mono-
lithic bloc of Communist nations, no effective worldwide
Communist conspiracy. Yugoslavia for one, Albania for
another, had resisted Russian domination. Communists in
those countries had achieved power on their own, and they
went their own way.

China was another example. According to revisionists,
the Russians neither liked nor understood the Chinese
version of communism. Orthodox communism, as practiced
by Russia, rested on industrial workers in the cities—the

[5] Rexford Guy Tugwell, *Off Course, from Truman to Nixon* (New York:
Praeger, 1971), pp. 189–190.

Generalissimo
Chiang Kai-shek.

proletariat. Mao Tse-tung based his movement and his revolution on the peasant farmers, a group the Russian Communists had never trusted or managed to convert to their beliefs. Far from aiding the Chinese Communists, say revisionists, Russia had gone along with the U.S. policy of supporting Chiang Kai-shek. After declaring war on Japan, the Soviet Union invaded the Chinese province of Manchuria. Upon the Japanese surrender, Soviet forces held Manchurian cities until Chiang, with American aid, could airlift troops to take them over. The Chinese Communists won their revolution on their own. And they won, say revisionists, because the Chiang government was so corrupt and oppressive that it lost the support of the people. Thousand of Chiang's Nationalist soldiers threw down their arms, refusing to fight for his regime. Thousands of others went over to the Communist side. Chiang himself lost China, not Communist sympathizers in the U.S. State Department. And who decided, ask revisionists, that China was Chiang's, or ours, to lose?

With respect to the Greek situation, revisionists cite the secret British-Russian agreement of October, 1944. They contend that Stalin deplored the left-wing uprising in Greece and wished it stopped because rumors of Russian aid to Greek Communists were harming the Soviet Union's relations with the United States and Western Europe. Stalin did not believe that Britain—or, as it turned out, the United States—would allow Greece to fall under left-wing control. To aid the rebels would be a waste of resources. Russia therefore gave the Greek Communists no help. Communist Yugoslavia did, principally by opening its borders to rebels seeking a temporary haven. Eventually Yugoslavia stopped sheltering the rebels, however, and this helped to bring about their defeat. According to revisionists, the United States simply replaced Britain as the protector of the Mediterranean. And further, they say, American aid to Greece enabled a reactionary and oppressive monarchy to retain control of a country in which a third or more of the people lived in abject poverty.

As to Russian designs on Western Europe, revisionists argue that Russia was in no position to be aggressive. The country had been too badly damaged by the war. Although the Soviet Union ended the conflict with some 260 divisions under arms, it quickly demobilized and cut military spending. Later it did rebuild its armed forces, but according to revisionists the buildup occurred only because Stalin came to perceive the United States and Western Europe as a threat to its own security—particularly after the establishment of the Marshall Plan and NATO. Revisionists do not deny that European Communist parties took orders from Moscow. But they contend that Stalin cautioned the strong Communist parties of France and Italy not to push for power but instead to go along with the moderate parties then in control. This, as much as the Marshall Plan, might explain why there was no attempted Communist takeover in Western Europe.

The United States presented the Cold War in terms of ideology—freedom versus communism. Revisionists suggest, however, that there were more important and less idealistic considerations behind the Cold War. One factor was Truman's inexperience in foreign affairs, and his desire to establish himself as a strong president. His "get tough with the Russians" attitude sprang as much from a personal need to prove himself as from any real threat to the national interest. A second factor, say the revisionists, was the desire of American businessmen and government officials to bolster capitalism in Europe. These people were not so much interested in promoting political freedom as they were in developing and monopolizing foreign markets for American goods. Furthermore, according to revisionists, the Cold War was good for business because it would lead to constant increases in the military budget, which would benefit industry in many ways. One revisionist historian, Lawrence S. Wittner, offers this point of view on the matter:

> The ebbing vitality of the liberal-Left, coupled
> with Truman's re-election in 1948, left the
> Administration a relatively free field in foreign affairs.
> Under the direction of [Dean] Acheson, appointed
> Secretary of State in early 1949, the Marshall
> Plan moved speedily along to bolster the forces of
> European and American capitalism. For chief
> administrator of the European Recovery Program
> [ERP], Truman named a Republican industrialist,
> Paul Hoffman, who according to Acheson preached a

"doctrine of salvation by exports with all the passion
of an economic Savonarola." In turn, Hoffman
appointed 400 lesser officials, primarily drawn from
business backgrounds. By the end of 1952, ERP
had distributed about $13 billion in American aid,
more than half of it to Germany, France, and
Great Britain. With this assistance, the nations of
Western Europe exceeded prewar production by 25 per
cent as early as 1950. But such economic recovery,
implemented by conservatives, left inequities in
wealth and income untouched and solidified Europe's
class structure. Journalist Theodore White observed:
"The workers could see only that what had been
saved was the *status quo*, that the recovery had
preserved their discomfort and given its fruits to the
privileged." Moreover, by propping up the old order,
the Marshall Plan encouraged the conservative
classes of Europe to attempt to maintain their colonial
empires. France fought the people of Algeria and
Indochina, the Netherlands battled Indonesian
nationalists, Belgium clung to control of the Congo,
and Britain suppressed colonial rebellions in Malaya
and Kenya. American corporations undoubtedly
benefited greatly from the program, for approximately
a third of American exports went to Marshall Plan
nations. Of the $4.6 billion worth of crude oil and oil
products Marshall Plan nations purchased between
April, 1948, and December, 1951, almost half
came from the five largest American oil companies,
with ERP financing the bulk of this. . . .

American business also gained significantly from
its expanding overseas operations, promoted and
protected by U.S. foreign policy. Between 1946 and
1960 the value of direct (or controlling) American
private investment abroad increased from $7
billion to $32 billion. Total U.S. investment abroad
increased between 1950 and 1960 from $19 billion
to $49 billion. During the 1950's the direct investment
outflow was $13.7 billion and the returned income
$23.2 billion—a handsome profit. About 75 per cent of
Standard Oil of New Jersey's profits in the late

1950's were derived from its foreign investments, while
Gulf derived two-thirds of its income from its
overseas operations. Reporting on a study in 1955, a
U.N. commission revealed that the net profit on a
barrel of Saudi Arabian oil selling for $1.75 was $1.40.
. . . The dominant position of American corporations,
particularly in the Third World, is illustrated by
the fact that in 1959 seven oil corporations,
five of them American, held two-thirds of the world's
recognized reserves, controlled the bulk of the world's
crude-oil production and refining, owned the major
pipeline systems, and controlled the tanker fleets.
The five American companies had overseas
investments of $9 billion, with contracts covering 64
per cent of the Middle East's oil reserves.

A growing volume of world trade proved equally
crucial to American corporations. Before World War
II, the net U.S. mineral imports amounted to less
than 1 per cent of domestic consumption, but in the
postwar years this pattern shifted significantly.
Between 1956 and 1960 the United States imported
over half its total metal consumption as well as
more than half its supply of fifty-four minerals and
crude commodities. A 1954 staff report of the
President's Commission on Foreign Economic Policy
noted that the "transition of the United States
from a position of self-sufficiency to one of increasing
dependence upon foreign supply is one of the
striking economic changes of our time." In return for
their vast imports of raw materials. U.S. corporations
inundated the markets of the "free world" with
the latest manufactured products. From 1950 to 1960
the value of American exports doubled to $20.6
billion, while American imports climbed by almost
two-thirds to $14.7 billion. Moreover, these figures
reflect only a declining fraction of total U.S.
overseas commerce, for America's rapidly growing
multinational corporations increasingly produced and
sold goods within foreign nations themselves.
Little wonder that the corporate elite took a keen
interest in American foreign policy. The United States

"must set the pace and assume the responsibility of the
majority stockholder in this corporation known as
the world," declared the treasurer (later chairman) of
Standard Oil of New Jersey in 1946. "American
private enterprise ... may strike out and save its own
position all over the world, or sit by and witness
its own funeral."[6]

The revisionist interpretation of the causes of the Cold
War rests at the opposite end of the scale from the conservative version. Conservative historians see Russia as a
ruthless aggressor and believe that postwar American
foreign policy was a necessary response to the Communist
drive toward worldwide domination. Revisionists fix much
of the blame on the United States, declaring that the Cold
War was almost a guarantee against a bad depression and
that for the most part Russian moves reflected a reaction
to those of the United States.

Still another point of view assigns less weight than the
revisionists to economics and less weight than the conservatives to ideology. To the so-called realist school of
historians, the Cold War simply demonstrated power
politics in action. Soviet objectives, they say, were limited
to Eastern Europe, where long rule by elitist classes had
failed to solve pressing economic and social problems. These
countries were ripe for change, for Communist governments. This was not the case in Western Europe. And the
Soviet Union recognized the difference, while the United
States did not. Realists consider Soviet activities in Eastern
Europe, and the Soviet desire to obtain free passage between
the Black and Mediterranean Seas, as extensions of traditional Russian policy.

Whatever the merits of these views, it is important to
remember that the Americans of the late 1940's did not
have the benefit of hindsight. Nor did the majority of them
have access to information on the possible reasons behind
Russia's policy in Eastern Europe, or on the divisions
within the Communist world. Even if they had, it might not
have mattered much. After all, Nazi Germany had offered
plausible reasons for expanding into Eastern Europe, and

[6] Lawrence S. Wittner, *Cold-War America: From Hiroshima to Watergate* (New York: Praeger, 1974), pp. 66, 118–119.

that expansion had proved merely to be the prelude to global war. And the Axis powers had fought with devastating effect despite the differences among them. Most Americans could judge the international situation only by what they read in the newspapers, and what they read frightened them. Country after country, including vast China, had fallen to Communists. And American citizens, including the prominent Alger Hiss, stood accused of aiding the Communist cause. The Cold War was distressing, but there were few people at the time who questioned its necessity.

As the 1950's opened, the Cold War abroad was already well underway. But the Cold War at home, pitting American against American, was only just beginning.

SUGGESTED READINGS

Ambrose, Stephen E. *The Rise to Globalism: American Foreign Policy, 1938-1976.* Rev. ed. Penguin Books.

Bernstein, Barton J., ed. *Politics and Policies of the Truman Administration.* Franklin Watts.

Freeland, Richard M. *The Truman Doctrine and the Origins of McCarthyism: Foreign Policy, Domestic Politics, and Internal Security, 1946-1948.* Schocken Books.

Goulden, Joseph C. *The Best Years: 1945-1950.* Atheneum.

Greenstone, J. David. *Labor in American Politics.* University of Chicago Press, Phoenix Books.

May, Ernest R. *The Truman Administration and China, 1945-1949.* J. B. Lippincott.

Miller, Merle. *Plain Speaking: An Oral Biography of Harry S. Truman.* Berkley, Medallion Books.

Stone, I. F. *The Truman Era.* Random House, Vintage Books.

Truman, Harry S. *Truman Speaks: On the Presidency, the Constitution, and Statecraft.* Columbia University Press.

Weinstein, Allen. *Perjury: The Hiss-Chambers Case.* Alfred A. Knopf.

Senator Joseph R. McCarthy has become symbolic of the fear of Communist subversion that haunted many Americans during the years 1949 to 1954.

3

THE KOREAN WAR

AND McCARTHYISM

The 1950's opened with the Cold War heating up. And the war in Korea, according to the Truman administration, offered another example of worldwide Communist aggression and conspiracy.

At the close of World War II, Russia had occupied Korea from its northern border to the 38th parallel. American forces occupied the territory south of the parallel. A Communist government was established in the north. In the south, the United States helped to set up a republican government which soon fell under the control of the conservative—some said reactionary and oppressive—Syngman Rhee. Adhering to agreements, both Russia and the United States withdrew their troops from Korea. It was hoped that the two Koreas would eventually be reunited, but instead they remained deeply divided over the type of government a united Korea should have.

Syngman Rhee employed strong-arm tactics and censorship to maintain his regime. Political opponents were jailed. Rhee's government, along with the Americans in South Korea who supported it, became increasingly unpopular. In May, 1950, Rhee's party was overwhelmingly defeated at the polls. Still, he remained in power.

On June 25, 1950, seeking to reunite the country by force, North Korea invaded the south without warning. Faced with heavy fire and superior mechanized forces, the defending Republic of Korea troops fell back.

On hearing the news of the North Korean attack, President Harry S. Truman quickly consulted advisers and then announced that the United States would aid South Korea against the aggressor. "The attack upon Korea," Truman stated, "makes it plain beyond all doubt that communism has passed beyond the use of subversion to conquer independent nations, and will now use armed invasion."

Next, the American delegate to the United Nations appeared before the Security Council with a resolution calling upon the U.N. to give "such assistance to the Republic of Korea as may be necessary to repel the armed attack and to restore peace and security in the area." The Security Council passed the resolution, establishing what President Truman later called a "police action." Truman declared, "For the first time in history the nations who want peace have taken up arms under the banner of an international organization to put down aggression." However, although many nations sent combat units, the vast majority of non-Korean troops were furnished by the United States.

Historians have since cast doubt on the idea that the Soviet Union was behind the North Korean move. Russia had helped to establish a Communist government in North Korea, and it had supplied that country with military hardware. But when the intervention resolution came before the Security Council, the Russian delegate was absent, having walked out some time before in protest over another matter. If the Russians had known about the North Korean plan to invade the South, asked the doubters, why didn't the Soviet delegate return to the Security Council meeting in time to veto the resolution? If he had returned, he could have prevented the U.N. action, forcing the United States to act alone. And this, as the Russians knew, would have presented Truman with a difficult political problem. Only a few months before, in January, 1950, Secretary of State Dean Acheson had drawn a line to indicate the perimeter of U.S. interests in Asia. Japan fell within the line, Korea outside of it. Even earlier, in 1947, the Joint Chiefs of Staff had declared Korea to be of little strategic value to the United States. If the Russians had blocked the U.N. resolution, the American public might have balked at the idea of carrying on a war independently to defend a country that had no real importance for U.S. national security. But the U.N. resolution put matters in a different light. With the

Unations

The Security Council votes on the resolution, introduced by Britain and France, to commit United Nations troops to the fighting in Korea under the unified command of the United States. The resolution, which was called "the gravest decision in United Nations history," was approved by seven favorable votes, with none against and three nations (Egypt, India, and Yugoslavia) abstaining. The empty seats visible in the photograph belong to the Russian delegation, which had walked out some time earlier in protest over the exclusion of Communist China from the United Nations.

resolution, Truman could and did present U.S. military involvement as a necessary measure to support and strengthen the United Nations, ensuring that the new international organization would not degenerate into uselessness as the old League of Nations had done following World War I.

Whether or not the Russians were really behind the North Korean attack, Truman and his advisers believed that they were. American involvement in Korea represented a continuation of the containment policy, but with an important difference. Now, for the first time, significant numbers of Americans were being asked to risk their lives in a full-scale military engagement in order to prevent the spread of communism.

Truman's call to arms was popular at first, and the initial objective of repelling the invaders from South Korea soil was achieved. But interest waned as the war bogged down into a frustrating stalemate. The conflict had nothing like the effect that World War II had on the home front. America fought the war with one hand; most people went about their business as though it did not exist. Korean veterans, on returning home, were shocked to find that there was so little concern.

The cost of the Korean War was high. About 54,000 Americans died as a result of the conflict; many more were seriously wounded. Between 1950 and 1952 the armed forces more than doubled, to a total of 3.6 million men. The defense budget increased from $13.1 billion in 1950 to $44.2 billion in 1952. Long-range costs were also high. The war did nothing to ease world tensions, and after its conclusion the United States felt compelled to maintain troops in South Korea and to spend billions of dollars supporting a South Korean government that was often accused of corruption, oppression, and disregard for human rights. The most fateful outcome of intervention in Korea was Vietnam. Korea marked the first step along a course that led to tragedy.

Back to the 38th Parallel

Under the command of General Douglas MacArthur, the hero of the Pacific in World War II, United Nations forces had pushed North Korean troops north of the 38th parallel by September, 1950. Originally, according to U.S. and U.N. statements, the purpose of the war had been simply to repel the invader. Now the objective broadened. United Nations troops pursued the enemy into North Korea, and it appeared that the country might be reunited by force— which is what North Korea had set out to do, only now the South would be the victor. But before that could happen, another factor emerged.

Because of America's failure to recognize Mao Tse-tung's government and its continued support of Chiang Kai-shek, the Chinese Communists regarded the United States as an enemy. And as U.N. forces approached the Yalu River, the border between Korea and China, the Chinese warned against proceeding farther. The Truman government ignored the warning. The advance continued. True to their word, on October 26, 1950, the Chinese moved more than three hundred thousand troops across the river. Soon the

U.S. Army

Men of the 187th Airborne make practice jumps at Taegu, Korea. The North Koreans, with heavy Russian-made tanks, proved a formidable enemy, and on July 8, 1950, General William Dean reported to MacArthur, "I am convinced that the North Korean Army . . . [has been] underestimated."

U.N. forces were in full retreat, falling back south of the 38th parallel. In the spring of 1951, the North Korean–Chinese advance was finally halted and pushed back just north of the 38th parallel. There the U.N. and Communist forces dug in, facing each other, to begin what would ultimately amount to more than two years of trench warfare. The war, now at a stalemate, could be won only by sacrificing many more thousands of U.S. and U.N. troops and by spending many more billions of dollars on equipment. Because the cost of total victory would be so high, and because the original objective of the "police action" had been met—that is, the North Koreans had been driven out of the South—Truman decided to negotiate a peace treaty. But the negotiations would drag on for many months, and during that time many more lives would be lost.

To conclude a war by negotiation was foreign to American tradition. As a victor, the United States had always been in a position to dictate terms. Truman's conservative critics deplored his decision to revert to the original war

U.S. Army

General Douglas MacArthur (right), commander of the United Nations forces, visits the front lines above Suwon, Korea, with his aides on January 28, 1951.

aim—repelling the invader. This, critics said, represented a "no-win" policy. Truman, however, was wary of the Chinese. He feared that a general war might develop with China, and if that happened the Russians might finally enter the conflict to support their Communist allies. He therefore continued to seek a negotiated peace.

General MacArthur also chafed under the "limited-war" policy. He publicly derided China's ability to wage an all-out war. He demanded authority to bomb targets within China or, at the very least, to bomb the bridges across the Yalu River in order to destroy the Chinese supply lines into North Korea. But Truman believed that such action would be too risky, and he stood firmly against MacArthur's urging.

MacArthur then began to make public statements criticizing the administration's policy. He even went so far as to write a critical letter to the House minority leader, Joseph Martin. Martin released the letter, which was the ultimate in insubordination. In April, 1951, Truman relieved MacArthur of his command—fired him.

Conservatives, still smarting over the fall of China to Mao Tse-tung's Communists, had almost idolized MacArthur. Truman's dismissal of the popular general touched off a storm of protest. Nearly eighty thousand telegrams poured into the White House, sixty-nine percent of them supporting MacArthur. The historian Eric Goldman summed it up:

> From San Gabriel, California, to Worcester,
> Massachusetts, Harry Truman was burned in effigy.
> In Los Angeles the City Council adjourned "in
> sorrowful contemplation of the political assassination"
> of the General. In Charlestown, Maryland, a woman
> tried to send a wire calling the President a moron,
> was told she couldn't, persisted in epithets until
> the clerk let her tell Harry Truman he was a "witling."
> In Eastham, Massachusetts, Little Rock, Houston,
> and Oakland, flags went down to half-mast. People
> savored scores of new anti-Truman stories. "This
> wouldn't have happened if Truman were alive,"
> the wisecracks went. Or "I'm going to have a Truman
> beer—you know, just like any ordinary beer except
> hasn't got a head."[1]

Dwight D. Eisenhower, serving as supreme commander of the Western European Defense Force, receives the news of MacArthur's dismissal.

MacArthur's return from abroad, for the first time since before World War II, was a catharsis for Americans frustrated and insecure over the course of world events. The general gave speeches in many cities. He was the object of a parade down Pennsylvania Avenue in the nation's capital which attracted three hundred thousand spectators. And he addressed a joint session of Congress, ending with these words:

> I am closing my fifty-two years of military service.
> When I joined the Army, even before the turn of
> the century, it was the fulfillment of all my boyish
> hopes and dreams. . . . The hopes and dreams have
> long since vanished, but I still remember the refrain of
> one of the most popular barracks ballads of that
> day, which proclaimed most proudly that old soldiers
> never die; they just fade away. And like the old
> soldier of that ballad, I now close my military career

[1] Eric F. Goldman, *The Crucial Decade and After: America, 1945–1960* (New York: Random House, Vintage Books, 1960), p. 203.

UPI

General MacArthur addresses a joint session of Congress on April 19, 1951. Vice-President Alben Barkley is seated to the left, Speaker of the House Sam Rayburn to the right. Altogether, the general's historic speech lasted thirty-four minutes and was interrupted by thirty ovations.

and just fade away, an old soldier who tried to do his duty as God gave him the light to see that duty. Good-by.[2]

A proud, imperious man who had won much acclaim for victories during World War II and who had run the postwar Japanese occupation single-handedly, MacArthur did not fade away quite yet. He continued his nationwide tour, delivering numerous speeches. And as a new-found rallying point for American patriotism, he attracted huge crowds. As Eric Goldman pointed out:

Apart from specific arguments about international or domestic affairs, MacArthur stood for an older America in a score of less tangible ways. His full-blown oratory recalled ten thousand Chautauqua

[2] Quoted in ibid., p. 205.

nights [a popular lecture series in the nineteenth and early twentieth centuries]. "Though without authority or responsibility, I am the possessor of the proudest of titles. I am an American," the General would say with a grandiose patriotism straight out of the days of William McKinley [president from 1897 to 1901]. In city after city MacArthur appeared with one arm around Mrs. MacArthur, another around his son Arthur, the unabashed symbol of Home and Motherhood and what he delighted in calling "the simple, eternal truths of the American way."

Like many Americans who were so disturbed by the dominant trends in the national life, the General moved closer to the theory of conspiracy in explaining the developments. An aura of dark conniving surrounded MacArthur's denunciations of "the insidious forces working from within," of those who would "lead directly to the path of Communist slavery." "We must not underestimate the peril," he cried out. "It must not be brushed off lightly. It must not be scoffed at, as our present leadership has been prone to do by hurling childish epithets such as 'red herring,' 'character assassination,' 'scandal monger,' 'witch hunt,' 'political assassination,' and like terms designed to confuse or conceal."[3]

General MacArthur eventually became president of Remington-Rand Corporation, and little more was heard from him. But his words concerning Communist conspiracy would continue to echo in millions of minds for some time to come, thanks to the activities of a senator from Wisconsin named Joseph R. McCarthy.

In February, 1950, shortly before the Korean War began, McCarthy kicked off what would become a virulent campaign against communism in America, making all the proceedings of the House Un-American Activities Committee look pale by comparison. Indeed, it would add a new word to the English language: McCarthyism. McCarthyism is defined as:

[3] Ibid., p. 208.

1. The political practice of publicizing accusations of disloyalty or subversion with insufficient regard to evidence.

2. The use of methods of investigation and accusation regarded as unfair, in order to suppress opposition.[4]

The names of United States senators have frequently been associated with important events and eras in American history. No one discusses the time of attempted North-South accommodation that led to the Compromise of 1850 without referring to the roles played by Senators John C. Calhoun, Daniel Webster, and Henry Clay. The Progressive era that spanned the first years of the twentieth century will always be associated with the names of Robert M. La Follette of Wisconsin and George Norris of Nebraska. It is impossible to recall the fight over the Treaty of Versailles at the end of World War I and the United States' decision not to join the League of Nations without remembering Senator Henry Cabot Lodge of Massachusetts. Senators have been influential in forming the foreign and domestic policies of the United States. Only one, however, has ever put his stamp on a period so indelibly that the era itself bears his name, and that one was Joseph R. McCarthy. The years of the early 1950's are not called the Korean War era. Instead, they are remembered as the McCarthy era or the era of McCarthyism.

The McCarthy Background

Joseph Raymond McCarthy was born in a rural area near the college town of Appleton, Wisconsin, on November 14, 1908, the fifth of seven children. McCarthy dropped out of school at the age of fourteen and went into the poultry business. Later he became manager of a chain store in a small Wisconsin town. At twenty he returned to high school, graduated, and entered Marquette University in Milwaukee. He began as an engineering student but switched to law after two years. Following a few years of practice in a small town, McCarthy ran for the office of district attorney of Waupaca County, Wisconsin, on the Democratic ticket. He

[4] *American Heritage Dictionary of the English Language* (New York: American Heritage, 1969), p. 809.

lost that election, but three years later he won the post of circuit judge, this time as a Republican. As a judge McCarthy earned notoriety for granting "quickie" divorces and for decisions that were overturned by the state supreme court. In 1942 he enlisted in the Marine Corps. He did not resign his judgeship, however; he simply took a leave of absence. The future senator later made much of his war record in the Pacific theater, referring frequently to himself as "Tail Gunner Joe." Actually he was an intelligence officer who never saw combat duty.

In 1944 McCarthy took a thirty-day leave of absence from the Marine Corps to enter the Republican senatorial primary contest against Alexander Wiley, then junior senator from Wisconsin. Although he lost the election, he polled a respectable number of votes. Two years later, by then out of the marines, McCarthy tried for the Senate again. This time his opponent in the Republican primary was Robert M. La Follette, Jr., who had first won office following his father's death in 1925. Contrary to all predictions, McCarthy won the primary. La Follette's long isolationist record, many observers believed afterward, worked against him. Also, La Follette had been a persistent critic of the Fascist dictator of Spain, Francisco Franco, and that probably cost him Catholic votes. McCarthy probably gained Catholic votes simply because he was a Catholic himself. It was a stunning victory for a relative newcomer to Wisconsin politics. McCarthy went on to win the general election in November, 1946, without difficulty.

McCarthy's Democratic opponent in the general election was Howard J. McMurray, a University of Wisconsin professor. During the campaign, McCarthy alleged that McMurray was supported by the Communist newspaper, *The Daily Worker*. McMurray could not overcome the effect of this allegation, and he lost badly.

McCarthy's early career as a freshman senator was unremarkable. Like many other senators, he lobbied actively for influential constituents. He made few Senate speeches and was not identified with any particular political issues. All this changed on February 9, 1950, when McCarthy made a Lincoln Day speech in Wheeling, West Virginia. In it, he said:

UPI

Although he was by then out of the service, Joseph R. McCarthy circulated this two-year-old photograph of himself in uniform to the press for publicity purposes during his 1946 campaign for the Senate.

Ladies and gentlemen, while I cannot take the time to name all the men in the State Department who have been named as active members of the Communist party and members of a spy ring, I have here in my hand a list of 205 [here some observers said he waved a piece of paper]—a list of names that were made known to the secretary of state as being members of the Communist party and who nevertheless are still working and shaping policy in the State Department.[5]

McCarthy's timing was excellent. Although he had produced no actual evidence for his accusations, they received indirect confirmation the following day when the arrest of Klaus Fuchs was reported in the newspapers. McCarthy's charges seemed credible, and millions of Americans—confused by the turn of postwar events—found in McCarthy's allegations a simple, satisfying explanation. Extremely pleased with the headlines he started to gather across the country, McCarthy went on to Denver. There he changed the 205 members of the Communist party to "205 security risks." Next day in Salt Lake City the 205 security risks became "57 card-carrying Communists." Ten days later, in a Senate speech, McCarthy transformed the 57 Communists into "81 cases." A numbers game began, and the phrase "card-carrying Communist"—whatever it meant—entered the language.

In Search of an Issue

So far as anyone knew, McCarthy had been little concerned with communism before February, 1950, and there was a great deal of speculation about why he had so suddenly and uncompromisingly identified himself with the issue. One widely told story of how McCarthy was launched on his anti-Communist campaign centered on a meeting he held in Washington with William A. Roberts, an attorney; the Reverend Edmund Walsh, a Catholic priest and teacher at Georgetown University; and Charles Kraus, a professor of

---

[5] No copy of the original speech exists. McCarthy spoke from rough notes only. People depended on newspaper reports and on McCarthy's own recollections for the content of his speech, and there was some confusion about what McCarthy actually said.

political science at Georgetown. McCarthy, the story went, stressed to his companions that he urgently needed an issue with which to capture national attention. After several issues were discarded, Father Walsh finally suggested an acceptable one—Soviet Russia as a threat to United States security through subversive activities.

Roy Cohn was a young lawyer who graduated from law school before he was twenty-one, too young to take the bar examination. For many months he was a close associate of McCarthy, serving as counsel on McCarthy's Senate investigative committee. While he admitted that the Washington meeting had occurred, Cohn declared that McCarthy had decided a month or two before that to emphasize the Communist issue. "McCarthy told me," wrote Cohn,

> that he had had no special interest in Communism
> prior to the late fall of 1949. He also had no special
> knowledge of the subject. He reacted in quite the
> same reflexive manner as most Americans to foreign
> "isms." He deplored them but saw no reason to
> become excited.[6]

But then, Cohn continued, just before Thanksgiving, 1949, three men came to see McCarthy. These men had a report allegedly prepared by the FBI showing in detail the extent to which Soviet spy networks were operating in the United States. The three men had decided that a member of the United States Senate might be persuaded to read the document and take action on it. They had selected four candidates. The first three senators they approached had refused to accept the document. McCarthy, fourth on the list, took the document home. He stayed up nearly all night reading it, and the next morning phoned his acceptance of the report and his decision to do something about it. Roy Cohn did not name the three men, or the three other senators who were approached. Nor did he suggest any reason why the men had selected those particular senators.

Cohn believed that McCarthy launched his campaign against Communists first of all because he was patriotic. McCarthy, wrote Cohn, "was worried about the threat to the

---

[6] Roy Cohn, *McCarthy* (New York: New American Library, 1968), p. 8.

UPI

Senator Joseph McCarthy and his committee counsel, Roy Cohn, share a lighter moment during one of the committee's hearings in 1954.

country posed by the Communist conspiracy, and he decided to do what he could to expose it." This worry apparently was ignited simply by reading the document, when for years the newspapers had been overflowing with discussions of Communist conspiracies. Cohn also said that McCarthy realized the political opportunities the cause presented. "He had found, he thought, a politically attractive issue he could sink his teeth into."[7] Earlier in his account, Cohn remarked,

> Joe McCarthy bought Communism in much the same way as other people purchase a new automobile. The salesman showed him the model; he looked at it with interest, examined it more closely, kicked at the tires, sat at the wheel, squiggled in the seat, asked some questions, and bought. It was just as cold as that.[8]

Cohn also quoted McCarthy on his phone call to one of the three men the morning after he had read the spy document. "I got him out of bed," McCarthy recalled, "and told him I was buying the package."[9]

[7] Ibid., p. 10.
[8] Ibid., p. 8.
[9] Ibid., p. 10.

McCarthy and His Methods

In a speech in Reno, Nevada, after Wheeling, McCarthy named some names. He cited them as specific evidence of Communist infiltration of the State Department and the continued presence of Communists there, although he actually called the persons neither Communists nor traitors. He simply wanted, he said, to "expose" them. The persons were John W. Service, Mary Jane Keeney, Gustavo Duvan, and Harlow Shapely.

Later, after someone straightened out the record, certain facts about these persons became clear. Service was a State Department expert on the Far East. He had been investigated as part of the *Amerasia* case and completely cleared. Mary Jane Keeney had worked for the State Department for less than four months. Gustavo Duvan had left the department in October, 1946. Harlow Shapely was an astronomer. He had supported some left-wing causes and at the time was serving as an American delegate to a UNESCO conference. Shapely had never worked for the State Department. From Reno, McCarthy wired President Truman that he could get more names from Secretary of State Dean Acheson. Truman did not respond.

McCarthy returned to Washington to an uneasy Senate awaiting a speech in which he had promised to discuss "eighty-one cases." Republican leaders were cautious. They realized that McCarthy was playing with fire and they were uncertain about his political value. Only later did they decide that he could be used to political advantage against the Democrats. Democrats were apprehensive, and growing angry. McCarthy had directly attacked the State Department. He had aroused doubts about the nation's Democratic leadership. And, although Democrats did not realize it at the time, he was building up his charge that for twenty years the Democratic party had been the "party of treason" in the United States. Senators on the Democratic side of the Senate were anxious that the man be slapped down, although they had worked out no plan to do so.

In his speech on the evening of February 20, 1950, McCarthy discussed his cases. He alleged that they proved that the State Department was full of subversives. In numerous instances he stumbled and retreated into vagueness. He made the hero of one case the villain of another. He named no names, and he allowed no senator to examine any of the documents from which he read.

Unfortunately, the Democrats did not respond in a way that would cast strong doubt on McCarthy's allegations. No one really bored in to pin him down and force him to produce his evidence for everyone to see. Instead, they concentrated on small points, interrupting McCarthy frequently with badgering questions, and helped create the impression that he was a lonely fighter battling for the salvation of the nation.

The same thing occurred during hearings of a Senate committee appointed to investigate McCarthy's charges. The committee, chaired by Millard Tydings of Maryland, opened hearings on March 8. Committee meetings were tumultuous. Democratic members quarreled with Republicans and vice versa, and all, at one time or another, became entangled with McCarthy. The hearings were so badly conducted and McCarthy was so frequently badgered that he was able to cast himself as a martyr, or at least as a tiny David fending off a huge Goliath. Although McCarthy accused certain persons of Communist affiliation or sympathy, once again he failed to produce evidence that would prove anything.

Senator Millard Tydings of Maryland.

In its final report, the Tydings Committee concluded that McCarthy had no list of names at all. What he had held in his hand that night in Wheeling was a three-year-old letter from former Secretary of State James Byrnes informing a congressman that permanent tenure for 205 unnamed State Department employees might be denied on various grounds, including drunkenness. The committee characterized McCarthy's charges and tactics as

> a fraud and a hoax perpetrated on the Senate of the United States and the American people. They represent perhaps the most nefarious campaign of half-truth and untruth in the history of this Republic.

Dean Acheson, whom McCarthy later attacked on several occasions for being "soft on communism" and called a traitor to his country, was even more blunt in characterizing McCarthy. Wrote Acheson in *Present at the Creation*:

McCarthy's Wheeling speech was not a brilliant
maiden effort in the traditional parliamentary or
senatorial style. It was the rambling, ill-prepared result
of his slovenly, lazy, and undisciplined habits with
which we were soon to become familiar. . . .[10]

The Tydings report had surprisingly little effect on
McCarthy's popularity and no effect whatever on his methods. In the fall of 1950, McCarthy went into Maryland to
campaign against Tydings' re-election. Using as evidence a
fraudulent composite photograph in which Tydings
appeared to be engaged in friendly conversation with Earl
Browder, the head of the American Communist party,
McCarthy succeeded in casting doubts on Tydings' loyalty
to the United States. Although he had earlier been considered invulnerable, Tydings was defeated. Politicians of both
parties began to develop a healthy respect for McCarthy's
power.

For the next two years, McCarthy continued to agitate the
Communist issue in the Senate and in speeches around the
country, and he continued to receive a great deal of publicity. Whenever a senator speaks, people—including newspaper reporters—listen, and McCarthy spoke about an issue
vital to the hearts of millions of Americans. Then, in 1952,
the American people elected a Republican president,
Dwight D. Eisenhower, and with him a Republican majority
in both houses of Congress. McCarthy became chairman of
the Senate Subcommittee on Investigations of the Committee on Government Operations. The position gave him a secure platform from which to carry on his crusade.

Congressional committees exist mainly for the purpose of
inquiring into the need for legislation and for examining
legislation that is proposed. Any interested citizen can
appear before a congressional committee to make known his
or her opinions on a particular issue. Committees possess
the power to subpoena witnesses to appear before them if the
committee members believe a person's testimony is needed
and if the person does not appear voluntarily. Congressional
committees are not judicial bodies. They are not bodies

Senator McCarthy
being interviewed by
the press after his
successful bid for
re-nomination to the
Senate in 1952.

[10] Dean Acheson, *Present at the Creation: My Years in the State Department* (New York: W.W. Norton, 1969), p. 362.

before which a person can be put on trial for an action or a belief. Although he was certainly not the first member of Congress to do so—or the last—McCarthy turned his committee meetings into courtroom sessions and, for all intents and purposes, accused and put witnesses on trial for their alleged parts in a Communist conspiracy. His language when examining witnesses was frequently intemperate and imprecise. His accusations were usually sweeping, and his proof often consisted of no more than rumor and hearsay. And his unwillingness to allow witnesses to give their testimony without constant interruption became notorious.

A great many people at the time said they agreed with McCarthy's aims but deplored his methods. They said they agreed that Communists and Communist sympathizers should be rooted out of the government, but they did not like the way McCarthy went about doing it. Treason and conspiracy to subvert a government are among the most serious charges that can be brought against a person. Simply accusing a person of treason or subversion can be tantamount to ruining his or her life. Such charges must be handled with caution and upheld by sound evidence and due process of law. If the end justifies the means, as many McCarthy supporters insisted was true, then government by law becomes a mockery.

Many people in the United States believed that all the talk about methods was a quibble. McCarthy, they said, was doing an important and patriotic job. Perhaps the lives of a few innocent persons were ruined and perhaps civil liberties were not nicely attended to, but all that was a small price to pay for ferreting out even one Communist. What good, they asked, would civil liberties do anyone if the Communists took over?

McCarthy's methods consisted of publicly accusing a person—directly or by implication—of having taken part in a Communist conspiracy. The "proof" might consist of the fact that during the 1930's a person had belonged, however briefly or tangentially, to an organization the United States attorney-general later cited as "subversive." Or a person might have written an article in a scholarly journal expressing disagreement with U.S. policy toward Russia or China. Or a person might have made a contribution, however small, to an organization which later appeared on the attorney-general's list of subversive groups, believing that the contribution went to support a worthy cause, which indeed it might have. An instance of this last type of accusation was related by Dean Acheson.

During the Tydings Committee hearings on McCarthy's Wheeling speech, Secretary of State Acheson held a press conference. He quoted from the press conference in his book *Present at the Creation*:

Secretary of State
Dean Acheson.

> Q: Are you aware, Mr. Secretary, that Senator McCarthy saw fit to inject Mrs. Acheson's name into the proceedings of the Tydings Committee?
>
> A: I understand that he made that contribution to the gaiety of the situation.
>
> Q: Do you have anything to say in that particular situation?

Acheson responded by saying that he had telephoned his wife to ask what the matter was all about.

> And she hadn't the faintest conception nor had she ever heard of the organization which Senator McCarthy accused her of belonging to. It was something like the Women's National Congress or something of that sort. So we looked up this organization and found that it was a merger of many others, among them one called the Washington League of Women Shoppers. That rang a bell. She said that ten years or so ago she had paid two dollars . . . and she was given a list of stores in Washington classified as fair or unfair to their employees. That was the extent of her recollection of this matter.
>
> I told her that it was charged that she was a sponsor of it. She said that was interesting and asked who were the other sponsors. So I read them to her and she said that sounded rather like the Social Register and she thought her position was going up, but she couldn't recall whether she had been a sponsor or not. . . .[11]

[11] Ibid., p. 363.

Mrs. Annie Lee Moss testifying before McCarthy's Senate investigating subcommittee in 1954.

UPI

Many others found it more difficult than Mrs. Acheson to "exonerate" themselves from McCarthy's charges. An implication of disloyalty, particularly when it was spread across the front pages of newspapers, was extremely difficult to combat. The American people, now soaked in the conspiracy theory, were willing to believe the worst of anyone. The experience of Annie Lee Moss was a case in point. Senator Charles E. Potter of Michigan described the case in his book *Days of Shame*:

First, in the morning, it was Annie Lee Moss who appeared before the McCarthy committee. She had once been employed by the Army Signal Corps but had been suspended from her job when called to a previous hearing by McCarthy and branded a Communist. She was being brought in now, McCarthy said, as an example of how the Army "coddled" Communists.

As the hearing opened, McCarthy told Mrs. Moss that he was curious to know why she had been shifted from working in the cafeteria in the Pentagon to Army code work when, Joe said, her superiors knew she had a Communist record. Here again was the routine distortion—the Army had no such record then nor at any other time. Mrs. Moss testified that she had not at any time been a member of the Communist party and that she didn't even know what the Communist party was until she had been called to the previous meeting. [Senator] Stuart Symington [of Missouri] told her that he believed she was telling the truth, and I think that summed up the feelings of all of us including Joe McCarthy.

Mrs. Moss faced him with dignity from the witness chair, and her all-out honesty and bewilderment at the charges, the grief at losing her government job, and Joe's realization that once again another of his balloons was about to be pricked, caused him to make up his mind to leave the room and the further questioning to Roy Cohn. Before he left, he was further humiliated by the loud applause of the audience after Symington told Mrs. Moss that he thought she was telling the truth.

Cohn tried to save something from this fiasco by saying that the subcommittee had substantiating testimony from an unidentified witness that Mrs. Moss had been a Communist in 1943. This was, of course, an underhanded and vicious attempt to use hearsay evidence, and Senator [John L.] McClellan [of Arkansas] protested vigorously. ...

It turned out that the "evidence" against Mrs. Moss was that a former undercover agent had testified that her name was one of many listed as members of Communist-front organizations. It was also brought out that there were three Annie Lee Mosses in Washington alone.

If any one of the three women named Annie Lee Moss who lived in Washington at that time was a Communist, research could certainly have determined which one it was; the hearsay evidence of a corroborating witness could have been produced by bringing in the witness to confront the suspect. Then, if this Annie Lee Moss who had been called in (or whichever one) might have been the true suspect, McCarthy would have had a case.

As it was done, this woman who did appear had been suspended from her job—and what person at her low-level income can afford to be out of work for even one day?—and the pattern of her life had been permanently damaged.[12]

McCarthy did not restrict himself to badgering small fry. He described President Truman and Secretary of State Dean Acheson as "the Pied Pipers of the Politboro," adding of the president, "The son of a bitch ought to be impeached." He called the distinguished General George C. Marshall, chief of staff during World War II and a former secretary of state, "an instrument of the Soviet Conspiracy." McCarthy labeled Owen Lattimore, a distinguished professor at Johns Hopkins University and an expert in Far Eastern affairs, "the architect of America's policy toward China," and the "number-one Soviet spy in the United

[12]Charles E. Potter, *Days of Shame* (New York: Coward-McCann, 1965), pp. 107–108.

States," alleging subversive activity by Lattimore as the cause for the "fall" of China. Although occasionally a consultant for the government, Lattimore had never been a member of the State Department.

Some Republican leaders saw McCarthy as a partisan instrument to use against Democrats, but the senator from Wisconsin spared not even members of his own party. He implied at one point that President Eisenhower too was a traitor, and he badgered Eisenhower's secretary of state, John Foster Dulles, into appointing a friend of his, Scott McLeod, as personnel chief of the State Department. Dulles had to clear all appointments with McLeod, who in turn cleared them with McCarthy. McCarthy was at the zenith of his power. Senator Margaret Chase Smith of Maine was one of the few Republicans to speak out against him, saying, "I do not want to see the Republican party ride to political victory on the Four Horsemen of Calumny—fear, ignorance, bigotry, and smear."

McCarthy wrote a book in 1952, defending his activities and his record. In it he explained a number of things, partially in a question-and-answer format:

Senator Margaret
Chase Smith.

UPI

Q. I have often heard people say "I agree with Senator McCarthy's aim of removing Communists from Government, but I do not agree with his methods." Senator why don't you use methods which could receive the approval of everyone?

A. I have followed the method of publicly exposing the truth about men who, because of incompetence or treason, were betraying this nation. Another method would be to take the evidence to the President and ask him to discharge those who were serving the Communist cause. A third method would be to give the facts to the proper Senate Committee which had the power to hire investigators and subpoena witnesses and records.

The second and third methods listed above were tried without success. The President apparently considered any attempt to expose Communists in the government as a cheap political trick to embarrass him and would not even answer a letter offering him evidence of Communist infiltration. The result of

THE KOREAN WAR AND McCARTHYISM

my attempt to give the evidence to a Senate
Committee [the Tydings Committee] is well known.
Every person I named was whitewashed and given a
clean bill of health. The list included one who has
since been convicted and others who have been
discharged under the loyalty program. . . .

One of the safest and most popular sports engaged
in today by every politician and office seeker is to
"agree with McCarthy's aim of getting rid of
Communists in government," but at the same time to
"condemn his irresponsible charges and shot-gun
technique." It is a completely safe position to take.
The Communist Party and their camp followers
in press and radio do not strike back as long as you
merely condemn Communism in general terms. It
is only when one adopts an effective method of
digging out and exposing the under-cover, dangerous,
"sacred cow" Communists that all of the venom and
smear of the Party is loosed upon him.

I suggest to you, therefore, that when a politician
mounts the speaker's rostrum and makes the statement
that he "agrees with McCarthy's aims but not his
methods," that you ask him what methods he himself
has used against Communists. I suggest you ask
him to name a single Communist or camp follower
that he has forced out of the government by his
methods. . . .

Whenever I ask those who object to my methods
to name the "objectionable methods," again I
hear parroted back to me the Communist *Daily
Worker* stock phrase, "irresponsible charges" and
"smearing innocent people." But as often as I have
asked for the name of a single innocent person who
has been "smeared" or "irresponsibly charged,"
nothing but silence answers. . . .

Q. Will you explain your use of the numbers 205
and 57 in your Wheeling speech?

A. At Wheeling I discussed a letter which Secretary
of State Byrnes wrote in 1946 to Congressman
Adolph Sabath [of Illinois]. In that letter Byrnes
stated that 284 individuals had been declared by the

President's security officers as unfit to work in the State Department because of Communist activities and for other reasons, but that only 79 had been discharged. This left a balance of 205 who were still on the State Department's payroll even though the President's own security officers had declared them unfit for government service.

In the same speech at Wheeling, I said that while I did not have the names of the 205 referred to in the Byrnes letter, I did have the names of 57 who were either members of or loyal to the Communist Party. The following day I wired President Truman and suggested that he call in Secretary of State Acheson and ask for the names of the 205 who were kept in the State Department despite the fact that Truman's own security officers had declared them unfit to serve. I urged him to have Acheson tell him how many of the 205 were still in the State Department and why. I told the President that I had the names of 57. I offered those names to the President. The offer was never accepted. The wire was never answered. . . .

Q. What is your answer to the charge that you employ the theory of guilt by association?

A. This should properly be labeled BAD SECURITY RISK BY ASSOCIATION or GUILT BY COLLABORATION rather than GUILT BY ASSOCIATION.

The State Department, whose publicity agents complained the loudest about guilt by association, has adopted in their loyalty yardstick what they condemn as the theory of guilt by association. . . .

Strangely enough, those who scream the loudest about what they call guilt by association are the first to endorse innocence by association.[13]

McCarthy and the Fifth Amendment

The Bill of Rights consists of amendments to the Constitution that guarantee certain personal liberties and spell

[13] Joseph R. McCarthy, *McCarthyism: The Fight for America* (New York: Devin-Adair, 1952), pp. 7, 8, 11.

out limitations on governmental power. The Fifth Amendment says:

> No person shall be held to answer for a capital, or otherwise infamous crime, unless on a presentment or indictment of a grand jury, except in cases arising in the land or naval forces, or in the militia, when in actual service in time of war or public danger; nor shall any person be subject for the same offense to be twice put in jeopardy of life or limb; nor shall be compelled in any criminal case to be a witness against himself, nor be deprived of life, liberty, or property, without due process of law; nor shall private property be taken for public use, without just compensation.

To charge a person with treason is to accuse him of a capital, infamous crime. Yet McCarthy sought no indictments by grand juries. And the section of the Fifth Amendment related to a person's right to refuse to testify if he believes that such testimony as he shall give might incriminate him was frequently brought to national attention during the McCarthy era. Several witnesses before the McCarthy Committee invoked the Fifth Amendment and refused to answer certain questions because they feared self-incrimination. This did not mean that such people were guilty of any crime. They were not even legally on trial for any crime. They were exercising a traditional and respected constitutional privilege. McCarthy quickly twisted a refusal to testify into *prima facie* evidence of an admission of guilt, and thus the phrase "Fifth Amendment Communist" was born. This phrase, like "card-carrying Communist," was patently absurd, but repeated over and over again it seemed to take on some kind of meaning, and it was used frequently to defame and smear those brought before the McCarthy Committee. Much of the dignity and value was drained from the Fifth Amendment as a consequence.

The Army Dentist: Irving Peress

By 1954 McCarthy was concentrating his attacks on the United States Army. He claimed to have discovered a spy

Dr. Irving Peress
testifying during
hearings on his
honorable discharge
from the army.

ring at an army radar laboratory at Fort Monmouth, New Jersey. As part of his investigation, McCarthy uncovered the fact that an obscure army dentist, Irving Peress, had been promoted from captain to major and shortly thereafter slated for discharge because there was reason to suspect that he might have had something to do with left-wing groups. The Peress case marked the beginning of McCarthy's downfall.

A New Yorker, Irving Peress was drafted into the army in 1952 and commissioned a captain. Like all new soldiers, Peress filled out and signed many forms, some of them containing disclaimers of membership in any organization considered at the time to be subversive. On one form Peress affirmed that he had not been a member of a subversive organization; on subsequent forms containing the disclaimer, he invoked the Fifth Amendment. Not until some months later was the discrepancy noticed, and no evidence was uncovered by the army that would have made it possible to take any legal action against him. Peress was promoted under an act of Congress which specified that dentists of his ability and experience should enter the service as majors, not captains.

McCarthy seized on the Peress case after the army had decided that Peress might have some connection with subversive activities and had made ready to discharge him, which was legally all that it could do. The army did, however, take a great deal of time in coming to this decision and so left itself open to the charge of bureaucratic bungling. McCarthy treated the episode as an opportunity to prove that the army was "soft on communism" and that someone with Communist sympathies had been responsible for Peress's promotion.

Peress appeared before McCarthy's committee in January, 1954. The following is a portion of the transcript of that hearing:

> *Chairman:* Did anyone in the Army ever ask you whether you were a member of the Communist party or a Communist party organizer?
> *Peress:* I decline to answer that question under the protection of the Fifth Amendment on the ground that it might tend to incriminate me.

UPI

Chairman: You decline to answer whether or not they asked you?

Peress: I again decline, claiming the privilege for the reason previously stated.

Chairman: Were you a member of the Communist party at the time you were inducted?

Peress: I again claim the privilege.

Chairman: Did any Communists intervene to have your orders changed so you would not have to leave the country? [Peress had been slated for shipment overseas. Illness in his family caused the army to change his orders at that time and subsequently he never left the United States.]

Peress: I again claim the privilege.

Chairman: You are entitled to the privilege. Is your wife a member of the Communist party?

Peress: I again claim the privilege.

And so the testimony went. McCarthy kept asking questions about Peress's association with the Communist party and Peress continued to invoke the Fifth Amendment, thirty-two times in all. The hearing made the headlines in many papers. McCarthy had, he said, uncovered another Fifth Amendment Communist.

A few days after the hearing, Peress requested from his commanding officer, Brigadier General Ralph W. Zwicker, an immediate discharge from the army. The request was granted and Peress returned to civilian life on February 2. Seeking to blame someone for Peress's promotion and the lack of any action against him, McCarthy summoned General Zwicker before his committee. A much-decorated officer, Zwicker had had a distinguished military career and was due for promotion to major general. In vain, under questioning by McCarthy and his counsel, Roy Cohn, Zwicker tried to make clear that the army had known about the Peress problem and had done all it could about the man—that is, it had discharged him. McCarthy was not to be deterred.

Brigadier General Ralph W. Zwicker. In private, McCarthy called Zwicker a "Fifth Amendment General."

Chairman: In other words, as you sat here this morning and listened to the testimony you heard nothing new?

Mr. Cohn: Nothing substantially new?

General Zwicker: I don't believe so.

Chairman: So that all of these facts were known at the time he was ordered to receive an honorable discharge?

General Zwicker: I believe they are all on record; yes, sir.

Chairman: Do you think, General, that anyone who is responsible for giving an honorable discharge to a man who has been named under oath as a member of the Communist conspiracy should himself be removed from the military?

General Zwicker: You are speaking of generalities now, and not on specifics—is that right, sir, not mentioning about any one particular person?

Chairman: That is right.

General Zwicker: I have no brief for that kind of person, and if there exists or has existed something in the system that permits that, I say that is wrong.

Chairman: I am not talking about the system, I am asking you this question, General, a very simple question. ... You will answer that question, unless you take the Fifth Amendment. I do not care how long we stay here, you are going to answer it.

General Zwicker: Do you mean how I feel toward Communists?

Chairman: I mean exactly what I asked you, General; nothing else. And anyone with the brains of a five-year-old child can understand that question.

The reporter will read it to you as often as you need to hear it so that you can answer it, and then you will answer it.

General Zwicker: Start it over, please. [The question was reread by the reporter.]

General Zwicker: I do not think he should be removed from the military.

Chairman: Then, General, you should be removed from any command. Any man who has been given the honor of being promoted to general and who says, "I will protect another general who protected Communists," is not fit to wear that uniform, General. I think it is a tremendous disgrace to the Army to

have this sort of thing given to the public. I intend
to give it to them. I have a duty to do that. I intend
to repeat to the press exactly what you have said.

At this point, McCarthy was at the peak of his popularity.
And yet, as Senator Ralph Flanders of Vermont remarked:

... He dons his warpaint. . . . He goes into his war
dance. He emits his war whoops. He goes forth to
battle and proudly emerges with the scalp of a
pink Army dentist. We may assume that this
represents the depth and seriousness of Communist
penetration at this time. . . .[14]

The Army-McCarthy Hearings

Badly stung by the public exposure of the length of time
it had required to dispose of the Peress case, as well as by
McCarthy's line of questioning and his condemnation of
General Zwicker, the army struck back.

Roy Cohn, McCarthy's committee counsel, had a young
friend named David Schine. Cohn brought Schine in to
work for the committee and, with McCarthy's blessing, the
two of them toured Europe to find out whether there were
any subversive books in United States Information Agency
libraries in various countries. Cohn and Schine found a
number of volumes they considered subversive—among
them John Steinbeck's *The Grapes of Wrath*—because the
books presented a not altogether pleasant picture of
America to European readers. Cohn and Schine—and
McCarthy—believed that only books with "positive" points
of view about the United States should be shelved in
American libraries overseas. What some observers called the
Cohn-Schine "book-burning expedition" received considerable attention in the press and was publicly condemned
by President Eisenhower in a speech at Dartmouth College.

When Schine was drafted into the army, both Cohn and
McCarthy exerted pressure on army officials to secure a
commission for the young man. Although they failed to
get him an officer's rank, Schine did seem to enjoy many
special privileges denied ordinary recruits undergoing basic

[14] Quoted in Goldman, *The Crucial Decade and After,* p. 270.

training. Stationed in New Jersey, Schine seldom served on KP duty, and he had frequent overnight and weekend passes that allowed him to spend a great deal of time in New York City.

In the spring of 1954, the army issued a report detailing Cohn's activities on behalf of Schine. The report alleged that Cohn, using the power of his position on the McCarthy Committee, had badgered and harassed army officials, including Secretary of the Army Robert Stevens, in order to obtain special treatment for his friend. According to the account of Senator Charles Potter of Michigan, the report prompted three members of McCarthy's committee—Karl Mundt of South Dakota, Everett Dirksen of Illinois, and Potter himself—to demand that McCarthy fire Cohn for improper conduct. McCarthy refused. He labeled the report an attempt to blackmail him into calling off further investigations into the army's "failure to root out subversives." The army then brought formal charges of improper attempts to influence the actions of its officers, and a Senate committee, chaired by Karl Mundt, was established. On April 22, 1954, the Army-McCarthy hearings opened.

One of the most significant things about the hearings, which went on for several weeks, was that they were televised. Day after day, millions of viewers could watch the members of their government in action, and they could make certain judgments for themselves. In particular, they could observe McCarthy at first hand and could see how he operated. No longer did they need to depend on what they read in newspapers and magazines in order to form an opinion of the man.

Few of the principals in the Army-McCarthy hearings emerged altogether unscathed. Secretary of the Army Stevens at first came across as a man who had simply knuckled under to Cohn and McCarthy. However, after several grueling days of testimony under questioning by the attorney for the committee, Ray Jenkins, and by committee members themselves, Stevens began to win the sympathy of television audiences and newsmen. Roy Cohn appeared as a dark young Svengali, a manipulator who had exerted unusual and nefarious influence on high officials to gain favors for Schine and who had threatened those

Joseph McCarthy interrupts proceedings during the Army-McCarthy hearings to make one of his numerous points of order.

officials with dire consequences should they refuse. McCarthy fared the worst of all. He badgered witnesses, gave obscure answers to questions, clowned, at times pretended indifference, delivered long and sometimes self-righteous harangues, and in general made an unfavorable impression on many viewers.

One notable exception in this rather unattractive cast of characters was Joseph Welch, the counsel for Secretary Stevens, who made a national name for himself during the hearings. Balding, with a long face and broad nose, Welch dressed and acted the part of a conservative Boston attorney, which he was. A masterful trial lawyer, Welch frequently disconcerted witnesses with quiet, penetrating questions. In what proved to be the climax of the hearings, Welch pinned the Wisconsin senator to the wall for all the nation to see.

On June 9, Welch questioned Roy Cohn about the fact that although he and McCarthy claimed to have had information about subversion at Fort Monmouth for weeks before their committee hearing on the subject, they had not brought the information to the attention of the secretary of the army or anyone else. Please, Welch said to Cohn, when you know about subversion and spying, quickly tell someone about it so that action can be taken. At that point McCarthy injected himself into the proceedings:

> *Senator McCarthy:* Mr. Chairman . . .
>
> *Senator Mundt:* Have you a point of order?
>
> *Senator McCarthy:* Not exactly, Mr. Chairman, but in view of Mr. Welch's request that the information be given once we know of anyone who might be performing any work for the Communist Party, I think we should tell him that he has in his law firm a young man named Fisher whom he recommended, incidentally, to do work on this committee, who has been for a number of years a member of an organization which was named, oh, years and years ago, as the legal bulwark of the Communist Party, an organization which always swings to the defense of anyone who dares to expose Communists. I certainly assume that Mr. Welch did not know of this young man at the time he recommended him as the assistant counsel for this committee, but he has such terror and such a great desire to know where anyone is located who may be serving the Communist cause, Mr. Welch, that I thought we should just call to your attention the fact that your Mr. Fisher, who is still in your law firm today, whom you asked to have down here looking over the secret and classified material, is a member of an organization, not named by me but named by various committees, named by the Attorney General, as I recall, and I think I quote this verbatim, as "the legal bulwark of the Communist Party." He belonged to that for a sizable number of years, according to his own admission, and he belonged to it long after it had been exposed as the legal arm of the Communist Party. . . .

Roy Cohn and others among McCarthy's supporters at the hearings tried to turn him off, realizing that he was going too far. But McCarthy would not be stopped:

> I am not asking you at this time to explain why you tried to foist him on this committee. Whether you knew he was a member of that Communist organization or not, I don't know. I assume you did not, Mr. Welch, because I get the impression that,

UPI

Army counsel Joseph Welch aggressively questions Roy Cohn, chief counsel for McCarthy. At first Welch seemed too self-controlled to cope with McCarthy's emotional tactics, but he soon proved to be a strong, effective opponent.

while you are quite an actor, you play for a laugh, I don't think you have any conception of the danger of the Communist Party. I don't think you yourself would ever knowingly aid the Communist cause. I think you are unknowingly aiding it when you try to burlesque this hearing in which we are attempting to bring out the facts, however. . . .

Mr. Welch: Senator McCarthy, I did not know— Senator, sometimes you say, "May I have your attention?"

Senator McCarthy: I am listening to you. I can listen with one ear.

Mr. Welch: This time I want you to listen with both.

Senator McCarthy: Yes.

Mr. Welch: Senator McCarthy, I think until this moment . . .

Senator McCarthy: Jim [James N. Juliana, a McCarthy aide], will you get the news story to the effect that this man belonged to this Communist-front organization? Will you get the citations showing that this was the legal arm of the Communist Party, and the length of time that he belonged, and

the fact that he was recommended by Mr. Welch?
I think that should be in the record.

Mr. Welch: You won't need anything in the record
when I have finished telling you this.

Until this moment, Senator, I think I never really
gaged your cruelty or your recklessness. Fred Fisher is
a young man who went to the Harvard Law School
and came into my firm and is starting what looks
to be a brilliant career with us.

When I decided to work for this committee I asked
Jim St. Clair, who sits on my right, to be my first
assistant. I said to Jim, "Pick somebody in the
firm who works under you that you would like." He
chose Fred Fisher and they came down on an
afternoon plane. That night, when he had taken
a little stab at trying to see what the case was about,
Fred Fisher and Jim St. Clair and I went to dinner
together. I then said to these two young men, "Boys, I
don't know anything about you except I have always
liked you, but if there is anything funny in the
life of either one of you that would hurt anybody in
this case, you speak up quick."

Fred Fisher said, "Mr. Welch, when I was in
law school and for a period of months after, I
belonged to the Lawyers' Guild," as you suggested,
Senator. He went on to say, "I am secretary of the
Young Republicans League in Newton [Massachusetts]
with the son of the Massachusetts Governor, and
I have the respect and admiration of the twenty-five
lawyers or so in Hale and Dorr [his law firm]."

I said, "Fred, I just don't think I am going to ask
you to work on the television and it will hurt like
the dickens."

So, Senator, I asked him to go back to Boston.

Little did I dream you could be so reckless and
so cruel as to do an injury to that lad. It is true
that he is still with Hale and Dorr. It is true that he
will continue to be with Hale and Dorr. It is, I regret
to say, equally true that I fear he shall always bear
a scar needlessly inflicted by you. If it were in my
power to forgive you for your reckless cruelty, I
would do so. I like to think I am a gentleman, but

your forgiveness will have to come from someone
other than me.

Senator McCarthy: Mr. Chairman.

Senator Mundt: Senator McCarthy?

Senator McCarthy: May I say that Mr. Welch talks
about this being cruel and reckless. He was just
baiting; he has been baiting Mr. Cohn here for hours,
requesting that Mr. Cohn, before sundown, get out
of any department of Government anyone who is
serving the Communist cause.

I just give this man's record, and I want to say,
Mr. Welch, that it has been labeled long before he
was a member, as early as 1944. . . .

Mr. Welch: Senator, may we not drop this? We
know he belonged to the Lawyers' Guild, and Mr.
Cohn nods his head at me. I did you, I think, no
personal injury, Mr. Cohn.

Mr. Cohn: No, sir.

Mr. Welch: I meant to do you no personal injury,
and if I did, I beg your pardon.

Let us not assassinate this lad further, Senator. You
have done enough. Have you no sense of decency, sir,
at long last? Have you no sense of decency?

Senator McCarthy: I know this hurts you, Mr.
Welch. But I may say, Mr. Chairman, on a point
of personal privilege, and I would like to finish it. . . .

Mr. Welch: Mr. McCarthy, I will not discuss this
with you further. You have sat within six feet of
me, and could have asked me about Fred Fisher.
You have brought it out. If there is a God in heaven,
it will do neither you nor your cause any good. I
will not ask Mr. Cohn any more questions. You,
Mr. Chairman, may if you will, call the next
witness. . . .

"It was over," Fred Cook summed up in his *Nightmare
Decade:*

It took a few seconds for the realization to sink in;
then the caucus room rocked with the thunder of
applause. Even the press photographers, for the first
time in the memory of Washington observers, were so

When Senator
McCarthy attacked
Welch's young
assistant, Fred
Fisher, Welch was
visibly shaken. But
he quickly recovered
and made a moving
defense, much to the
delight of the hearing
room audience.
Welch later said that
America was
protected from
demagogues by
"immense reservoirs
of common sense."

moved that they dropped their cameras and clapped for Welch. Senator Mundt, who had tried to prevent such demonstrations in the past, bowed his head to the gale as this one swept the hearing room—then quickly called a five-minute recess.

Joe McCarthy slouched in his chair, breathing hard. Spectators and reporters shunned him. Feeling the universal hostility, he looked around, spread out his hands in puzzlement, and asked as if to himself, "What did I do wrong?"[15]

The hearings dragged on after that, but for all real purposes they had ended. On August 31 the Mundt Committee issued its report. Republican members, while they chastised McCarthy for not controlling his staff more closely, concluded that he had personally done nothing on Schine's behalf. Democrats on the committee condemned McCarthy for condoning Cohn's conduct with respect to Schine, and for all his actions in smearing individuals with unfounded, unproved accusations.

On June 1 Senator Ralph Flanders of Vermont, in a Senate speech, had called for a thorough investigation of McCarthy and his activities. Leaders of both parties feared that nothing good for them could come of such action. Many still feared McCarthy's influence and his popular support. The Senate leaders tried to put Flanders off, but he persisted. Finally, after extensive debate, the Senate decided that it would lose considerable public respect and confidence if it did not do something about McCarthy. It did not entertain a motion of censure, however. The Senate merely established a six-member committee to hear the case against the senator from Wisconsin. No senator volunteered for a place on the committee, so its members were appointed.

Several days of testimony in the fall of 1954 indicated that a censure of McCarthy would have been justified. But, after the committee finished its work, the Senate did not follow that course. He lost none of his privileges nor any of his committee assignments. He was no longer a committee chairman, but that was because control of Congress had

Senator Ralph Flanders called for the censure of his fellow Republican, Senator McCarthy. Flanders, who once said he was "anti-pink, anti-mink, and anti-stink," was labeled "senile" by McCarthy, but the Senate supported Flanders and McCarthy was on his way out.

UPI

[15] Fred J. Cook, *Nightmare Decade* (New York: Random House, 1971), p. 519.

shifted to the Democrats after the 1954 congressional elections.

Yet McCarthy had lost his power. A Gallup poll in the late summer of 1954 showed that more than a third of the people still supported him, and he still had many powerful backers among right-wing groups. But he was no longer newsworthy. Reporters and photographers, who had formerly clustered about him eagerly awaiting the next revelation of subversion, now shunned him. When he arose to speak, the Senate chamber emptied. For months President Eisenhower had held himself aloof from the controversy over McCarthy, only bringing the influence of his office to bear against the senator at the outset of the army hearings. Now he let it be known that McCarthy was not welcome in the White House or at any presidential reception. Once McCarthy had been almost daily in the headlines. He had been, in the eyes of Republican leaders, a wonderful weapon in political wars against the Democrats. He had been a fearsome and dangerous enemy. Now McCarthy was nothing. He was not even worthy of criticism. Influential figures and the news media dismissed him, and he rated scarcely a small notice on page 10 of any newspaper.

Physically and mentally, McCarthy was a shattered man. He went rapidly downhill, drinking more and more heavily. He died on May 2, 1957, in Bethesda Naval Hospital in Maryland, near Washington, D.C. McCarthy ended his life a tragic figure, yet the tragedy for the nation had been much more immense. In summing up McCarthy's career, the historian Samuel Eliot Morison provided what is perhaps the best epitaph for the man: "For success in dividing a country by sowing suspicion of treason in high places, there has been no one to equal Joe McCarthy since Marat in the French Revolution."[16]

The Fruits of McCarthyism

There were many fruits of McCarthyism, all of them bitter. McCarthy set up an underground of civil-servant informers, exercised a virtual veto over State Department hiring and firing, dictated to a considerable extent the foreign policy of

[16] Samuel Eliot Morison, *The Oxford History of the American People* (New York: Oxford University Press, 1965), p. 1084.

the United States, humiliated the secretary of the army, drove from Washington four senators who opposed him, hinted that two presidents were guilty of treason, and demoralized officials and employees on all levels of the federal government. The man created havoc in the American political system and did great damage to the American concept of justice and civil liberties. And for more than three years, responsible national leaders and the general public let him get away with it.

The McCarthy era spawned many radical right-wing organizations, perhaps the best known being the John Birch Society, founded by candy manufacturer Robert Welch in 1958. Others included the American Nazi party, Minutemen, Christian Crusade, Christian Anti-Communist Crusade, Young Americans for Freedom, Americans for Constitutional Action, and the National Americanism Commission of the American Legion, to name but a few. Some of these organizations were anti-black, some were anti-Semitic, all were anti-liberal and rabidly anti-Communist. All shared a simplistic view of history and current problems. All subscribed to the "conspiracy theory" as a means of explaining past and present misfortunes. Whatever had gone wrong in American foreign policy, whatever had happened in the world that seemed in any way detrimental to American interests, whatever adversities appeared at home—all were the result of a worldwide Communist conspiracy. As Robert Welch of the John Birch Society put it:

Communism is not a political party, nor an ideological crusade, nor a rebirth of Russian imperialist ambitions, though it comprises and uses all of these parts and pretenses. Communism, in its unmistakable present reality is wholly a conspiracy, a gigantic conspiracy to enslave mankind; an increasingly successful conspiracy controlled by determined, cunning and utterly ruthless gangsters, willing to use any means to achieve its end.[17]

[17] Robert Welch, *The Blue Book of the John Birch Society* (Belmont, Mass.: John Birch Society, 1961), pp. 30–31.

In the opinion of Welch and other right-wing leaders, there could be no accommodation with communism anywhere in the world.

In some respects—their willingness to suspend certain civil liberties, for example, and their attempts to censor opposing points of view—the leaders of right-wing groups resembled the leaders of the Communist countries of which they were so fearful. In *The Strange Tactics of Extremism,* Harry and Bonaro Overstreet examined this resemblance. "The Radical Right," they wrote,

> is by no means a mirror-image of the Communist Left. Its contempt for "reformism" is almost Leninist in character. To a striking degree, its organizations are built on the principle that wisdom resides in a leader or elite group, and that it must be dispensed to the masses in predigested, capsule form. It thinks in absolutes and conquers the complexities of problems by means of pat over-simplifications. Also, it borrows many communist tactics and stratagems. But, for all this, it is by no means simply Communism moved over to the opposite extreme.
>
> For one thing, and an important one, it is an indigenous movement; not part of an international conspiracy. Its roots are here; not abroad. Thus, it can best be understood, in many of its aspects, as an nth degree exaggeration of traits common among us in many gradations.
>
> For another thing, while a considerable machinery has developed for the exchange of materials among far-right groups and for the overlapping of their Boards, the Right extreme is still occupied by a host of organizations—each of these having its own leadership. There is no single form of discipline; nor is there any one "top" from which directives can be handed down.
>
> Lastly, while Communism can be studied as a definable theory-practice system, it is often hard to draw the line between Radical Rightism and the farthest right type of legitimate conservatism. This line cannot be drawn, we think, on the simple basis of

UPI

Slogans such as this one advocating the impeachment of Supreme Court Chief Justice Earl Warren were popular among some groups, especially in the South following the Court's decision on integration in the schools.

where people stand on this or that particular issue. If we start cataloguing complex problems as ones about which there can be no legitimate differences of opinion, we play the extremist game—and out goes the baby with the bath. . . .[18]

Activities on the extreme right in America worried such public figures as Senator Stephen Young of Ohio. In the early 1960's he addressed himself to those activities in a speech in the Senate, saying, in part:

Although the danger from internal communism has been lessening, the radicals of the right—in Europe they would be called fascists—now pose a dangerous threat in trying to destroy the civil liberties and institutions which are the foundations of freedom. They accuse everyone who disagrees with their brand

[18] Harry and Bonaro Overstreet, *The Strange Tactics of Extremism* (New York: W.W. Norton, 1964), pp. 19–20.

of "Americanism" of being a Communist or Communist sympathizer. They question the integrity of our Supreme Court. [The John Birch Society, in its publications and on billboards and bumper stickers, demanded the impeachment of Chief Justice Earl Warren because of liberal Court decisions.] They stir resentment against our participation in the United Nations. They want the income tax repealed.

They try to block all foreign aid programs. They vilify foreign-born and minority-group American citizens. They spread seeds of suspicion in communities throughout the nation.

The greatest danger today arises from the fact that millions of well-meaning Americans embrace their programs as valid solutions to the deeply complex problems which confront our nation in an age of swift change and social upheaval. . . .[19]

Right-wing groups have had their greatest impact on the local level. Their members have prowled public libraries in search of books that might in any way, in their opinion, be tainted by left-wing thought. They have kept a constant and owlish watch on schools, closely examining curriculums and textbooks for "Communist" tendencies. They have been particularly upset about courses and materials that enable students to learn something about the United Nations, which in the right-wing view is a vehicle for the international Communist conspiracy.

In addition to encouraging the growth of extreme right-wing organizations, McCarthyism effectively damaged the Foreign Service of the United States. Many of McCarthy's targets were members of that service, some of them highly placed officers, others on the lower levels. Recruitment for the Foreign Service fell off after it was placed under deep, though totally erroneous, suspicion of harboring subversive and disloyal persons.

During the McCarthy era, many ordinary and a number of well-known people lost their jobs and had their lives altered as a result of suspicion of disloyalty. One such person

[19] *Congressional Record,* Eighty-eighth Congress, First Session, p. 15178.

Owen Lattimore in 1952. When the photograph was taken, Lattimore had just completed twelve difficult days of testimony before the Senate Internal Security Committee.

was Owen Lattimore, whom McCarthy had finally named as a Soviet agent after several days of teasing hints to build up headlines. Lattimore fought back vigorously, but it was a bitter, uphill struggle and for many months his good name and his career were in jeopardy. He was indicted for perjury, but the government's case was so weak that it was almost immediately thrown out of court. Numerous people working in government jobs and in defense industries, many of them performing tasks that had nothing to do with security, were ousted on flimsy or totally unsupported charges of disloyalty.

In the entertainment industry, the blacklists established during the late 1940's grew in size and scope. They spread from the movies to radio, television, legitimate theater, concert halls, lecture circuits, and even nightclubs. They included the names of producers, directors, writers, actors, announcers and news commentators, comedians, musicians, singers, and even technicians. These people were deprived of their livelihoods, and the general public was deprived in turn of artistic contributions and critical insights that might have gone far to relieve the cultural aridity of the 1950's.

The McCarthy era fastened loyalty oaths on the nation. College and university faculty members, public school teachers on all grade levels, and many other public employees such as social workers, librarians, and firemen were forced to sign loyalty oaths as a condition of employment. Affirming loyalty to the Constitution was not sufficient. Public servants had to sign special oaths disclaiming membership in organizations judged, frequently with no particular evidence offered, as subversive. Refusal to sign was *prima facie* evidence of disloyalty and grounds for dismissal. Few people stopped to reflect that real Communists bent on subverting American institutions would have been among the first to sign.

According to Fred Cook, possibly the most damaging effect of McCarthyism was that it forced the nation to continue in its unrealistic Cold War policy toward China. On the one hand, the United States pretended that China's Communist regime did not exist and, on the other hand, attempted to "contain" it. Fearing charges of being "soft on communism," no administration dared adopt any other policy during the 1950's and 1960's. And the nation's China policy, in Cook's opinion, led first to the tragedy of a stalemate war in Korea and then to the even greater tragedy of Vietnam.

McCarthyism did not die with the man. As Samuel Eliot Morison observed, "the poisonous suspicion that he injected into the body politic will take many years to leach out."[20] McCarthyism left as a heritage a large body of laws and administrative practices based upon the notion that there were tests for such things as loyalty, security, and Americanism. Elaborate security screenings became commonplace. Blacklists begun in the late 1940's and early 1950's were still operating effectively in the 1960's, barring creative and competent people from employment in their chosen fields. University professors, who were among McCarthy's favorite targets, retreated into non-controversial research and political non-involvement, and a major theme of the student protest movement of the 1960's was the ivory-tower isolationism of faculty members. In private industry no less than in government and education, a person's intellectual interests, political ideas, and personal associations were often scrutinized with a thoroughness that would have been considered an intolerable invasion of privacy in past decades. More than twenty years after the man himself was discredited, a great many Americans were still living psychologically in the McCarthy era.

Throughout the 1960's and even into the 1970's, echoes of McCarthyism—anti-intellectualism, smear techniques, strident demands for law and order, wholesale condemnations of groups of people who differed noticeably from the mainstream of Americans—could be heard in the speeches of representatives of both major political parties.

McCarthyism will live as long as people accept simplistic solutions for complex problems, as long as the conspiracy theory for explaining all adverse events retains credence in anyone's mind. It will remain alive as long as change is feared, and as long as faith in the American system of democracy is less than complete.

Reflecting upon the impact of McCarthy and his methods, John Cogley offered this warning:

[20] Morison, *The Oxford History,* p. 1084.

Such attacks can always be made and will have a certain validity. For it is in the nature of democracy that the wrong-headed will get a hearing with the wise; that the guilty will have the refuge of civil liberties along with the innocent; that the liar will share the platform with the truth-teller. Democracy is a dangerous business, and we should have known this before Senator McCarthy dramatized it. We should have known that we cannot have democracy without constant hazard. . . . The abuse of democratic institutions should have been taken for granted. The price should have been paid willingly. But as long as people think that democracy is "safe" and fool-proof, ripe pickings for the next Senator McCarthy who comes along will remain.[21]

A Footnote

Two decades after the death of Joe McCarthy, his name still could stir interest and even controversy. Early in 1977, millions of Americans watched *Tail Gunner Joe,* a television film about McCarthy's career. Trying to cover too much, the film was superficial, and even staunch McCarthy-haters of long standing granted that it was terribly slanted against him. Roy Cohn responded a few weeks later with *The Answer to "Tail Gunner Joe,"* an instant book purporting to tell the truth, or at least to present another side of the picture. Cohn offered nothing new.

The McCarthy file in the library of the Madison, Wisconsin, *Capital Times,* which opposed McCarthy from the beginning, continues to grow. Scanning the clippings, one finds at least one mention of the late senator a year. And a small group of people, known as the McCarthy Foundation and centered at Milwaukee, seeks to keep his memory alive. Each spring since Joe McCarthy died, on the Saturday nearest to the date of his death, members of the group have gathered in a Milwaukee church for a memorial mass. The following day they meet once again, at Joe's grave, on a grassy knoll overlooking the Fox River at Appleton. Then they join together for a meal and to hear a speech. And

---

[21] John Cogley, "McCarthyism Revisited," *The Commonweal* 62 (1961): 151.

the speaker always hews to the vintage line: Communist conspiracy, still pervading America.

Members of the foundation probably need not worry about McCarthy's memory remaining alive. The textbooks will see to that, for it seems unlikely that Joseph R. McCarthy will ever be relegated to the status of a mere footnote to American history.

SUGGESTED READINGS

Acheson, Dean. *Present at the Creation: My Years in the State Department.* W. W. Norton.

Buckley, William F., Jr., ed. *American Conservative Thought in the Twentieth Century.* Bobbs-Merrill.

Goldman, Eric F. *The Crucial Decade and After: America, 1945-1960.* Random House, Vintage Books.

Latham, Earl. *The Communist Controversy in Washington: From the New Deal to McCarthy.* Atheneum.

Latham, Earl, ed. *The Meaning of McCarthyism.* D.C. Heath.

Lipset, Seymour, and Raab, Earl. *The Politics of Unreason: Right-Wing Extremism in America.* 2nd ed. University of Chicago Press, Phoenix Books.

McCarthy, Joseph R. *America's Retreat from Victory.* Robert Welch, Inc., Western Islands Books.

Overstreet, Harry and Bonaro. *The Strange Tactics of Extremism.* W. W. Norton.

Spanier, John W. *The Truman-MacArthur Controversy and the Korean War.* W. W. Norton.

Waitley, Douglas, *America at War: Korea and Vietnam.* Glencoe.

The effects of racism—which the Swedish sociologist Gunnar Myrdal called the "American dilemma"—are dramatically illustrated in this view of Washington, D.C., photographed on August 15, 1940.

4

THE STIRRING

OF BLACK REVOLT

Until the war years pointedly exposed the extent of racism in America, there was no recognized "Negro problem" in the United States. Relegated to second-class status shortly after Reconstruction, and constituting about ten percent of the total population in 1940, black Americans experienced injustice—socially, politically, and economically. Yet it never occurred to most whites that this state of affairs was anything but normal. Declared the black hero of Ralph Ellison's 1952 novel, *The Invisible Man,* "I am invisible, understand, simply because people refuse to see me." And what most people refused to realize was that this frustration lay like a ticking time bomb beneath the surface of black American life. As the philosopher William James once observed:

> No more fiendish punishment could be devised
> than that one should be turned loose in a society and
> remain absolutely unnoticed by all the other
> members thereof; if no one turned round when we
> entered, answered when we spoke, or minded what
> we did, but if everyone we met cut us dead, and
> acted as if we were nonexistent, a kind of rage and
> impotent despair would well up in us, from which the
> cruelest bodily tortures would be a relief; for these
> could make us feel that, however bad our plight, we
> had not sunk to such a depth as to be unworthy
> of attention.

Ralph Waldo
Ellison, the author of
Invisible Man, wrote
of the despair of
black intellectuals,
whose opportunities
for education and
employment were
sharply limited and
whose contributions
to scholarship and
the arts were so
often ignored or, if
noticed, scorned.

Whites sometimes did notice blacks—when they got into trouble. Bigger Thomas, the central character in Richard Wright's novel *Native Son,* felt totally alienated from society. Doors of opportunity were closed to him, his existence went unnoticed, until he murdered a white woman. Then society quickly marshalled its forces to destroy him, but at least it recognized his presence. "I didn't know I was alive in this world," Bigger told his lawyer shortly before his execution in the electric chair, "but I'm alright now. I feel alright when I look at it that way." Bigger had identity at last.

UPI

Gunnar Myrdal was a Swedish sociologist who thoroughly documented the prevalence of racism in every aspect of American life during the 1940's. But his conclusions were hopeful. He believed that the American commitment to equality was an even stronger force than racism and that it would ultimately prevail. In *An American Dilemma,* Myrdal wrote:

> The bright side is that the conquering of color caste is America's own inherent desire. The nation early laid down as the moral basis for its existence the principles of equality and liberty. ... The great reason for hope is that the country has a national experience of uniting racial and cultural diversities and a national theory, if not a consistent practice, of freedom and equality for all. What America is constantly reaching for is democracy at home and abroad. The main trend in its history is the gradual realization of the American creed.[1]

Still, the road to realization of that American creed would prove to be a long one, even after blacks began speaking up for their rights.

Segregation and Discrimination

By custom, housing was segregated in the North, and whites usually resisted any black attempt to moved beyond well-defined boundaries. So did real estate salesmen. According to the code of ethics of the National Association

[1] Gunnar Myrdal, *An American Dilemma: The Negro Problem and Modern Democracy* (New York: Harper, 1944), p. 1021.

UPI

A street in East Harlem, the major black area of New York City, photographed in 1952.

of Real Estate Boards, "A realtor should never be instrumental in introducing into a neighborhood . . . members of any race or nationality . . . whose presence will clearly be detrimental to property values." Whites sincerely believed that a black family moving into a white neighborhood, regardless of the family's income, would immediately depress the value of property. And since value is mostly in the mind, the lowering of property values became a self-fulfilling prophecy. Blacks maintained their own communities, such as New York City's Harlem and Chicago's South Side, and they were served by their own doctors, lawyers, and other professionals. Most blacks were confined to substandard housing, and their landlords, black and white, often took advantage. Black author Richard Wright once described conditions in Chicago, and told how whites

> react emotionally as though we had the plague when we move into their neighborhoods. Is it any wonder, then, that their homes are suddenly and drastically reduced in value? They hastily abandon them,

Library of Congress

This children in this photograph, taken in 1941, belonged to a family of ten who were being forced to move from their home in Caroline County, Virginia, because the land was to be taken over by the government for use as an army base. It is probable that their parents, like thousands of other black Southerners during the war years, moved North in search of a better life.

sacrificing them to the Bosses of the Buildings, the men who instigate all this for whatever profit they can get in real-estate sales. And in the end we are the "fall guys." When the white folks move, the Bosses of the Buildings let the property to us at rentals higher than those the whites paid.

And the Bosses of the Buildings take these old houses and convert them into "kitchenettes," and then rent them to us at rates so high that they make fabulous fortunes before the houses are too old for habitation. What they do is this: they take, say, a seven-room apartment, which rents for $50 a month to whites, and cut it up into seven small apartments, of one room each; they install one small gas stove and one small sink in each room. The Bosses of the Buildings rent these kitchenettes to us at the rate of, say, $6 a week. Hence the same apartment for which white people—who can get jobs anywhere

and who receive higher wages than we—pay $50 a
month is rented to us for $42 a week! And because
there are not enough houses for us to live in,
because we have been used to sleeping several in a
room on the plantations in the South, we rent
these kitchenettes and are glad to get them. These
kitchenettes are our havens from the plantations in
the South. We have fled the wrath of Queen
Cotton and we are tired.

Sometimes five or six of us live in a one-room
kitchenette, a place where simple folk such as we
should never be held captive. A war sets up in our
emotions: one part of our feelings tells us that it
is good to be in the city, that we have a chance at
life here, that we need but turn a corner to become a
stranger, that we no longer need bow and dodge
at the sight of the Lords of the Land. Another part of
our feelings tells us that, in terms of worry and
strain, the cost of living in the kitchenettes is too high,
that the city heaps too much responsibility upon us
and gives too little security in return.

The kitchenette is the author of the glad tidings
that new suckers are in town, ready to be
cheated, plundered, and put in their places.[2]

Segregated housing meant segregated schools. And the
schools that blacks attended in the North were almost
always inferior to those in white neighborhoods.

Housing aside, for the most part the hundreds of thousands of blacks who migrated from the South during the two
world wars considered themselves better off in the North.
They could vote, and there were employment opportunities
at higher wages than where they had formerly lived. Still,
the vast majority of jobs available to blacks were menial—
maid, janitor, elevator operator, waiter, bellhop, and the
like.

The South remained Jim Crow—rigidly segregated, by
law as well as by custom. Blacks attended their own schools,
from elementary grades through college. If they were

[2] Richard Wright, *Twelve Million Black Voices: A Folk History of the
Negro in the United States* (New York: Viking Press, 1941), pp. 104–105.

allowed to use public facilities enjoyed by whites—such as movie theaters, restaurants, buses, or trains—they were forced into segregated sections. The Supreme Court of the United States had found "separate but equal" facilities constitutional, in the *Plessy* v. *Ferguson* case in 1896. However, although rigidly separate, the facilities were seldom equal. And any black who strayed from his place, who in any manner indicated that he considered himself equal to whites, was viewed as "uppity." He also placed himself in danger. As late as the World War II years, lynchings still occurred in the South.

Poll taxes were an effective means of preventing blacks from voting. In some areas, blacks could not register to vote unless they passed literacy tests or tests on the Constitution. These tests could easily be rigged to the disadvantage of blacks. Congressional bills to abolish the poll tax, like anti-lynching bills, regularly failed. On more than one occasion, southern senators resorted to the filibuster to kill them.

Richard Wright told how it was to grow up under Jim Crow conditions:

I was learning fast, but not quite fast enough.
One day, while I was delivering packages in
the suburbs, my bicycle tire was punctured. I walked
along the hot, dusty road, sweating and leading
my bicycle by the handlebars.
    A car slowed at my side.
    "What's the matter boy?" a white man called.
    I told him my bicycle was broken and I was walking
back to town.
    "That's too bad," he said. "Hop on the running
board."
    He stopped the car. I clutched hard at my bicycle
with one hand and clung to the side of the car
with the other.
    "All set?"
    "Yes, sir," I answered. The car started.
    It was full of young white men. They were drinking.
I watched the flask pass from mouth to mouth.
    "Wanna drink, you?" one asked.
    I laughed as the wind whipped my face.

Instinctively obeying the fresh planted precepts of
my mother, I said:

"Oh, no!"

The words were hardly out of my mouth before I
felt something hard and cold smash me between
the eyes. It was an empty whiskey bottle. I saw stars,
and fell backwards from the speeding car into the
dust of the road, my feet becoming entangled in the
steel spokes of my bicycle. The white men piled
out and stood over me.

"Nigger, ain' yeh learned no better sense 'n tha'
yet?" asked the man who hit me. "Ain' yeh learned
t' say *sir* t' a white man yet?"

Dazed, I pulled to my feet. My elbows and legs
were bleeding. Fists doubled, the white man
advanced, kicking my bicycle out of the way.

"Aw, leave the . . . alone. He's got enough," said
one.

They stood looking at me. I rubbed my shins,
trying to stop the flow of blood. No doubt they felt a
sort of contemptuous pity, for one asked:

"Yuh wanna ride t' town now, nigger? Yuh reckon
yuh know enough t' ride now?"

"I wanna walk," I said, simply.

Maybe it sounded funny. They laughed.

"Well, walk, yuh black . . .!"

When they left they comforted me with:

"Nigger, yuh sho better be . . . glad it wuz us yuh
talked t' tha' way. Yuh're a lucky . . . 'cause if
yuh'd said that t' somebody else, yuh might've been
a dead nigger now."[3]

The World War II Experience

The advent of the draft and the beginning of a wartime
economic boom spotlighted the lowly position of blacks in
America. The armed forces had long been Jim Crow. The
navy used blacks mainly as mess attendants and stewards.
The army employed them as truck drivers and laborers.
No black had ever graduated from the naval academy at

[3] Richard Wright, *The Ethics of Jim Crow* (New York: Harper, 1948),
pp. 25–26.

Dr. Charles Richard Drew, an Amherst graduate who earned his medical degree at McGill University in Canada, was largely responsible for the success of the American Red Cross in saving thousands of lives, on and off the battlefields, through transfusions from the blood banks that he developed. In 1950 Drew was injured in an automobile accident and, although bleeding profusely, was refused treatment at a white hospital in North Carolina. He bled to death, at age forty-six, before he could be moved elsewhere.

American Red Cross/
Painting by Betsy Graves
Reynean

Annapolis, and only four had graduated from the army's West Point. Many southern draft boards refused to induct blacks, partly because of prejudice and partly because they did not wish to drain off the source of cheap labor in their communities. Only pressure from the federal government forced them to modify that policy. Most of the blacks who were drafted, North and South, were assigned to menial jobs in segregated units commanded by white officers. In the armed services, even blood plasma was segregated—black and white. This was supreme irony, for it was the work of a black surgeon, Dr. Charles R. Drew, which led to the development of plasma and blood banks in 1940 and 1941.

In civilian life blacks had trouble finding jobs, even as defense production began to increase. Many whites refused to work with them. The American Federation of Labor, a national association of crafts unions, had discriminated against blacks for years, allowing only a few to join. In the newer Congress of Industrial Organizations, which took in both skilled and unskilled labor, conditions were little better. The United Auto Workers, under the direction of Walter Reuther, was among the few unions to admit blacks in any significant number.

In shipbuilding and in the iron, steel, and refining industries, blacks found it easier to get jobs. Many skilled occupations, however, remained off-limits even in those industries.

Such black leaders as Walter White of the National Association for the Advancement of Colored People and A. Philip Randolph, head of the Brotherhood of Sleeping Car Porters, protested vigorously against discrimination in industry and in the armed forces. Injustice of this kind, they argued, ought not to be tolerated in a country representing itself as a bastion of democracy for the world. Randolph threatened to lead a black march on Washington on July 1, 1941, unless the government acted before that time.

To avert a prominent display of national disunity during this critical period, President Roosevelt did act. He issued an executive order, No. 8802, which stated: "There shall be no discrimination in the employment of workers in defense industries or Government because of race, creed, color, or national origin. . . ." The Fair Employment

Practices Committee was established soon after. The committee could order employers to comply with its guidelines on job discrimination and could cancel government contracts if they refused. It could not, however, take court action or levy fines. And, in the rush to rearm, it was unlikely that the public would support cancellation of defense contracts on the grounds of racial discrimination. In fact, it was not until 1943, when a labor shortage developed, that blacks gained general entry into the job market. About discrimination in the armed forces, Roosevelt did nothing.

Still, the leaders of the March on Washington movement had made some progress. In 1942 they issued a more comprehensive set of demands:

Walter White chose to identify himself closely with black Americans and their struggle for equality even though he was only one sixty-fourth Negro and could easily have passed for white. He served as secretary of the NAACP from 1931 to his death in 1955. He also wrote a number of books including an autobiography, *A Man Called White.*

1. We demand, in the interest of national unity, the abrogation of every law which makes a distinction in treatment between citizens based on religion, creed, color, or national origin. This means an end to Jim Crow in education, in housing, in transportation and in every other social, economic and political privilege; and especially, we demand, in the capital of the nation, an end to all segregation in public places and in public institutions.

2. We demand legislation to enforce the Fifth and Fourteenth Amendments guaranteeing that no person shall be deprived of life, liberty or property without due process of law, so that the full weight of the national government may be used for the protection of life and thereby may end the disgrace of lynching.

3. We demand the enforcement of the Fourteenth and Fifteenth Amendments and the enactment of the . . . Poll Tax bill so that all barriers in the exercise of the suffrage are eliminated.

4. We demand the abolition of segregation and discrimination in the Army, Navy, Marine Corps, Air Corps and all other branches of national defense.

5. We demand an end to discrimination in jobs and job training. Further we demand that the FEPC [Fair Employment Practices Committee] be made a permanent administrative agency of the U.S.

Asa Philip Randolph
founded the
Brotherhood of
Sleeping Car
Porters—the first
strong national labor
union with a
predominantly black
membership—in
1925. He continued
as its leader until
1968, when he retired
at the age of eighty.

Government and that it be given power to enforce its decisions based on its findings.

6. We demand that federal funds be withheld from any agency which practices discrimination in the use of such funds.

7. We demand colored and minority group representation on all administrative agencies so that these groups may have recognition of their democratic right to participate in formulating policies.

8. We demand representation for the colored and minority racial groups on all missions, political and technical, which will be sent to the peace conference so that the interests of all people everywhere may be fully recognized and justly provided for in the postwar settlement.[4]

But 1942 was the darkest year of the war for the Allies. Roosevelt and his advisers were preoccupied with events far from home—in Europe, the Middle East, and the Pacific. And black leaders, for patriotic reasons, refrained from organizing any further large-scale marches or demonstrations that might have diverted attention to their demands.

In some northern cities where blacks migrated seeking war-related jobs, racial tensions found release in violence. A particularly bloody riot occurred on a hot summer night in Detroit in 1943. It took several lives, black and white. This and similar incidents suggested that white northerners were not ready to accept blacks with equality. Neither were some white soldiers. There were ugly racial incidents in many army camps during the early years of the war.

Even though draft boards were often slow to conscript them, blacks were free to enlist. By the end of 1941, more than a hundred thousand blacks were in the army, most of them volunteers. By the end of 1942, the number had grown to nearly half a million, with about eighty thousand in the air force (then part of the army). Blacks were housed in segregated barracks at training camps, and according to army policy only a small number of blacks was assigned to any one camp. This policy meant that units which would eventually fight together as part of the same division received separate training, hampering the development of

[4] Quoted in *Survey,* November 1942.

UPI

Black women assemble cartridges at a government arsenal in South Carolina in 1942. At the start of the war there were few jobs open to blacks in the growing defense industries, but by the summer of 1944 some 100,000 blacks were working in the aircraft industry and by October of that year more than 300,000 had received training for defense industry employment.

effective coordination and *esprit de corps.* And many units received combat training that was sketchy at best, being assigned instead to service or supply duties.

But for the great majority of blacks in the army, combat was not an immediate worry. By late 1942, only about one-eighth of the army's black soldiers—54,000 out of 467,000—were deployed overseas, and most of them were in labor battalions. Many field commanders were reluctant to use black troops in any capacity, often revealing bigotry when pressed by black leaders for explanations. Blacks, they said, would be unreliable under fire and difficult to discipline even in non-combat situations; they would be resented by white soldiers, causing morale problems; and they would be unacceptable to the people of foreign countries, causing diplomatic problems. One important exception in this military parade of prejudice was General Douglas MacArthur, who informed Chief of Staff George C. Marshall in March, 1942:

I will do everything possible to prevent friction or resentment on the part of the Australian government and people at the presence of American colored troops. Please disabuse yourself of any notion that I might return these troops after your decision to dispatch them.[5]

The situation in the air force was not much better. In the uncertain months after Pearl Harbor, most black "airmen" were assigned to security battalions posted at air bases around the United States, their responsibility being to defend the bases against enemy sabotage, parachute, or bombing attacks. But no such attacks occurred—luckily, since very few security battalions were equipped with anti-aircraft weapons or even trained to use them. After about a year, nearly all of the black units were broken up and their members were reassigned to service and supply duties. A limited program for training black pilots was set up at Tuskegee Institute, but that too ran into problems. The air force would not assign the pilots to white squadrons, but a black squadron could not be formed because no black support specialists, such as aircraft mechanics, had been trained. Unwilling to send blacks to white specialist schools, the air force dithered for a while and then, in a wasteful duplication of effort, set up separate training facilities for blacks. That decision triggered the resignation of William H. Hastie, a distinguished black judge who had been serving as civilian aide to the secretary of war.

During the early months of war, blacks in the navy were restricted to duty as servants. But, from the beginning, there were blacks on the nation's ships who performed far beyond the call of such humble duties. Dorie Miller, the hero of Pearl Harbor, was a mess attendant who had never been trained in the use of a machine gun. Under fire, he replaced a dead gunner and shot down four Japanese aircraft, an act for which he received the Navy Cross. Two years later, still a mess attendant, he was killed in the South Pacific. Charles Jackson French, another mess attendant, distinguished himself after his ship was abandoned during the Battle of the Coral Sea. With a rope tied around his body, he

Dorie Miller received the Navy Cross for his heroic actions in World War II.

The Associated Publishers, Inc.

[5] Quoted in John P. Davis, ed., *The American Negro Reference Book* (Englewood Cliffs, N.J.: Prentice-Hall, 1966), p. 637.

swam for two hours hauling a raft bearing fifteen men, not pausing to rest until he was beyond the range of enemy fire. Dozens of other black mess attendants, cooks, and stewards were decorated for equally courageous acts.

As the war went on, cracks in the wall of segregation began to appear. This was largely the result of concentrated efforts by black leaders such as White, Randolph, and Hastie, plus a few sympathetic whites such as Congressman Hamilton Fish of New York, who had learned the value of black combat troops as an officer in World War I. But it was also partly the result of a shift in public attitude. To an increasing number of civilians in and out of government, it seemed just plain silly to exclude thousands of men from the fighting—men who were able and willing to fight— merely because of their color.

The first breakthrough came in the navy, in 1942, when blacks were accepted for general service. Although restricted to shore duty and trained and housed in segregated facilities, they could now acquire skills that would lead to advancement. In 1944 the shore rule was lifted, and blacks were finally permitted to serve on naval vessels in specialist and combat positions. Rigid segregation was impractical in the close quarters of a ship, and before the war's end black and white sailors were sharing the same mess halls and recreation areas. By that time, too, blacks had been accepted for general service in the Marine Corps (a branch of the navy) and in the Coast Guard.

The air force, stung by Judge Hastie's resignation, modified its policies early in 1943 by integrating blacks into most of its training programs, including those for officers. A few months later, the all-black 99th Pursuit Squadron, trained at Tuskegee and commanded by Captain Benjamin O. Davis, Jr., left for the Mediterranean Theater of Operations. In less than a year, the squadron posted an impressive record—500 combat missions representing 3,277 sorties against enemy targets. In June, 1944, the 99th was incorporated into the 332nd Fighter Group, also a black unit, and equipped with long-range fighter-bombers. Led by Davis (now promoted to colonel), the 332nd demolished any lingering doubts about the role of blacks in the air force. By March, 1945, when the group received the Distinguished Unit Citation, it had flown 1,578 combat missions for a total of 15,553 sorties. After the war Davis

U.S. Army

Brigadier General Benjamin O. Davis, Sr., the first black general in the army, at the front lines in France, 1944.

UPI

Members of the first all-black air force unit prepare to join the fighting in Italy in 1944. Walter White, who assisted the group, wrote, "Whatever prejudice . . . existed on either side . . . began to seem . . . superfluous and silly in the face of death and danger. . . . The experience gained in North Africa, Sicily, and now Italy had earned them the reputation of being 'the hottest fighting unit in Italy.'"

was promoted to general. He was the first black to hold that rank in the air force, just as his father had been the first black general in the army. During the Korean War he served as chief of staff of the United Nations command.

The army, with the most black manpower, was the last to change. At the beginning of 1944 there were more than seven hundred thousand black GI's, but still only a small percentage had been sent overseas. A War Department memorandum summarized the army's situation:

1) Having a backlog of [black] combat units in the United States;

2) Having to deplete or inactivate these units to provide personnel for service units to avoid wasting manpower;

3) Having to answer numerous queries from Negro organizations without having definite justification

for failure to commit Negro personnel in combat units.[6]

The break came in the early spring of 1944, and it began with a query from Congressman Fish. Fish demanded to know why a fully trained and equipped black combat unit in the South Pacific was being used only for labor duties. He received the following reply from the office of Secretary of War Henry L. Stimson:

A soldier manning the cannon of an M-4 tank near Nancy, France, 1944.

U.S. Army

> It so happens that a relatively large percentage of the Negroes inducted into the Army have fallen within the lower educational qualifications, and many Negro units accordingly have been unable to master efficiently the techniques of modern weapons.[7]

The "Stimson letter," with its plain implication that blacks were too dumb to fight, stirred up a storm of protest following its publication in the black press. At last the War Department was forced to act. In March, the 24th Infantry was released for combat at Bougainville in the Solomon Islands. A few months later a larger black combat unit, the 92nd Division, was shipped to Italy. Then, early in 1945, a shortage of riflemen developed in the European Theater of Operations. Black troops serving in non-combat units were permitted to volunteer for retraining as infantrymen to fill the need. About five thousand did volunteer, some men accepting a reduction in rank in order to get into the fighting. The black riflemen were organized into segregated ten-man platoons, but each platoon was assigned to a predominantly white infantry group—an important step toward integration. By the war's end, black soldiers had effectively disproved all the army's old arguments against the use of black combat troops. They had fought bravely and with discipline; they had lived and worked alongside white soldiers with remarkably little friction; and they had been well accepted by the people of foreign countries, particularly in Europe.

[6] Quoted in ibid.
[7] Quoted in ibid., p. 638.

Altogether, World War II operated to raise the expectations of black Americans. In war-related jobs or in the armed forces, many experienced a degree of equality and economic independence they had never known before. And from patriotic propaganda, all of the nation's black population heard a great deal about democracy and freedom and why America was fighting dictatorships. As a black newspaper columnist wrote in 1945:

> I do not believe that Negroes will stand idly by and see these newly opened doors of economic opportunity closed in their faces. Negro women will not be content to toil in other people's kitchens again for $3, $4, or $5 a week and a bag of left-over food scraps to take home to their poorly fed young ones.
> Nor will Negro GIs permit our propaganda machine to forget that it did the world's best job when it sought to convince these same Negro GIs that this was really a war for democracy and against fascism.[8]

Returning Home

The GI Bill aided blacks considerably. It helped produce an average of ten thousand black college graduates a year during the 1950's, thus creating a new black leadership. It also focused attention on segregated schools, which were the only schools that blacks could attend in the South.

In other respects, segregation in the South remained the same. Whether a black was or had been in uniform did not matter. Blacks had their "place," and they had best stick to it.

There were some shocking incidents. In Mississippi, in 1946, a black tenant farmer accused of stealing a saddle was set upon by a band of whites and flogged to death. In Louisiana, two young blacks were arrested on a charge of trying to break into a white person's house. A mob killed one and beat the other nearly to death. In South Carolina, a black soldier argued with a bus driver who refused to allow him to use a restroom at a stop. The young man was arrested and taken to jail—where, during "interrogation,"

---

[8] *Michigan Chronicle,* 22 December 1945. Quoted in Joseph C. Goulden, *The Best Years: 1945-1950* (New York: Atheneum, 1976), p. 354.

a police officer ground out his eyes with a billy club. No white involved in these or other incidents suffered punishment.

Several years after the war, the black newspaperman Carl T. Rowan returned to his hometown of McMinnville, Tennessee, then a community of about five thousand people. He had this to report:

Carl T. Rowan first became known as a writer and newscaster. Later he served under President Kennedy as deputy secretary of the State Department and ambassador to Finland, and under President Johnson as director of the United States Information Agency.

> Buttressed by self-caution and a feeling that I knew my way around the devious halls of Jim Crow, I returned to McMinnville, to the familiar gravel streets that I had walked for almost two decades. I returned to frame houses with decaying foundations, to yards barren of grass; and even the tiniest hovel with the farthest-away privy had its nostalgic meaning. Some were houses where human beings—people I knew—lived like rats, and where rats outnumbered the people. Some were houses I knew by starred flags of World War II, which still hung dusty in windows. They were houses where my schoolmates lived, or once had lived. . . .
>
> I went to a dumpy little café that townspeople call "The Slobbery Rock." That name aptly describes the shaky old structure, which sits on a rocky ledge just two blocks from the heart of downtown. A jukebox blared out a blues tune. High school youngsters of fourteen to sixteen, and a drunken woman of at least fifty-five, dragged across the sawdust-strewn dance floor. The air was thick with greasy smoke, heavy with the mingled odors of laborers and school-girl perfumes. There, at the Slobbery Rock, gathered ninety-nine per cent of Negro McMinnville's youth, out for their weekend entertainment.
>
> When I was a youth, Negro youngsters had two choices for away-from-home entertainment. They went to one of the two segregated movies, where they sat in a balcony not even provided with a restroom; then they either went home or to "The Rock." It takes no sociologist to guess which course they usually chose. McMinnville did have one other Negro café, but it was too small for dancing and usually

UPI

National Archives

An example of a "for colored only" restaurant in the South in the late 1940's. Segregation extended to most public facilities, including transportation, movie theaters, and even drinking fountains.

closed very early. There was a skating rink—barred to Negroes. There was a tax-supported swimming pool—barred to Negroes. . . .

The McMinnville of 1951 was little different, I found. "The Rock" was still "the place to go." There was one new place, Harvey's Bar B-Q Stand. Harvey's was clean and the food delicious, but a resentful Negro community talked of boycotting it because the place, run by Harvey Faulkner, a Negro, was segregated. Negro youngsters complained that when they asked for straws in their soft drinks they were told none was available. On the other side of Harvey's, however, whites sipped through straws.

"Worst insult of all," said a Negro teacher, "are the signs put up on the colored side: 'NO DRINKING, NO CURSING, NO MATCHING' " [a form of gambling

with coins]. Faulkner had put up no such signs on
the white side.

I asked Faulkner why he ran a Jim Crow place.
Most cafés run by whites bar Negroes entirely, a
few allowing them to enter by the back door for food
to take out. A Negro ordering hamburgers at the
Serv-All [sic] must stand on the street and wait until
they are cooked. Harvey Faulkner knew all this as well
as I. He leaned on the counter, studying my question;
then, as if the answer had popped out of nowhere,
snapped: "I've got to live; white folks represent
nearly half my trade."

What McMinnvillian could condemn Faulkner?
He had set no precedent; Negro McMinnville had
done that in many ways. Had not Bernard High
School annually set aside front seats for whites who
came to see our closing-of-school plays? Had not the
Church of Christ reserved many of the front seats
for whites who came to its tent revivals? I stood
in Harvey's on the colored side, peeking around the
counter into the white side, and I realized that his Jim
Crow establishment was just another sacrifice offered
up to the Southland's deity, segregation. Faulkner,
like myself and millions of other Negroes, had made
concessions to Jim Crow in adjusting his life to the
South's double standard. The signs on the colored
side of Harvey's were a manifestation of that double
standard. In a few misty seconds, I seemed to
recall countless incidents in my relatively short
lifetime that were manifestations of that double
standard.

Against this background, I could understand
Faulkner's decision, even if I could not justify it. He
had learned the who, what, when, where, and why
of the South the same way I had, and the nucleus of
every lesson was strict compliance with the mores of
the particular community; above this there was neither
justice nor common sense. That made running a cafe
something like going home from school—the way
I went home from school in the early thirties.
You learned to put up a partition so white and black
hands never lifted a glass from the same counter,
though it be the same piece of wood, and you learned

the same way I learned the ABC's of Dixie race
relations: words like nigger, redneck, darky,
peckerwood, shine, cracker, eight ball, snowflake. . . .
The way I learned them, these were third-grade words.

McMinnville's Negro school was located in such a
way that a group of white children had to pass it on
their way home from their school. They met
homebound Negro children, and each afternoon there
would come the chant:

"Eeeny, meeny, miny, mo; catch a nigger by the
toe. . . ."

And a Negro youngster would reply:

"We've got cheese at home; all I need is a cracker
to go with it. . . ."

Since no group could clearly establish dominance by
hurling epithets, the issue was resolved into who
should use the sidewalks, and the conflict assumed
physical proportions. Young fists, propelled by hatreds
of past generations, hatreds no youngster could give
reason for, would fly at young faces of opposite color,
churning blood from noses and feeding grist to the
mills of hatred for another generation. But this could
not go on indefinitely—not in McMinnville. White
parents apparently complained to the school
superintendent, who called the Negro principal. Soon,
a swollen lip betraying me as a participant in the
strife, I stood before the Negro principal with several
schoolmates.

With the wisdom of a man who has been burned,
lecturing children against playing with fire, the
principal explained that we could not win. "If the
whites want the sidewalks, get off. Walk in the street,"
he ordered. With those words, words I dislike to
remember, "peace" came to McMinnville to the extent
that nobody fought over sidewalks. This was because a
few youngsters walked in the street; the indomitable
among us climbed fences and went home across fields
rather than face the youngsters for whom we had had
to give up the sidewalks. "Peace" remains with
McMinnville in that sense.

It is this capacity for change that has made
McMinnville a "good Southern town," in the words of
her Negro citizens. They mean that for a quarter

century there have been no lynchings, no race riots.
Policemen do not "pick on" Negro neighborhoods.
There are no Ku Klux Klan pogroms [massacres], no
bigots shouting in the streets that all Negroes must be
shipped back to Africa. In that negative sense—
because it is better than a lot of small Southern
communities—McMinnville is a "good town."

But McMinnville is a peaceful town, I found in
1951, because, in the words of a former river-buddy,
"no Negro in his right mind" would show up at the
city swimming pool with trunks and the intention of
swimming. And McMinnville Negroes still do not go
to the tax-supported public library, ask for a book,
and sit down and read. If Negro pupils want books,
their teachers must go get the books and bring them
out to the pupils. Skating is still something Negroes do
on sidewalks or not at all. And when a street is
blocked off for square dancing, Negroes watch from a
distance.[9]

Although discrimination continued to limit the everyday
lives of most black Americans, at least two important
breakthroughs were achieved during the late 1940's which
promised enlarged opportunities for the future. The first
was the official desegregation of the armed forces. When the
Eightieth Congress refused to enact civil rights legislation,
President Truman bypassed the legislature in one area and
excercised his presidential power as commander-in-chief.
In July, 1948, he issued Executive Order No. 9981, which
stated: "It is the declared policy of the president that there
shall be equality of treatment and opportunity for all
persons in the Armed Services without regard to race, color,
or national origin." A seven-member committee was
appointed to make sure that the order was carried out, and
a deadline of June 30, 1954, was set for complete integration.
With the Korean War to speed things up, and with very
little conflict, that goal was largely met. Segregation,
however, proved easier to eliminate than discrimination.
Some progress was made, but black leaders during the 1950's

[9] Carl T. Rowan, *South of Freedom* (New York: Alfred A. Knopf, 1952),
pp. 19–27.

Ralph Johnson Bunche was probably the best-known black American in the years immediately following the war. A graduate of UCLA (like Jackie Robinson), he went on to further study at Harvard and in London, becoming a teacher at Howard University in Washington, D.C. In 1944 he joined the State Department, where his abilities were quickly recognized. He helped to organize the United Nations and in 1947 began two years of negotiations which led eventually to peace in Palestine, an effort that won him the Nobel Peace Prize in 1950. He served as undersecretary of the UN from 1955 until his death in 1971.

Jackie Robinson helped the Dodgers to win six National League pennants and to defeat the Yankees in the 1955 World Series. He retired from baseball in 1957, going on to a successful career in business.

had ample reason to complain that blacks did not receive equal opportunities for training and advancement.

Professional sports remained as segregated as anything else until 1947. That year, General Manager Branch Rickey brought a gifted athlete named Jackie Robinson to the Dodgers, then in Brooklyn. Introducing a black to white professional baseball was unprecedented, and it caused no end of talk and apprehension. Robinson withstood abuse from spectators and rival players, and he was denied hotel accommodations in many cities. All the while, he kept silent. Then, one summer day in 1949, he achieved complete equality. An umpire made a call on Robinson that he considered wrong. In the past, he had quietly accepted all decisions. This time he lost his temper and shouted and threatened, just as any white ballplayer would do. Baseball finally had become color-blind. The bar which had held black athletes back for so long had fallen.

The 1952 Election

Harry Truman's executive order desegregating the armed forces helped him politically among blacks. His Korean war policy and the internal Communist issue, however, worked against him. With his popularity rating at a low twenty-six percent in the spring of 1952, Truman decided not to seek re-election. The race for the Democratic nomination narrowed down to two candidates: Governor Adlai Stevenson of Illinois and Senator Estes Kefauver of Tennessee. Both men were considered liberals.

In the meantime, Dwight D. Eisenhower had left Columbia University in 1950 to assume command of the NATO forces in Europe. There, wooed ardently by minority party leaders, Eisenhower at last decided that he was a Republican and would like to be president. While not even in the country, he overwhelmingly won the New Hampshire presidential primary early in 1952. He then swept on to primary victories in Minnesota, New Jersey, Pennsylvania, Massachusetts, and Oregon. And in July at Chicago, defeating all other contenders including Ohio's conservative Senator Robert A. Taft, Eisenhower received the nomination for the presidency on the first ballot. The Republicans then put together what was to be an unbeatable combination by nominating Richard M. Nixon for the vice-presidency. Nixon's role in the Hiss case had made him a bona fide Communist hunter, and his stock had accordingly risen among those who saw a Communist conspiracy everywhere. In 1950, Nixon had defeated Helen Gahagan Douglas for one of California's Senate seats, conducting what most people agreed was a campaign of innuendo, smearing Douglas with the "soft on communism" brush.

Governor Adlai Stevenson welcomed Democrats to Chicago later in July. Referring to the Republican convention in his speech of greeting, he said, "For almost a week, pompous phrases marched over this landscape in search of an idea, and the only idea they found was that the two great decades of progress in peace, and of victory in war, and of bold leadership in this anxious hour, were the misbegotten spawn of bungling, of corruption, of

Adlai Stevenson, when approached by Truman to be the next Democratic candidate for president, was stunned. He said, "I've just come from Blair House and the President wants me to save the world from Dwight Eisenhower."

UPI

Estes Kefauver often wore a coonskin cap to emulate Davy Crockett in his campaign for the Democratic nomination, but his advocacy of civil rights cost him Southern support and he was disliked by some big-city bosses in the North because of his association with the fight against organized crime.

socialism, of mismanagement, of waste, and of worse." He continued, "I guess our Republican friends were out of patience, out of sorts, and, need I add, out of office."

Southern Democrats were now back in the regular fold. To make sure they did not bolt again, the convention adopted a weak and ambiguous civil rights platform plank. This time, black delegates walked out.

Eisenhower allowed Nixon to lead the attack on the Democrats' alleged "softness on communism," an issue at which Nixon was a master. The general himself conducted a lackluster campaign, speaking dully but earnestly, frequently with mixed syntax. Listening to one speech, a reporter groaned, "He's crossing the 38th platitude again!" But what Eisenhower said, or how he said it, really didn't matter. People liked Ike—his famous grin, his steadiness, his conservatism. He came across more like a father than a leader, offering the country security rather than challenge.

Stevenson carried on a brave campaign, but it was no time for liberalism. Eisenhower's was a great victory—33.9 million popular votes to Stevenson's 27.3 million. The general took 442 electoral votes to the governor's 89. Four years later, Eisenhower won an even greater victory over Stevenson—35.5 to 26 million popular votes.

Brown v. Board of Education of Topeka

During the campaign Eisenhower had promised that, if elected, he would go to Korea to look into the situation personally. He did that, and in 1953 weary negotiators completed their task and the war finally ended. Eisenhower made one other significant move. He nominated the liberal Republican governor of California, Earl Warren, as chief justice of the Supreme Court, and the Senate confirmed him. Ike later regretted the nomination, calling it "the biggest damfool mistake I ever made." No court did more for civil rights than the Warren Court, beginning with *Brown* v. *Board of Education of Topeka* in 1954.

Over the years, the Supreme Court had chipped away at segregation and discrimination. It had struck down city ordinances forbidding blacks or whites from moving into housing on blocks occupied predominantly by members of the other race. It had struck down state laws barring blacks

UPI (both)

In both well-equipped urban schools, like that at the left, and in poor rural schools, like that at the right, segregation was either required by law—as in seventeen of the Southern states—or achieved by less formal means, such as discriminatory school board policies.

from voting in primary elections. There had been some cases involving education. The Court said, for example, that Missouri could not fulfill the separate-but-equal doctrine by paying tuition to an out-of-state school for a black applicant to the University of Missouri law school. In 1950 the Court ruled that the law school established by Texas for blacks was not equal to the white school. Then, in the fall of 1952, similar cases arrived from Kansas, South Carolina, Delaware, Virginia, and the District of Columbia. The Court lumped them all together under the Kansas case, *Brown* v. *Board of Education of Topeka.*

The *Brown* case had begun in 1951 when the Reverend Oliver Brown tried to enroll his daughter Linda in a white school because it was closer to home and because he judged the black school she attended to be inferior. The enrollment was denied. Brown, aided by the NAACP, filed suit in a federal court, charging a violation of the equal protection clause of the Fourteenth Amendment. The ruling went against him, and he appealed to the Supreme Court, which heard arguments late in 1953.

In the past, the Court had turned away such cases. It had abided by the 1896 ruling in *Plessy* v. *Ferguson,* which held that constitutional rights were not impaired if states, counties, or muncipalities provided Negroes with facilities that were "separate but equal." The *Plessy* decision read in part:

> If the two races are to meet on terms of social
> equality, it must be the result of natural affinities,
> a mutual appreciation of each other's merits and a
> voluntary consent of individuals. . . . Legislation
> is powerless to eradicate racial instincts or to abolish
> distinctions based upon physical differences.[10]

At 12:52 P.M. on May 17, 1954, more than three hundred years after the first Negro slaves arrived in America and ninety-one years after the Emancipation Proclamation, Chief Justice Earl Warren began reading a unanimous decision that would abolish the *Plessy* ruling. Said the Court, in *Brown*:

> Does segregation of children in Public Schools solely
> on the basis of race, even though the physical
> facilities and other tangible factors may be equal,
> deprive the children of the minority group of equal
> educational opportunities? We believe that it does.
> . . . To separate them from others of similar age
> and qualifications solely because of their race
> generates a feeling of inferiority as to their status in
> the community that may affect their hearts and minds
> in a way unlikely to be undone.
> . . . We conclude that in the field of public education
> the doctrine of "separate but equal" has no place.
> Separate educational facilities are inherently unequal.
> Therefore we hold that the plaintiffs and others
> similarly situated for whom the actions have
> been brought are by reason of the segregation
> complained of, deprived of the equal protection of the
> laws guaranteed by the Fourteenth Amendment.[11]

[10] *Plessy* v. *Ferguson,* 163 U.S. 537 (1896). Quoted in Henry Steele Commager, ed., *Documents of American History* (New York: Appleton-Century-Crofts, 1963), p. 178.

[11] *Brown* v. *Board of Education of Topeka,* 347 U.S. 483 (1954). Quoted in ibid., pp. 621–622.

UPI

Mrs. Nettie Hunt explains the importance of the Supreme Court's ruling on integration to her three-year-old daughter on the steps of the Court building.

In a related case the following year, the Court ordered that schools be desegregated "with all deliberate speed."

Reacting to the *Brown* case, critics charged that the Court had relied more on sociological and psychological data than on firm law in reaching its decision. It was true that the Court had drawn on the works of such scholars as Gunnar Myrdal. That did not, however, make the decision any less binding. Nor was it the first time that the court had based its arguments on psychology. In fact, in denying the appeal of Plessy, the plaintiff who had challenged a Louisiana statute concerning separate transportation in the 1896 case, the Court had said:

> The underlying fallacy is the assumption that the enforced separation of the two races stamps the colored race with a badge of inferiority. If this be so, it is not by reason of anything found in the act

In 1956, children and their mothers in Hillsboro, Ohio, express their feelings in signs after being turned away from school. The Supreme Court had ordered immediate integration at the school, but school board members said they were awaiting "official notification" before taking any action.

but solely because the colored race chooses to put that construction upon it.[12]

Although there were complaints, response from the border states was relatively mild, and prompt. Within two years, Maryland and West Virginia had each integrated schools in all but two counties. Missouri had moved beyond the two-thirds mark in its desegregation efforts. Kentucky had integrated all but seven of its schools by 1960.

The picture was different in the Deep South, the former Confederate states. They moved much more slowly, and with greater resistance. By 1960, Alabama, Mississippi, Georgia, and South Carolina had not integrated at all. Louisiana, Virginia, North Carolina, and Florida had integrated less than one-tenth of one percent of their black school populations by the same date.

[12] *Plessy* v. *Ferguson.* Quoted in ibid., p. 178.

Resistance to desegregation took many forms. Some state legislatures passed resolutions declaring the Supreme Court's decision unconstitutional. Other states authorized school boards to close the public schools and to use private funds to establish segregated private schools. White supremacists in some communities revived the Ku Klux Klan, and White Citizens' Councils sprang up. Violence became commonplace. By the first of January, 1959, 530 incidents of racial violence, reprisal, and intimidation had been recorded. The list included beatings, murders, and bombings of houses and churches.

There was no national leadership on the issue. The Supreme Court only decides—it does not enforce the law. The president holds that responsibility, and Eisenhower was not enthusiastic about desegregation. Asked if he endorsed the *Brown* decision, the president replied, "It makes no difference whether or not I endorse it." He implied, in fact, that he disapproved of it. Although he was urged to take a stand, to call for national unity and compliance with the law, Eisenhower did nothing. Then he was forced to act.

Little Rock

The most spectacular and prolonged conflict over desegregation began in September, 1957, at Little Rock, Arkansas. The school board had approved a plan for high school desegregation. But a group of citizens obtained a court injunction to prevent integration in the city's Central High School. Arkansas Governor Orval Faubus supported the group. He ordered National Guard units to surround the school, supposedly to "maintain order." When Negro students approached on the first day of school, they were confronted by a noisy and hostile white crowd. Guardsmen turned the students away. A federal judge then granted an injunction against Governor Faubus. Under court order, he removed the National Guard troops on September 20. The following Monday, September 23, nine black students entered the school. According to a *New York Times* reporter, this is what happened next:

Governor Orval E. Faubus of Arkansas.

UPI

> A mob of belligerent, shrieking and hysterical demonstrators forced the withdrawal today of nine Negro students from Central High School here.

Despite a heavy turnout of local and state police to see that the Negroes were not molested in Little Rock's newest attempt to integrate the high school, city authorities bowed to the fury of about one thousand white supremacists. They ordered the Negro students to leave the school about noon. The integration attempt had lasted three hours thirteen minutes.

While fringe fights broke out and several persons were roughed up by irate segregationists, the mob shouted insults and obscenities against the "niggers" and "nigger-lovers." Groups of white students who had walked out of the school after the nine Negroes entered chanted: "Two, four, six, eight, we ain't gonna integrate." ...

For a time this morning it appeared as though integration would take place smoothly in this city of 102,213 population. A few persons had arrived at the high school by six o'clock. By seven, with the sun just beginning to break through the clouds, only one hundred or so had gathered at both ends of the street leading to the two-block-long school. Wooden barricades, placed at either end of the street, stopped them at those points.

Eighty members of the local police force, some on motorcycles and in squad cars, but most on foot, were on the school grounds or in the vicinity. Fifty state troopers were in the area, ready to help if needed.

At eight o'clock it was evident that the violence that Governor Faubus had predicted would take place. By this time some five hundred persons had gathered. They appeared in a fighting mood.

"The niggers won't get in," members of the crowd said, time and again.

At eight forty-five the school buzzer could be dimly heard. School was in session.

"Where are the niggers?" One person asked another. "Let them try to get in. ...."

"We'll lynch them all," several yelled.

"Sure, and all you Yankee newspapermen with

UPI

Heavily guarded black students are escorted into Little Rock Central High School on September 26, 1957. President Eisenhower had to send federal troops to the Arkansas school to enforce the Supreme Court ruling on integration.

them," a gravel-voiced man shouted. This was met with a howl of approval.

The police tried to keep the crowd off the street. The surging angry mob kept pushing forward. "Please keep back, step back," the police said politely at first, then with more authority.

"Don't you dare lay your hands on me," one woman screamed as a police officer asked her to move away.

"Lady," he pleaded, "I'm not going to touch you. I'm just doing my duty."

Suddenly a yell went up: "There they are, they're coming."

The crowd rushed after four men who turned out to be Negro newspapermen. They were manhandled by the crowd, but managed to escape.

A man yelled: "Look, they're going into our school."

Six girls and three boys crossed over into the schoolyard. They had arrived in two automobiles and had driven to the side of the school. Mrs. [Daisy] Bates [president of the Arkansas NAACP] accompanied them.

Slowly, almost as though they were entering a normal classroom on a normal school day, the students walked toward the side door of the school. The boys, in open shirts, and the girls, in bobby-socks, joked and chatted among themselves. They carried armfuls of textbooks.

The crowd now let out a roar of rage. "They've gone in," a man shouted.

"Oh, God," said a woman, "the niggers are in school."

A group of six girls, dressed in skirts and sweaters, hair in pony-tails, started to shriek and wail.

"The niggers are in our school," they howled hysterically.

One of them jumped up and down on the sidewalk, waving her arms toward her classmates in the school who were looking out of the windows, and screamed over and over again: "Come on out, come on out."

Tears flowed down her face, her body shook in uncontrollable spasms.

Three of her classmates grew hysterical and threw their arms around each other. They began dancing up and down.

"The niggers are in," they shrieked, "come on out of the school. Don't stay in there with the niggers. Come on out. Come on . . . ."

Hysteria swept from the shrieking girls to members of the crowd. Women cried hysterically, tears running down their faces.

"I'm going to get the niggers out," said Mrs. Clyde Thomason, recording secretary of the Mothers League of Central High, a segregationist group.

She started toward the school. Two policemen blocked her way.

"Please go back to the sidewalk," one begged
quietly.

"Go on and hit me, just go and hit me," Mrs.
Thomason, who had been enjoined by [federal] Judge
Davies not to interfere with the integration program,
said. She became hysterical.

A man walked over to the policemen who were
struggling to restrain Mrs. Thomason. "This is my
wife, officer," he said. "I'll take her with me."

An elderly man jumped upon the barricade. "Let's
go over the top," he shouted. "Who's going over
with me?"

"We'll all go," the crowd yelled.

Over the wooden barricade they went. A dozen
policemen stood in the way. Slowly the crowd
gave way.

The police were taunted by the mob, well out of
hand by now. Instead of tapering off, as it had
at previous morning demonstrations, the crowd grew
in numbers. By ten o'clock it had grown to about
one thousand.

"Turn in your badge," the crowd yelled at the
police.

One of the policemen said, apologetically: "I'm
only doing my duty. If I didn't I'd lose my job."

Another one, Thomas Dunaway, took off his badge
and walked away.

"Hurray! Hurray!" the crowd cheered.

"He's the only white man on the force," a young
man in a plaid shirt shouted.

"Let's pass the hat around," someone suggested.

In a moment several persons went through the
crowd, collecting money. Dollar bills were tossed into
the hat. It was estimated that about two hundred
dollars had been collected for the policeman who
gave up his badge.

The men and women, augmented by students,
surged over the "off limits" line and spread into
the street facing the school grounds. For a time it
appeared as though the local police would be

Nine black children enter Central High School accompanied by a detachment of the 101st Airborne Division. Eisenhower had ignored the issue so long that the *New York Times* was prompted to write, "The President did, belatedly and powerfully, what he might not have had to do at all if he had previously made his position unmistakably and publicly known."

completely overwhelmed by the angry crowd.

"Come on out of school, come on out, the niggers are in there," the crowd yelled.

Four girls slowly walked down the side steps of the high school.

A tremendous cheer echoed through the crowd.

"They're coming out," was shouted time and again.

Soon a group of six left. The students began to leave the school at more frequent intervals. At first the police did not permit adults to enter the school. They were acting under order of Virgil T. Blossom, Superintendent of Schools.

"I'm going to get my child," one parent said defiantly.

"Sorry, you'll stay right here," the policeman answered.

Quickly this order changed. One by one, mothers and fathers walked up to the school steps, and then returned with their children. Each time a student walked out of the school the cheers increased.

"Mother, come and get me," a girl telephoned. "They're fighting something awful here inside the school."

By twelve o'clock the mob had reached its greatest strength, and by now completely ignored the local police. The crowd remained behind the barricade, but it did not maintain order there. Several newsmen were attacked and beaten. A Negro reporter was kicked and manhandled.

Threats, jeers, and insults became more ominous.

"Let's rush the police," a ringleader shouted. "They can't stop us."

At noon the police received this message on their shortwave radios: "This is the Mayor. Tell Principal Jeff Matthews [of Central High] that the Negroes have been withdrawn. Tell Mr. Matthews to announce that to the student body. I've talked with Virgil Blossom and Negroes have been withdrawn."

At twelve-fourteen Lieutenant Carl Jackson of the Little Rock police force stood on the school grounds facing the crowd. Over a loudspeaker set up

UPI

on the sidewalk in front of the school the officer said, "The Negroes have been withdrawn from school."

"We don't believe you," the crowd yelled back. "That's just a pack of lies."

"Is there anyone whom you would believe?" he asked.

"I saw a nigger standing in the doorway just now," a woman yelled.

"Let's go in and see," another shouted.

"If you have any one person in the crowd you believe, he can go in and see, then report to you," Lieutenant Jackson said.

Mrs. Allen Thevenet, of the Mothers League of Central High School, stepped forward across the street.

"Will you accept Mrs. Thevenet's word?" the Lieutenant asked. The crowd gave a reluctant approval.

Accompanied by a policeman, Mrs. Thevenet went into the school. On her return she came to the loudspeaker and said: "We went through every room in the school and there are no niggers there."

The Negro students, meantime, had been taken out through a side door and escorted in two police cars to their homes. Despite the rumors that had been flying through the crowd that the students "had been beat up," they were not molested while in school.

"They were surprised when they were told to leave at noontime," Mrs. Bates said later.

"Nothing much happened at all," Thelma Mothershed, one of the nine Negro students, said.

"Nothing really happened," agreed Terrance Roberts, age sixteen. "We went to classes as scheduled. After the third period we were taken out and driven home. Some school officials came to see us." He added: "I was pushed once but I wasn't hit. It was quiet after we got into our classes. A few white students walked out."

Another of the girls, Elizabeth Eckford, said: "I was the only Negro girl in my class."

Would they want to come back?

"Yes," they agreed, "if we can come here without causing any trouble. The students will accept us once we go with them for a while."[13]

Kept informed of events in Little Rock, President Eisenhower denounced the mob action there and issued an order that the law be obeyed. The next morning a crowd gathered at Central High once again. The president now took stronger action. He federalized the Arkansas National Guard and ordered the 101st Airborne Division into Little Rock. Under military protection, the nine black students re-entered the school on September 25. Paratroopers patrolling the school prevented a crowd from forming.

Soldiers remained at Central High throughout the 1957–58 school year. Tensions ran high within the school, and there were many incidents involving black and white students. During the 1958–59 term, Central High was closed. Under court order, it reopened in the fall of 1959. This time Little Rock police maintained order, and tension gradually faded. Little Rock had been integrated, but the price had been high.

"I don't believe you can change the hearts of men with laws or decisions," President Eisenhower was quoted as saying, his words echoing those of the Supreme Court in the 1896 *Plessy* case. But as Martin Luther King, Jr., pointed out, laws and decisions that are properly enforced change behavior, and a change of heart might follow. Enforced, laws and decisions can guarantee the rights of minorities and curb the tyranny of the majority.

Today, with integration commonplace, one might view the events in Little Rock in 1957 with wonder, and find it difficult to believe they ever happened. Why should people grow so emotional and ugly over the thought of black and white students attending school together? The answer lies in the influence schools have on students, from kindergarten through graduation, or in what parents perceive that influence to be. Schooling is compulsory. Few can escape it. Children begin attending at an impressionable age. Southern whites had grown up in a segregated culture; they considered segregation justifiable and natural, a means

[13] *New York Times,* 24 September 1957, pp. 1, 34.

UPI

The University of Oklahoma, forced by a Supreme Court ruling to accept fifty-four-year-old G. W. McLaurin as a student, abides by the letter of the law—but not the spirit—by placing him in an ante-room apart from the other students.

of dealing with a people they considered inferior. Mixed schooling could not help but damage that myth of inferiority. And racial mingling in school might lead to mingling elsewhere. Perhaps above all else, southern whites feared that integration would lead to racial intermarriage. Little Rock was a prime example of how deeply the idea of integration could stir emotions. Attitudes on the issue were much the same throughout the Deep South.

Feelings toward integration were not confined to the lower schools. Whites felt the same about higher education. In the winter of 1956, under a federal court order, Autherine Lucy was admitted to the University of Alabama. This entrance of a single black student to an all-white university triggered rioting. The university administration solved the problem by expelling Autherine Lucy for an alleged "outrageous" statement in her suit against the institution. This time the federal government did nothing.

The Montgomery Bus Boycott

On December 1, 1955, a year after the *Brown* decision, black seamstress Rosa Parks boarded a bus in Montgomery, Alabama, to return home after a long day on her feet at her

One evening in 1955, after a hard day's work, Rosa Parks refused to give up her seat on a Montgomery, Alabama, bus to a white man. At that moment, wrote Eldridge Cleaver later, "somewhere in the universe a gear in the machinery had shifted."

job in a downtown department store. She sat down in the first seat behind the section of the bus reserved for whites. The bus gradually filled, and more white passengers got on. The driver ordered Mrs. Parks and three other blacks to move farther back to accommodate them. Although the others moved immediately, Mrs. Parks did not. The bus was full. To move back to allow a white male to have her seat meant that she would have to stand. That, Mrs. Parks decided, was too much. She refused to move.

Rosa Parks' act was personal. She was not a member of an organization seeking to challenge the legality of segregated transportation. She had simply had enough. But her single act proved to be the spark which touched off a black civil rights movement that would last well into the 1960's.

Mrs. Parks was arrested and taken to jail. There E. D. Nixon, head of an organization called Progressive Democrats, signed her bond and she was released. That, however, was not the end of it.

Word of the incident got around Montgomery's black community, particularly within the Women's Political Council. Conferring by phone, a number of members decided that blacks should organize a boycott against the Montgomery bus line to protest segregation. They passed on the suggestion to Nixon, who agreed with it and further agreed to lead the boycott. Nixon then got in touch with the Reverend Martin Luther King, Jr., and related the incident to him. "We have taken this type of thing too long already," Nixon told King, his voice trembling. "I feel that the time has come to boycott the buses. Only through a boycott can we make it clear to the white folks that we will not accept this type of treatment any longer."[14]

Both Nixon and King then conferred by phone with the Reverend Ralph Abernathy, minister of the First Baptist Church in Montgomery. They agreed to rally support among black ministers and civic leaders, and to hold a meeting the following night. "As the hour for the evening meeting arrived," King later wrote,

> I approached the doors of the church with some
> apprehension, wondering how many of the leaders

[14] Martin Luther King, Jr., *Stride toward Freedom: The Montgomery Story* (New York: Harper & Row, 1958), p. 45.

UPI

would respond to our call. Fortunately, it was one of those pleasant winter nights of unseasonable warmth, and to our relief, almost everybody who had been invited was on hand. More than forty people, from every segment of Negro life, were crowded into the large church meeting room. I saw physicians, schoolteachers, lawyers, businessmen, postal workers, union leaders, and clergymen. Virtually every organization of the Negro community was represented.

The ministers endorsed the plan with enthusiasm, and promised to go to their congregations on Sunday morning and drive home their approval of the projected one-day protest. Their cooperation was significant, since virtually all of the influential Negro ministers of the city were present. It was decided that we should hold a citywide mass meeting on Monday night, December 5, to determine how long we would abstain from riding the buses. . . .[15]

Martin Luther King, Jr., an unknown twenty-six-year-old clergyman in 1955, had become a world-famous civil rights leader by the end of the Montgomery boycott.

The group put together a statement, which they agreed to have printed and distributed to the black community of Montgomery:

Don't ride the bus to work, to town, to school, or
    any place Monday, December 5.
Another Negro woman has been arrested and put in
    jail because she refused to give up her bus seat.
Don't ride the buses to work, to town, to school, or
    anywhere on Monday. If you work, take a cab,
    share a ride, or walk.
Come to a mass meeting, Monday at 7:00 P.M., at the
    Holt Street Baptist Church for further instruction.[16]

As he reflected on the proposed boycott, King had disturbing second thoughts, moments of uneasiness. Was this the proper thing to do? Wouldn't blacks be imitating the White Citizens' Councils, which also used boycotts to gain their ends? Was a boycott unethical, perhaps immoral? But, he wrote,

[15] Ibid., pp. 46–47.
[16] Ibid., p. 48.

As I thought further I came to see that what we were really doing was withdrawing our cooperation from an evil system, rather than merely withdrawing our economic support from the bus company. The bus company, being an external expression of the system, would naturally suffer, but the basic aim was to refuse to cooperate with evil. At this point I began to think about Thoreau's essay on civil disobedience. I remembered how, as a college student, I had been moved when I first read this work. I became convinced that what we were preparing to do in Montgomery was related to what Thoreau had expressed. We were simply saying to the white community, "We can no longer lend our cooperation to an evil system."

Something began to say to me, "He who passively accepts evil is as much involved in it as he who helps to perpetrate it. He who accepts evil without protesting against it is really cooperating with it." When oppressed people willingly accept their oppression they only serve to give the oppressor a convenient justification for his acts. Often the oppressor goes along unaware of the evil involved in his oppression so long as the oppressed accepts it. So in order to be true to one's conscience and true to God, a righteous man has no alternative but to refuse to cooperate with an evil system. This I felt was the nature of our action. From this moment on I conceived of our movement as an act of massive noncooperation. . . .[17]

The Montgomery *Advertiser* obtained a copy of the appeal and ran it as part of a front-page story on Saturday morning. The paper printed the story mainly to inform whites of the blacks' plans, but it turned out to be excellent publicity for the boycott and the Monday mass meeting.

On December 5, fully ninety percent of the members of the black community of Montgomery who ordinarily rode buses chose instead to walk, bicycle, hitch a ride, or stay home. Although this demonstration of black solidarity was completely ignored by the white authorities, its importance

[17] Ibid., pp. 51–52.

UPI

A scene outside the Montgomery County Courthouse during Martin Luther King's trial. After the Supreme Court's ruling declaring segregation on public transportation illegal, King rode a bus in Montgomery. "It was a great ride," he said.

did not escape black leaders. Their demands, originally limited and local in nature, escalated into an all-out campaign for desegregated public transportation. They extended the boycott, set up picket lines, solicited donations to underwrite costs, and organized a two-hundred-car motor pool for those who lived too far from work, school, or shopping areas to walk.

The boycott proved too effective for the white community to ignore for long. The bus company lost money and was forced to lay off drivers and cut back schedules. The success of the boycott, and its implications for the future, frightened whites throughout the South. Ninety black leaders were indicted under an old anti-union law prohibiting conspiracy to obstruct the operation of a business. King, the first to be tried and convicted, paid a $500 fine. Charges against the others were dropped. Other blacks were arrested on a variety of charges, and all those who participated actively in the boycott were harassed continually by white authorities. Finally, on December 13, 1956, in a suit brought by the NAACP, the Supreme Court of the United States declared

UPI

The Reverend Ralph Abernathy arrives at the courthouse in Montgomery on March 19, 1956, for the bus boycott trial.

that the Alabama state law requiring segregation on public buses was unconstitutional.

Throughout the year-long ordeal, the black residents of Montgomery had honored King's pleas for nonviolence. "Nonviolence," he had said, "is the most potent technique for oppressed people. Unearned suffering is redemptive." Nonviolent direct action, combined with litigation in the courts, had indeed proved to be a potent technique for the civil rights movement. King soon became nationally prominent, and his strategy gained wide acceptance among black leaders.

Born in Atlanta, Georgia, in 1929, King was only twenty-six when he became involved in the Montgomery bus boycott. He was a graduate of Morehouse College, Crozer Theological Seminary, Boston University, and the Chicago Theological Seminary. An ordained Baptist minister, King became pastor of the Dexter Avenue Baptist Church in Montgomery. He became and remained foremost among the new black leadership in America, and he spent the remainder of his life in the civil rights movement. He was awarded the Nobel Peace Prize in 1964. Four years later, while in Memphis, Tennessee, to aid in a garbagemen's strike, King was assassinated.

The Technique of Nonviolence

In his account of the Montgomery boycott, *Stride toward Freedom,* Martin Luther King, Jr., traced his intellectual antecedents to a number of philosophers and religious thinkers. In addition to Henry David Thoreau, whose essay "Civil Disobedience" influenced his attitude toward the boycott, King drew particular inspiration from Reinhold Niebuhr, the American theologian, and Mohandas K. Gandhi, the Indian nationalist leader who was assassinated in 1948. King stated that since nonviolence played such a positive role in the Montgomery movement, he felt obligated to discuss the basic characteristics of his philosophy.

First, he said, "It must be emphasized that nonviolent resistance is not a method for cowards: it does resist. Gandhi often said if cowardice is the only alternative to violence, it is better to fight."[18]

[18] Ibid., p. 101.

Second, King asserted, an outstanding characteristic of nonviolence is that it does not seek to defeat or humiliate the opponent, but to win his friendship and understanding. The nonviolent resister, King went on to say, must often express his protest through noncooperation or boycotts. But these are merely means to awaken a sense of moral shame in the opponent—the end is redemption and reconciliation. The aftermath of nonviolence is the creation of the beloved community, while the aftermath of violence is tragic bitterness. As he told a mass meeting of blacks in Montgomery in February, 1956:

> If we are arrested every day, if we are exploited
> every day, if we are trampled over every day, don't
> ever let anyone pull you so low as to hate them.
> We must use the weapon of love. We must
> have compassion and understanding for those who
> hate us. We must realize so many people are taught to
> hate us that they are not totally responsible for
> their hate. But while we stand in life at midnight, we
> are always on the threshold of a new dawn.[19]

A third characteristic of this method, according to King, is that the nonviolent attack is directed against *forces* of evil rather than against *persons* who happen to be doing evil. It is evil that the nonviolent resister seeks to defeat, not the person victimized by it. Elaborating on this concept, King told the people of Montgomery:

> The tension in this city is not between white
> people and Negro people. The tension is at bottom,
> between justice and injustice, between the forces
> of light and the forces of darkness. And if there is a
> victory, it will be a victory not merely for fifty
> thousand Negroes, but a victory of justice and the
> forces of light. We are out to defeat injustice and
> not white persons who may be unjust.[20]

Fourth, King said, nonviolent resistance is characterized by the fact that it avoids not only external physical violence

[19] *New York Times,* 23 February 1956.
[20] King, *Stride toward Freedom,* pp. 106-107.

Southern Christian
Leadership Conference

The Reverend Martin Luther King, Jr.

but also internal violence of spirit. Until his death, King believed that nonviolence was the way.

In another of his books, *Why We Can't Wait,* King asserted that the Negro method of nonviolent direct action by its very nature challenges the myth of inferiority. Even the most reluctant were forced to recognize that blacks—a supposedly inferior people—could choose and successfully pursue a strategy requiring such extensive sacrifice, bravery, and skill.

Dr. King also noted that one aspect of the civil rights struggle which received little attention was its contribution to the whole society. In winning rights for themselves, Negroes produced substantial benefits for the nation. The revolution for human rights opened for scrutiny other unhealthy areas in American life, and permitted a new and wholesome healing to take place. Eventually, King believed, the civil rights movement would contribute infinitely more to the nation than simply the eradication of racial injustice. It would enlarge the concept of brotherhood to a vision of total interrelatedness. Nonviolence, the answer to the blacks' need for a means to achieve equality, wrote King, might become the answer to the most desperate need of all humanity.

The Close of a Decade

The episode at Little Rock placed the federal government firmly in the area of race relations. It became more deeply involved in 1957 when Congress passed the first civil rights legislation since 1875. The Civil Rights Act of 1957 created a Civil Rights Commission as well as a Civil Rights Division in the Justice Department. Further, it empowered the Justice Department to bring suit on behalf of blacks denied the right to vote.

This legislation, however, proved hardly a start. Few suits were filed under the act during the remainder of the decade. Nor were there any more dramatic incidents like Montgomery as the 1950's passed into history.

During the 1950's, the black population had increased twenty-five percent, compared to an eighteen-percent increase among whites. More than half of America's blacks now lived outside the South, slightly more than seventy percent of them in urban areas, an increase from sixty-three percent in 1950. Black housing remained poor. Nationwide, in 1960 one out of six non-white families lived in housing units that were dilapidated, in comparison to one out of thirty-two among whites. And discrimination remained the rule, especially with respect to employment. According to a 1961 Civil Rights Commission report:

Although their occupational levels have risen considerably during the past 20 years, Negro workers continue to be concentrated in the less skilled jobs. And it is largely because of this concentration in the ranks of the unskilled and semi-skilled, the groups most severely affected by both economic layoffs and technological changes, that Negroes are also disproportionately represented among the unemployed. ... Negroes continue to swell the ranks of the unemployed as technological changes eliminate the unskilled or semi-skilled tasks they once performed. Many will be permanently or chronically unemployed unless some provision is made for retraining them in the skills required by today's economy. The depressed economic status of Negroes is the product of many forces, including the following:

Discrimination against Negroes in vocational as well as academic training.

Discrimination against Negroes in apprenticeship training programs.

Discrimination against Negroes by labor organizations—particularly in the construction and machinists' crafts.

Discrimination against Negroes in referral services rendered by State employment offices.

Discrimination against Negroes in the training and "employment" opportunities offered by the armed services, including the "civilian components."

Discrimination by employers, including Government contractors and even the Federal Government.[21]

A beginning had been made in the 1940's and 1950's. But the road to equality stretched well into the future.

[21] U.S. Commission on Civil Rights, *Civil Rights U.S.A.: Public Schools, Cities in the North and West* (Washington, D.C.: U.S. Government Printing Office, 1962).

SUGGESTED READINGS

Baldwin, James. *Go Tell It on the Mountain*. Dell.

Du Bois, W. E. B. *The Souls of Black Folk*. New American Library.

Ellison, Ralph. *The Invisible Man*. Random House, Vintage Books.

King, Martin Luther, Jr. *Stride toward Freedom: The Montgomery Story*. Harper & Row.

King, Martin Luther, Jr. *Why We Can't Wait*. New American Library.

Myrdal, Gunnar. *An American Dilemma: The Negro Problem and Modern Democracy*. 2 vols. Pantheon.

Wright, Richard. *Black Boy*. Harper & Row, Perennial Library.

Wright, Richard. *Native Son*. Harper & Row, Perennial Library.

Lakewood Park, California, a typical new suburb of the 1950's, was built on land which had been bulldozed flat and shorn of all vegetation by the subdividers. As these suburbs sprang up, they brought with them other hallmarks of the decade, including the backyard barbeque, Little League, and the station wagon.

5

THE 1950'S

IN RETROSPECT

During the fifteen years following World War II, personal incomes rose, population mobility increased, and urbanization continued at a rapid pace. On the whole it was a conservative time, as one might expect after a period of depression and war. As president during most of the 1950's, Dwight D. Eisenhower set the national tone, describing himself at different times as a "moderate conservative" or a "conservative moderate." The Eisenhower administration created a new cabinet department, the Department of Health, Education and Welfare. As its first secretary, Eisenhower appointed Oveta Culp Hobby, who had headed the Women's Army Corps during World War II. The administration also supported a progressive public housing bill. And before Eisenhower left office Congress passed the Kerr-Mills Act, the first federal measure to provide medical aid for the poor and aged.

Mostly, however, the administration rocked no boats. Perhaps the most significant phenomenon of the time was the rehabilitation of big business. In the 1930's, after the bottom dropped out of the economy and depression set in, businessmen—and the whole capitalist system—fell into low repute. But American industry had redeemed itself during the war, and it rose still higher in public esteem as the technological revolution continued during the postwar years. Eisenhower's first cabinet appointments reflected the position of big business in America. As one observer remarked, the cabinet was composed of "eight millionaires and a plumber." Martin Durkin, president of

Dwight D.
Eisenhower
expressed the
sentiment of millions
of Americans during
the 1950's when he
said that the path to
the future was "down
the middle."

the United Association of Journeyman Plumbers and Steamfitters, became secretary of labor. Charles Wilson, president of General Motors before his appointment as secretary of defense, was one of the millionaires. Wilson, a blunt and outspoken man, soon became the victim of misquotation. While testifying before a congressional committee about the possibility of a conflict of interest if he retained his General Motors stock while serving as defense secretary, Wilson said he believed that "what was good for the country was good for General Motors, and vice versa." This got shortened into "what's good for GM is good for the country," and the remark aroused considerable controversy. Adlai Stevenson, however, remained calm. "While the New Dealers have all left Washington to make way for the car dealers," he said, "I hasten to say that I, for one, do not believe the story that the general welfare has become a subsidiary of General Motors."

But many companies did become subsidiaries of others, another phenomenon which marked the time and which continues to the present. Competition in nearly all areas of business diminished as corporations moved toward conglomeration—the merger of diverse and unrelated industries under the same ownership. An oil company might acquire a motion picture studio, for example, or a food processing company might acquire a publishing house. Each firm within the conglomerate is managed separately, but all report to a single head. A trend toward oligopoly—the domination of an industry by a few firms—also gained strength during the 1950's. Eventually there were only four automobile companies, for example. Ford, General Motors, Chrysler, and American Motors controlled the market for domestically produced cars. And General Motors, with 54.5 percent, enjoyed the largest slice of that market.

As a businessman's administration, Eisenhower and his advisers valued a balanced budget. The administration did achieve balanced budgets in some years by cutting defense and other spending. But reduced federal outlays helped bring on three recessions—in 1954–55, in 1957–58, and in the fall of 1960.

A "youth culture" developed in the 1950's, in the sense that the teen-age years became generally recognized as a

separate stage of existence, between childhood and adulthood. This was something of a departure for American
society, and it was largely the result of economic prosperity—more and more young people, supported by their
families, could afford to prolong adolescence in high school
and college. Some aspects of the new teen-age culture—
clothing styles and musical tastes, for example—aroused
great concern among adults at the time. In retrospect,
however, the youth of the decade seems on the whole to have
been conservative and conformist, reflecting the contemporary mood.

The 1950's marked a period of transition—in part a
looking back to attempt to recapture and re-emphasize old
values, but at the same time a breathing space, a period of
calm before the decade of turmoil which, as it turned out,
lay ahead. There was much that was old, even stodgy,
about the 1950's. But there was also much that was new,
especially in the realm of technology.

Technology and Prosperity

As the United States emerged from World War II, no one—
friend or foe—doubted that it was the most technologically
advanced and most powerful nation on earth. The ability of
the United States to combine science and industry for the
mass production of the machines of war had no historical
precedent. And as factories converted their technology
and industrial capacity to peacetime markets, the American
consumer was dazzled by the number of new products. Cars
now could be purchased with all kinds of accessories,
functional or merely decorative. For the house there were
dish washers, clothes washers, clothes dryers, air con-
ditioners, water softeners, and many smaller appliances
such as food blenders and electric toothbrushes. For entertainment there were AM-FM radios, long-playing records,
high-fidelity record players, tape recorders, home movie
equipment, and—most exciting of all—television sets. The
consumer was equally overwhelmed by the number of
products made with synthetic materials, such as rayon,
nylon, dacron, orlon, vinyl, polyester, plastic, plexiglass,
fiberglass, acrylic, and so on. As the new technology continued to be refined, and as new products continued to

appear in the marketplace, Americans indulged themselves in luxuries—luxuries that many would soon come to regard as neccessities.

To Americans with money to spend, the 1950's must have seemed like a kind of earthly paradise, full of material delights. But to those who worked on assembly lines to produce the new consumer goods, the 1950's must have seemed like a decade of dehumanization. These Americans now performed single, machine-like tasks on assembly lines. Their work had become routine, uninspiring, and dull. They no longer worked on a product until it was finished. There was no longer an opportunity to be creative, or to take initiative, in their work. They felt no personal pride in a mass-produced product. And many felt insecure, knowing their present jobs probably would be taken over by machines, which would perform with one hundred percent efficiency and would not become bored, inefficient, or prone to make human errors.

As industry became more automated during the 1950's, some employees were trained for new jobs while others were left to seek new jobs on their own. But, despite the loss of some jobs to automation, steadily growing industrial production provided for more employment than unemployment during the decade. And this increased productivity made the economy healthy. The United States became the most affluent society in history.

Most Americans had little contact with the seemingly miraculous process of industrial automation, but many in their daily lives became acquainted with various types of new machines. In *Travels with Charley,* John Steinbeck reflected on this feature of American life:

> I had neglected my own country too long. Civilization had made great strides in my absence. I remember when a coin in a slot would get you a stick of gum or a candy bar, but in these dining palaces were vending machines where various coins could deliver handkerchiefs, comb and nail-file sets, hair conditioners and cosmetics, first-aid kits, minor drugs such as aspirin and pills to keep you awake. I found myself entranced with these gadgets. Suppose you want a soft drink; you pick your kind—Sungrape or

Cooly Cola—press a button, insert the coin, and stand back. A paper cup drops into place, the drink pours out and stops a quarter of an inch from the brim—a cold, refreshing drink guaranteed synthetic! Coffee is even more interesting, for when the hot black fluid has ceased, a squirt of milk comes down and an envelope of sugar drops beside the cup. But of all, the hot-soup machine is the triumph. Choose among ten—pea, chicken noodle, beef and vegetable, insert the coin. A rumbling hum comes from the giant and a sign lights up that reads "Heating." After a minute a red light flashes on and off until you open a little door and remove the paper cup of boiling hot soup.

It is life at a peak of some kind of civilization. . . .[1]

The machines Steinbeck described are commonplace now, but in the 1950's they were something new and remarkable.

Automobiles grew larger and longer in the 1950's. Some sprouted tail fins. But automotive design, and automobiles themselves, had their critics. John Keats, in his book *The Insolent Chariots,* claimed that American cars were too big, too expensive, too impractical, and too numerous. Keats criticized the poor fuel economy of the gasoline-guzzling cars, quoting an automotive official on the subject: "Oh, we're helping the gas companies, same as our competitors." He blasted the wide, low-slung, and gaudy design of the decade as unnecessary and wasteful. He decried the annual model change and "planned obsolescence"—the deliberate manufacture of cars that would become unfashionable or even nonfunctional within a few years. He lampooned the American "love affair" with the automobile. He scoffed at a public which preferred large cars loaded with "extras," and deplored the lack of safety features in automotive design. And who was to blame for the situation? Keats wrote,

I am painfully aware that I have not supplied a satisfactory answer to the question of whether it is Detroit or the public that makes our automotive taste.

[1] John Steinbeck, *Travels with Charley in Search of America* (New York: Viking Press, 1961), pp. 82–83.

General Motors

The 1954 Cadillac Eldorado convertible boasted a number of fashionable features, including an exhaust outlet built into the bumper, hand-brushed aluminum rear trim, a curved, tinted glass windshield, and, of course, tail fins.

Nearly all Americans have convinced themselves that they each need an automobile—a proposition as open to question as the theory that since everyone drinks milk, everyone should keep a cow. Since Americans must generally buy from Detroit, buy they do, so it doesn't seem to make much difference what Detroit sees fit to produce—the public will be stuck with it in any case. On the other hand, a large part of the public does seem to want fripperies, as any dealer will tell you, so we can say Detroit has this fact in mind.

Perhaps we come closer to the truth when we say there is an interaction here, and we can understand it better when we realize that Detroit does not produce cars for reasonable people like thee and me, but for that vast section of the American public that presumably has something radically wrong with it. If our cars were only minutely different, perhaps this bespeaks the fact that little things loom large in little minds. At all events, every automobile advertisement tells the reasonable man that the advertisement was written for someone suffering from a severe character defect, and it is not surprising to discover that this is true in literal fact. The wording is deliberate, and the car described is deliberately designed for the nut that is eventually to hold the wheel. If Detroit is right in this matter, there is little wrong with the American car that is not wrong with the American public. Now this

is quite an assumption, but it is the one upon which
Detroit has built its shabby fortunes. . . .[2]

By inaugurating a vast highway building program, the
federal government helped the auto industry as well as other
industries that depended on automobiles—oil companies,
for example, and motel chains. With the federal government
footing ninety percent of the bill, construction of the
interstate highway system began in the 1950's. The purpose
of the program, which has continued up to the present,
was to link all parts of the nation with four-lane roads.
But while this helped some segments of the economy, it
harmed others. Railroad passenger service deteriorated,
as did other forms of public transportation. Considerable
land, once tax-productive, soon lay under concrete. But
the highway program increased American mobility and,
along with television, helped to eliminate regional differences. Food served in restaurants along the interstates,
for example, looked and tasted the same in California as
it did in Maine.

Although there were some observers like John Keats who
worried about the side effects of prosperity—the squandering of natural resources and the deterioration of the
environment—most people during the 1950's regarded the
products of the new technology as a blessing and accepted
them without question. Most Americans, comfortable for
the present and optimistic about the future, did not regard
smog or other forms of pollution as worthy of serious con-
sideration. If the situation was as bad as the doomsayers
claimed, surely the leaders of government and industry
would correct it. Nor were most Americans concerned about
conditions in the inner cities, where overcrowding and
unemployment were facts of life. Surely, they thought, the
poor would improve their lot as they became more prosperous along with the rest of American society. And Americans were becoming more prosperous. It seemed that
families everywhere were buying new cars and commuting to
new homes in the suburbs, homes that were filled with

[2] John Keats, *The Insolent Chariots* (Philadelphia: J.B. Lippincott,
1958), pp. 14, 56–57.

dish washers, television sets, and other proofs of the nation's ever-increasing affluence.

Unfortunately, the optimism of the 1950's was not borne out in the 1960's. Then Americans learned that environmental conditions were fast approaching a crisis stage, that the squandering of oil and other natural resources would have to be checked, and that many Americans had not been able to claim their share of the nation's wealth. These and other oversights and inequities would become some of the political issues of the 1960's.

An Increase in Leisure Time

The belief that there is virtue in hard work has a long tradition in the United States. And throughout most of the nation's history it has been a useful belief, one that transformed the country from a wilderness to an industrial society capable of supporting more people in greater comfort than anywhere else in the world. Yet there is an irony in that fact. In the industrial society created by so much hard work, there has been less need for people to work hard. With all the productive capabilities that automation provides, it has become economically less important for individuals to work and more important for them to consume. But consumption—and particularly the consumption of goods and services one could easily do without—had traditionally been regarded not as a virtue but as a vice.

One characteristic of the industrial-technological society of the 1950's was the increased amount of leisure time available to people in lower socio-economic levels. This was new in the history of a nation in which industrial employees as well as farmers had long spent most of their waking hours at work. The average work week for manufacturing employees during the 1950's was between thirty-five and forty hours, with two to three weeks' annual paid vacations. Holidays, paid sick leave, and the institutionalization of the "coffee break" further extended workers' benefits. Much more leisure time became available than ever before, and producers of goods and services provided means to fill it. In 1953, *Business Week* reported:

> The average man can, in his spare time, dig in the garden (with a motorized tool), fly across the Atlantic, go swimming in a plastic pool, fish in the

Adirondacks, ski in Sun Valley, winter in Florida, hear chamber music on his hi-fi phonograph, look at Cinerama, make a coffee table (with an electric saw), read a 35¢ edition of Shakespeare. The National Recreation Association distinguishes no less than 81 different organized activities offered by U.S. municipal parks. One hobby expert ... has figured that there are some 200 recognizable "creative activities" in the United States today.[3]

By the mid-1950's, Americans were spending $800 million a year on powerboats alone. Another sign of the new leisure was the variety of special-purpose clothing for camping, fishing, skiing, or just relaxing to be found in the wardrobes of more and more ordinary citizens. Travel and sightseeing businesses contributed a considerable amount toward the Gross National Product.

Americans seemed to have insatiable appetites for labor-saving devices. A wide variety of such electrical tools as food mixers, can openers, knife sharpeners, and shoe shiners were snapped up when introduced to the market. Prepared foods, including frozen juices, prebaked and frozen breads and pastries, cake mixes, whole frozen dinners, and pre-mixed cocktails were equally well accepted. Even the work associated with baby care was reduced by commercially prepared baby food and by diaper services, the markets for which boomed during the 1950's.

Devices that saved labor usually saved time. Skeptics wondered if Americans were doing worthwhile things with the time they saved, or if they were merely spending more hours in front of television sets. Certainly they were consuming more products, and this seemed to help the economy. But people who had endured the depression years held a different attitude toward work. They found it incomprehensible that a person might contribute more to society by consuming than by producing. Yet even these people did not, it appeared, really wish to return to pre-automation days. Deploring what seemed a growing softness in the American character, they voiced a deeply ingrained American worry: if you do not work hard for something, is it really good for you?

Even Mom's traditional apple pie went "instant" during the 1950's, as this advertisement for a product called Pyequick demonstrates. The package contained dehydrated apple slices ("add water and a little sugar") and premixed pie crust ("just add water").

---

[3] *Business Week*, 12 May 1953, p. 13.

UPI

In 1951, when this photograph was taken, television was well on its way toward becoming the dominant medium in the communications industry. Even Senator Estes Kefauver and his family, shown in the picture, appear to have fallen under the spell of the tube's hypnotic eye. Kefauver became nationally known largely as a result of television, when many of the hearings of his Senate Crime Investigating Committee were broadcast live.

Mass Culture

Throughout most of Western history, culture—in the sense of literature, the fine arts, and the performing arts—has been accessible to a relatively small segment of society. It was defined, produced, and enjoyed by the educated few who had time and money to spend. In America in the mid-twentieth century, however, several factors combined to change this picture. American society in the 1950's was characterized by high productivity, expanding leisure time, increased mobility, higher college enrollments, a growing middle class, and rapidly developing communications technology. These factors helped to create a much larger audience for entertainment of all kinds, including cultural pursuits. What has been called "mass culture" blossomed in the 1950's.

Television led the way. Experiments with the medium of television went back to the 1920's. The first commercial program originated at the New York World's Fair in 1939.

At that time, five-inch and nine-inch sets were available at prices ranging from $200 to $600. By the end of 1941, there were about ten thousand sets operating in the country. Then, with the nation at war, further television activity ceased.

Development resumed at the end of the war, and by 1947 a number of models were on the market. Networks were now on the air thirty hours a week. The price of sets remained high, and a good many people saw television only in taverns whose owners had installed sets to attract customers. The popular comedian Fred Allen joked: "There are millions of people in New York who don't even know what television is. They aren't old enough to go into saloons yet."

Some observers saw great educational and cultural benefits stemming from television. They proved more hopeful than accurate, however, at least according to television's critics. Like radio before it, television became primarily a means of selling products, and commercials took up considerable time. Advertising revenues climbed as the medium gained in popularity, reaching $100 million a year in 1950.

The early television programs were mostly adaptations of popular radio entertainment. Soap operas had been standard daytime radio fare. Now they were on television. Quiz shows jumped from radio to the tube. Weekly radio programs featuring such comedians as Jack Benny and Burns and Allen now became television shows. The old radio standby "Amos 'n' Andy" also made the move to television, with black actors replacing the white actors whose voices had been heard in a caricature of black speech on radio. The new show, like the old, perpetuated unflattering racial stereotypes, and it was removed from the air after the civil rights movement gained strength.

Television also introduced some comedians who were new to the mass audience. Among the most successful was Milton Berle, whose tendency to adopt old material originated by others earned him the nickname "The Thief of Badgags." Sid Caesar and Imogene Coca created more sophisticated comedy on "Your Show of Shows," as did Jackie Gleason and Danny Kaye on their own shows. There were also a number of variety programs. The most popular of these was "The Toast of the Town," hosted by a rather

Jack Benny was one of the stars of radio who managed to make a successful transition to television. This may have been partly because he continued to rely on his audience to use their imaginations. For example, his money vault, around which recurring jokes were built, never appeared on the small screen.

UPI

Ed Sullivan hosted
"The Toast of the
Town" for twenty
years. The variety
show featured a wide
range of entertainers,
from a talking mouse
to (in the 1960's) the
Rolling Stones.

awkward newspaperman named Ed Sullivan, which appeared every Sunday night for twenty years. In addition to presenting established singers, dancers, and comedians, Sullivan regularly introduced newcomers. One newcomer created an enormous stir on his first appearance in 1956. He was Elvis Presley, who sang what was becoming known as "rock and roll." Adults were highly critical of Presley's flashy clothes, his long, slicked-back hair, the sensual, slurring quality of his voice, and the disturbing, pulsating beat of his music. And they were appalled by his body movements. As he strummed the guitar and belted out the lyrics, he swiveled his hips suggestively—some thought obscenely. After his first few moments on stage, the cameramen discreetly focused above his waist.

Baseball games and other sports events attracted millions of viewers. So did televised wrestling matches, which were more for entertainment than for real. *Time* magazine reported early in 1950:

> Television was promising either to kill or cure the sports world. Wrestling had a sweaty, dying pallor until it was hurried onto TV as an inexpensive fill-in. So astounding was its success that when Promoter Ned Irish put a wrestling match into Madison Square Garden last month, he grossed over $50,000—$10,000 more than any boxing card had drawn all season. Said Irish: "At least 40% of the customers were women—there's nothing you can attribute it to but television."[4]

Television programming was not all light entertainment. There were some strong and timely documentaries, such as those produced by Edward R. Murrow on "See It Now." There were some penetrating interviews, such as those conducted by Mike Wallace, which exposed public figures to the public view in a way that had never been possible before. And there was some fine drama—Paddy Chayefsky's *Marty* and Rod Serling's *Requiem for a Heavyweight*, to name only two important original plays—presented on such programs as "Playhouse 90," "Studio One," and "The Goodyear Playhouse."

But, in the opinion of many critics, the worthwhile

[4] *Time Capsule: 1950* (New York: Time-Life, 1967), pp. 179–180.

programs were few and far between, oases in the "waste-land" of television. Referring to television as the "boob tube," they saw it as a promise unfulfilled. Television, they said, was a medium held captive by hucksters peddling their wares, hucksters who judged the merit of a program solely on the basis of the audience it attracted for their commercials. Some critics feared television's effect on children who, it seemed, spent more time in front of the set each week than they did in school. Mothers, on the other hand, saw advantages. One mother in New York said, "The hours between play and bed used to be the most hectic part of the day. Now I know where the children are. The television set is the best nurse in the world."[5]

As far as the public was concerned, critics of television talked only to themselves. The sale of sets continued to climb until more than ninety percent of American homes had at least one. And faithfully, each week, millions of people watched programs that the critics considered worth-less. The tendency of so many people to stay at home for entertainment forced thousands of movie theaters to close. With attendance off, Hollywood produced fewer movies, and a number of studios fell into financial trouble. Even-tually, however, the movie industry struck a truce with television and became the source of programs made especially for the small screen.

Regardless of how one felt about it, television was a wholly new and wholly different form of communication. No one knew precisely its gross effects, to say nothing of its subtle effects, on viewers. The printed word is no more than a symbol. Motion pictures of momentous events essentially present history, things that occurred more or less recently but always in the past. Television, on the other hand, could bring *now* into the living room. One could be caught up in a televised event almost as though one were actually there. It was that *now* characteristic of television that was different, and people watching an event as it occurred had an inkling of what this meant—even though they might be totally unable to explain its effect on them, particularly when it happened day in and day out.

But television was not the only purveyor of "mass culture"

[5] Quoted in Joseph Goulden, *The Best Years: 1945-1950* (New York: Atheneum, 1976), p. 170.

to develop in the 1950's. The highly productive American economy offered other and better ways for people to expand their cultural horizons.

Unbreakable, long-playing 33^{1}/$_{3}$-rpm phonograph records appeared in 1948. Far superior in sound quality to the old 78's, and far more convenient to play and to store, the new records encouraged the collection of home music libraries. And soon there were thousands of records available for every musical taste, from the heaviest classical to the lightest pop. Stereophonic equipment, which further enhanced the quality of sound reproduction, was introduced in 1957. Stereo sets were expensive status symbols at first, but within a few years competition among manufacturers had made them as affordable, and as commonplace, as television sets.

Refinements in color printing made the visual arts more accessible. Through good prints and reproductions in art books, a person could become acquainted with the collections of the world's finest art museums without ever leaving home.

Then there was the paperback revolution in book publishing. Paperbound books had been around for nearly a century, but they were mostly "pulp" fiction—tales of romance, crime, and Wild West adventure that hardly counted as literature. In the 1930's, Penguin Books in England and Pocket Books in the United States tried reprinting good books in a paperback format, with some success. But it was during World War II that paperback publishing really took off. People lonely at home and far from home turned to books for entertainment and self-education. Hardbound books were too expensive for most of these new readers; they also used up too much paper (which was rationed like everything else) and took up too much space in shipment. The result was a paperback explosion. The publishing industry provided the armed forces with about 125 million paperbacks for distribution to servicemen, and many millions more were produced for sale in the domestic marketplace.

Contrary to expectations, the coming of peace and even the coming of television did not diminish the demand for inexpensive books. And, with the development of more economical methods of printing and binding, publishers were able to offer an ever-widening list of paperback titles, from the classics to contemporary best-sellers and "how-to" books. The new method of mass marketing—selling paperbacks in grocery stores, drug stores, and so on—recruited even more readers. In a hardbound edition, a new book might make the best-seller lists with a sale of about thirty thousand copies. In a paperback reprint, that same book might easily sell three hundred thousand copies.

During the 1950's, nearly seven thousand magazines turned out a total of 3.5 billion copies each year. Individual television programs counted their viewers in the millions. With the same books, magazines, and television programs consumed daily by large numbers of people, American culture achieved a degree of homogeneity, or sameness, never before envisioned. A man from a small town in Nebraska meeting a man from New York City could discuss a television program or an issue of a news magazine that each had seen or read in his own home the day before. Experiences in common produced homogeneity, which critics deplored just as they deplored the low-level content of those experiences. More than anything else, television and population mobility diminished—some say destroyed— diversities of speech, dress, manner, and style of life that once set off one section of the country, like the South, from others. Steinbeck commented on this aspect of American culture in *Travels with Charley*:

> It seemed to me [in my travels] that regional speech is in the process of disappearing, not gone but going. Forty years of radio and twenty years of television must have this impact. Communications must destroy localness, by a slow, inevitable process. I can remember a time when I could almost pinpoint a man's place of origin by his speech. That is growing more difficult now and will in some foreseeable future become impossible. It is a rare house or building that is not rigged with spiky combers of the air. Radio and television speech becomes standardized, perhaps better English than we have ever used. Just as our bread, mixed and baked, packaged and sold without benefit

John Steinbeck in 1962, the year he won the Nobel Prize for literature for his rich portrayal of American life in such novels as *The Grapes of Wrath, Cannery Row,* and *East of Eden.*

UPI

of accident or human frailty, is uniformly good and uniformly tasteless, so will our speech become one speech.[6]

Americans had created a high degree of political and economic democracy. Now they seemed to have developed a cultural democracy as well. People were experiencing more in the way of culture, but—critics asked—were they better off for it? Was the country better off? Were literature, the theater, and the arts in general better off? Did the flow of words and images to which people were so constantly exposed help them to arrive at a deeper understanding of themselves or their society?

Conformity in a Mass Society

In order to function, any society must demand some degree of conformity from its members. But during the 1950's, many observers believed, Americans became more conformist than was necessary or even healthy in a free society. Individualism, although still a highly valued trait in theory, seemed to be fading out in practice.

McCarthyism and the Cold War were responsible to a great extent for the political conformity of the decade. Television and the other mass media, which presented middle-class values almost exclusively, influenced people's ideas about how they ought to live, look, speak, and think. Another factor was population mobility—people moving from places where they and their families had been known, perhaps for generations, to new suburbs around urban areas. In those communities of strangers, people tended to judge each other on the basis of appearances, with the result that conformity in clothing styles, hair styles, and other superficial matters became more important in gaining social acceptance and even in finding employment. The growth of bureaucratic organizations, both in government and in private enterprise, also contributed. William Whyte expanded on this last factor in a widely read book, *The Organization Man*:

This book is about the organization man. If the term is vague, it is because I can think of no other

[6]Steinbeck, *Travels with Charley,* p. 86.

UPI

Representatives of labor and representatives of management are virtually indistinguishable in this photograph taken during bargaining talks between officials of the United Auto Workers and executives of the Ford Motor Company.

way to describe the people I am talking about. They are not the workers, nor are they the white-collar people in the usual, clerk sense of the word. These people only work for The Organization. The ones I am talking about *belong* to it as well. They are the ones of our middle class who have left home, spiritually as well as physically, to take the vows of organization life, and it is they who are the mind and soul of our great self-perpetuating institutions. ... They have not joined together into a recognizable elite—our country does not stand still long enough for that—but it is from their ranks that are coming most of the first and second echelons of our leadership, and it is their values which will set the American temper.

The corporation man is the conspicuous example, but he is only one, for the collectivization so visible in the corporation has affected almost every field of work. Blood brother to the business trainee off to join DuPont is the seminarian who will end up in the church hierarchy, the doctor headed for the corporate clinic, the physics Ph.D. in a government laboratory, the intellectual on the foundation-sponsored team project, the engineering graduate in the huge drafting room at Lockheed, the young apprentice in a Wall Street law factory.

They are all, as they so often put it, in the same boat. Listen to them talk to each other over the front lawns of their suburbia and you cannot help but be struck by how well they grasp the common denominators which bind them. Whatever the differences in their organization ties, it is the common problems of collective work that dominate their attentions, and when the DuPont man talks to the research chemist or the chemist to the army man, it is these problems that are uppermost.[7]

Even those who did not commit themselves psychologically to "the organization" found their professional and personal lives more and more hemmed in by rules and regulations as American institutions of all kinds grew in size and bureaucratic complexity during the 1950's. On the job, for white-collar and blue-collar workers alike, there were detailed written procedures—often prepared by executives unfamiliar with day-to-day operations—covering everything from parking spaces in the company lot to the types of clothing considered suitable for male and female employees. Dealing with insurance companies, unions, banks, and government departments at all levels, from the Social Security Administration to the dog catcher, became a matter of paperwork rather than personal contact. Income tax forms became more complicated, and new deductions kept showing up on the stubs of paychecks—deductions often mysterious to the wage earner. Year by year, it seemed, more and more people had less and less control over important aspects of their lives. Many people accepted the pressures to conform without much conscious thought, glad perhaps to have some guidelines in a society that was becoming increasingly impersonal. Others were aware of the pressures and resented them, but most conformed anyway, finding resistance impractical.

In 1950, a book called *The Lonely Crowd* by David Riesman, with Nathan Glazer and Reuel Denney, was published by Yale University Press. It was a small, hardcover

This photograph, taken in Washington, D.C., in 1949, symbolizes the pressures for conformity that Americans would find increasingly strong over the next decade.

National Archives

[7] William H. Whyte, Jr., *The Organization Man* (New York: Simon & Schuster, 1956), pp. 3–4.

edition designed for a tiny, scholarly audience. Then in 1953, *The Lonely Crowd* was picked up and abridged by Doubleday Anchor Books. In that edition it became the first of a whole series of best-selling "quality" paperbacks on sociology that included Vance Packard's *The Hidden Persuaders* and *The Status Seekers,* Whyte's *The Organization Man,* and C. Wright Mills' *The Power Elite.*

What people thought Riesman was saying in *The Lonely Crowd* offers an even better clue to the 1950's than what he actually did say. Riesman was talking about the different ways in which social conformity occurs. He noted what seemed to him to be an historical difference between "inner-directed" conformity and "other-directed" conformity. Inner-directed people, according to Riesman, received their goals and their ideas of right and wrong behavior from their parents. These goals and values—being successful, being religious, being honest, and so on—were drilled into the inner-directed person so thoroughly that they became a sort of internal compass which kept that person on course throughout life, no matter how the conditions of life might change. Other-directed people, by contrast, received their goals and ideas of proper conduct from a much wider source—from parents, school, friends, the mass media, and so on. The other-directed person continued throughout life to respond to the actions and wishes of others, and to take behavioral clues and set goals in accordance with the ever-changing social context. Thus the other-directed person's goals and ideas of right and wrong were less fixed and unchangeable. In part, at least, they were continually created and revised by sensitive interaction with other people.

But many readers of *The Lonely Crowd* heard Riesman saying something else entirely. They thought he was praising the inner-directed person as a rugged, individualistic non-conformist and putting down the other-directed person as a glad-handing conformist with no real personal identity. In the fifties, people read Riesman's book as a way of improving their characters, or at least as a way of reassuring themselves that they had the "right" rather than the "wrong" character. This in itself was ironic, for no nineteenth-century inner-directed type would ever do such a thing. Such a type would already *know* that his or her character and behavior were exactly what they should be.

In 1961, in a preface to the new edition of *The Lonely Crowd*, Riesman took pains to correct this widespread misunderstanding of his book. He said, in part:

> The other-directed person wants to be loved rather than esteemed; he wants not to gull or impress, let alone oppress, others, but, in the current phrase, to relate to them; he seeks less a snobbish status in the eyes of others than assurance of being emotionally in tune with them. . . . No lover of toughness or invulnerability should forget the gains made possible by the considerateness, sensitivity, and tolerance that are among the positive qualities of other-direction. . . .[8]

This emphasis on being emotionally in tune with others became increasingly important in the 1960's, and it carried over into the 1970's with books like Charles Reich's *The Greening of America.* In the 1950's, however, "other-directness" was almost totally misunderstood as being a weak, undesirable kind of "conformity," and this misunderstanding is a very good indicator of where, in a later phrase, that decade's head was at. It was an example of a defense mechanism that psychologists call "reaction formation." Sensing themselves to be increasingly conformist, yet unwilling to accept or alter that fact, many people in the 1950's compensated by adopting a tough, unemotional, pragmatic attitude which gave them the illusion of being rugged individualists in control of their own lives. At the same time, using another defense mechanism known as "projection," they were quick to pin the "conformist" tag on others.

Artists and writers of the period also felt the conflict between a desire to assert their individuality and a desire to share in such rewards of conformity as social acceptance and material prosperity. And, being more self-aware than the average "organization man," they found it more difficult to take refuge in defense mechanisms. The conflict they felt in themselves and saw in others made its way into literature. A dominant literary theme of the 1950's was the individual's struggle to achieve a personal identity in the face of pressures

[8] David Riesman et al., *The Lonely Crowd: A Study of the Changing American Character,* rev. ed. (New Haven: Yale University Press, 1961), preface.

from an impersonal society. But few authors suggested how that struggle could be won. Some fictional characters (like Bigger Thomas in Richard Wright's *Native Son*) achieved a kind of identity through violence. Others chose escapism, using alcohol or drugs to retreat into their own private worlds of fantasy and sensual gratification. Either way, the cost to the individual was usually madness, death, or both. Still other characters gave up the struggle and chose to live as pawns completely controlled by circumstances, wallowing in self-pity the while. For example, a character in Paddy Chayefsky's *The Goddess* had this to say:

> We are a gutted generation, born in the depression
> and obsessed with prosperity. Well, we got prosperity,
> and what have we got? A hysterical woman asleep
> upstairs who needs barbiturates to put her to
> sleep, Dexedrine Spansules to wake her up, and
> tranquilizers to keep her numb, who has a nervous
> breakdown once a year and has tried to kill herself
> at least four times that the public knows. I don't
> want my daughter to grow up like that. Or like me.
> A twisted, loveless man patched together by
> psychoanalysis. My daughter was a very strange little
> girl for a long time, well on her way to continuing
> the desolate pattern of her parents, her grandparents,
> and all the generations before her, the long
> parade of history that has brought us to this year of
> suicide and insanity.
>   Life is unbearable, if you don't love something. ...
> People like us can never love anything but our
> children. But that's something. She's given me
> moments of pleasure—moments when I can see that
> life is fine.[9]

Religion and the Church

After declining throughout much of the twentieth century, interest in religion revived during the 1950's. Actually, the revival began during World War II, and during the 1950's church membership and attendance rose. Religious institutions grew in strength, and their publications achieved wide

[9] Paddy Chayefsky, *The Goddess* (New York: Simon & Schuster, 1958), pp. 156, 163–164.

circulation. More people chose to be married in church than by a judge or justice of the peace, and the place of the minister in American society improved considerably. By the late 1950's, the churches were probably stronger than at any time during the century.

According to some observers, however, the mass of men and women who returned to the churches in the 1950's did so more for social than for theological reasons. "Joining the church" insured the enjoyment of rites for recognizing the important emotional crises of life—birth, marriage, and death. At the same time, in an uncertain social environment people perhaps sought an external source of discipline and a group in which children and adults could freely associate. While faith or belief may have made few demands on individuals, it did give them a sense of security. The church, to some extent, became a stabilizing force for the family.

Dr. Norman Vincent Peale.

During the 1950's, Protestant minister Norman Vincent Peale's *The Power of Positive Thinking* was the most popular religious reading. The magnetic preacher Billy Graham filled athletic stadiums and meeting halls with people seeking religious revival and wishing to make "decisions for Christ." Faith healer Oral Roberts staged tent shows and performed healing rites that attracted huge television, as well as live, audiences.

Churches also made some notable advances as social institutions during the postwar years. The ecumenical movement was one of the most positive forces in Christendom by the 1950's. The National Council of Churches was formed in 1950, and a number of denominational mergers followed. Catholic Archbishop Patrick A. O'Boyle, Methodist Bishop John Wesley Lord, and other leaders, such as James Pike and Malcolm Boyd, insisted that the voice of the church must be heard on the great issues of the time—that churches must be active in the world and must serve people, as well as God. An increasing number of churchpeople sought to relate their religion and the institutional church to the complex problems of modern society.

The Family

During the 1940's and 1950's, as during earlier generations, the family was the core around which most Americans planned their lives. Early marriage and parenthood were generally encouraged. Indeed, they were regarded as the criteria by which to measure personal stability and social responsibility.

Yet, despite its highly valued position in American society, the family suffered setbacks. Because of the uncertainties of life during wartime and the resulting social disruptions, the divorce rate nearly doubled between 1940 and 1946. By the mid-1950's it declined to the early 1940 rate and remained fairly constant for the remainder of the decade. But, owing to socio-economic changes in the postwar years, the family would never again offer the security it represented in times past.

Perhaps the biggest factors affecting the family in the 1950's were population mobility and the expansion of suburbs. Young men from rural areas, having learned new skills in the service or on the G.I. Bill, moved their families away from the communities where they had grown up and sought employment in the large industrial centers. Economic opportunities attracted thousands of families from all over the country to California and the Southwest, where vast suburban housing tracts were built to accommodate them. At the same time, increasing affluence made it possible for workers who had lived in city apartments to move out to the suburbs. This, too, meant leaving relatives and old neighborhoods behind. White-collar workers moving up the organizational ladder could expect to be transferred several times during their careers, and they moved with their families from suburb to suburb around the country. By the end of the decade, more than half the nation's population lived in suburban areas.

In *Travels with Charley,* John Steinbeck recorded a conversation with a mobile-home dweller on the subject of stability. "After dinner," wrote Steinbeck, "I brought up a question that had puzzled me."

These were good, thoughtful, intelligent people. I said, "One of our most treasured feelings concerns roots, growing up rooted in some soil or some community." How did they feel about raising their children without roots? . . .

The father, a good-looking, fair-skinned man with dark eyes, answered me. "How many people today have what you are talking about? What roots are there in an apartment twelve floors up? What roots are there in a housing development of hundreds and thousands of small dwellings almost exactly alike? My father came from Italy," he said. "He grew up in Tuscany in a house where his family had lived maybe a thousand years. That's roots for you, no running water, no toilet, and they cooked with charcoal or vine clippings. They had just two rooms, a kitchen and a bedroom where everybody slept, grandpa, father, and all the kids, no place to read, no place to be alone, and never had had. Was that better? I bet if you gave my old man the choice he'd cut his roots and live like this." He waved his hands at the comfortable room. "Fact is, he cut his roots away and came to America. Then he lived in a tenement in New York—just one room, walk-up, cold water and no heat. . . ."

"Don't you miss some kind of permanence?"

"Who's got permanence? Factory closes down, you move on. Good times and things opening up, you move on where it's better. You got roots you sit and starve. You take the pioneers in the history books. They were movers. Take up land, sell it, move on. I read in a book how Lincoln's family came to Illinois on a raft. They had some barrels of whisky for a bank account. How many kids in America stay in the place where they were born, if they can get out?"[10]

The sentiments expressed by Steinbeck's host were probably more common among men than among women. Men, after all, spent most of the day at work, in their own world of social contacts. In the evenings they were glad enough to return to the quiet comfort of the suburbs. But for women who had moved from small towns or older city neighborhoods, suburban life could be lonely. There were no relatives nearby to share in housework or child care, only an army of appliances. There were no adjoining porches, or communal laundry rooms, or other places where women might meet for casual conversation during the course of the day. The pleasant green lawns that separated suburban houses created psychological as well as physical distances, and neighbors often remained only nodding acquaintances. There were no small shops where one's name

[10] Steinbeck, *Travels with Charley*, pp. 91–92.

UPI

New home owners checking the progress of construction on their tract houses in Levittown, New York, in 1949. Levittown became the model for thousands of similar housing developments in the 1950's. A four-room house like those in the picture sold for $6,990, and even when closing costs, landscaping, and kitchen appliances were added the total cost was still well under $10,000. Each house in the tract was scheduled to have five trees planted on its grounds. Residents agreed, on purchase, to abide by certain tract-wide regulations, including no laundry hung out on Sundays, lawns mowed regularly, the installation of door chimes (no buzzers), and no alterations to house or grounds that would detract from the uniform appearance of the development.

and preferences were remembered, only huge impersonal shopping centers which—like the school and nearly everything else—could be reached only by car. There were no community activities dedicated to adult interests, only child-centered activities like the PTA, Girl Scouts, and Little League.

To make matters worse, most suburban women felt guilty about admitting, even to themselves, that there was something lacking in their lives. They were living what they had learned to regard as the ideal existence for an American woman. To question that ideal would have seemed disloyal to husband and children, even unpatriotic. And besides, what alternatives were there? Seeing the housewife's role glorified in women's magazines and on television, many women found it easier to believe that their dissatisfaction stemmed from some flaw within themselves. So they worked harder at the role, following the advice of magazine writers on how to be creative in cooking and interior decoration, how to make their husbands happier and their children smarter. Still, for many women it was not enough. By the end of the decade more and more married women were entering the work force, and many were seeking not merely money but also a greater measure of independence and fulfillment.

Youth

For children, particularly those in the teen years, suburban life was also limiting in many ways. Activities tended to be organized and supervised, and even during free time the suburb was less interesting to explore than either the country or the city would have been. The labor of young people was not needed to help support the family as it had been in times past. Indeed, apart from babysitting and mowing lawns, there was little work available for those who wished to gain some independence and experience. Because the suburbs were populated mostly by white middle-class "nuclear" families (parents and children only), there was little opportunity to become acquainted with elderly people, or with people of other social classes or ethnic groups. There was not even much meaningful contact with middle-class adults, apart from an occasional interested teacher and one's own parents.

One result of this state of affairs was that middle-class young people had a very narrow range of adult role models to choose among. Limited in experience, largely unaware of alternative life-styles, such teen-agers tended to conform to their parents' expectations without much protest. This acquiescence earned them the label "the silent generation," and social critics accused them of being overly cautious, complacent, and concerned chiefly with homing in on comfortable, secure jobs. A *Life* magazine editorial writer, commenting on the college graduating class of 1957, quoted some of the critics:

"Youth," James Thurber observed in his fable about
the young turkey who wanted to be cock of the
walk, "will be served, frequently stuffed with
chestnuts."

The U.S. had a lot of eager youth waiting to be
served this week, when some 300,000 men and women
came tripping out of graduating classes, their ears
ringing with commencement oratory. Seldom had a
graduating class come in for so much keel-hauling by
the orators, who seemed to feel that many of
the Class of '57, unlike the gobbling rebellious young
turks of the past, were a silent generation—perhaps
even prefabricated "organization men" only too
eager to claim faceless and voiceless roles in a world
whose besetting sin was unprotesting conformity.
The conformity by the orators was a demand
for revolt against conformity. Their exhortation, far
from being "Disperse, ye rebels!" was more an almost
anguished plea to "Rebel, ye dispersers!" But listen
to the indictments.

Here is that grave theologian and philosopher,
Paul Tillich, who, at New York's New School for
Social Research, bespeaks a fear of "patternization"
in a technical civilization which "tends to make
man into an object, caught in the machine of
production and consumption." Manipulation is
omnipresent—"economic manipulation in the way
executives are chosen and patterned according to the
needs of big business and administration," consumer
manipulation by mass communications, a
manipulation of culture in which "children receive
much too early the status of adults and adults remain
children." Dr. Tillich deplores a state of mind which
betrays "an intensive desire for security both internal
and external, the will to be accepted by the group
at any price, an unwillingness to show individual
traits, acceptance of a limited happiness without
serious risks."

Here is Yale's President A. Whitney Griswold who
in his baccalaureate asserts there is less danger of
"political subversion" than of "cultural submersion—
that the tide of organization in our private life
may engulf the last surviving instinct to preserve the
safeguards of individual freedom." He attacks "the
endless, sterile, stultifying conferences held in
substitution ... for individual inventiveness; the

public opinion polls whose vogue threatens even our moral and esthetic values with the pernicious doctrine that the customer is always right; the unctuous public relations counsels that rob us both of our courage and our convictions, the continuous daily deferral of opinion and judgment to someone else. . . . It conjures a nightmare picture of a whole nation of yesmen, of hitch-hikers, eavesdroppers and peeping Toms, tiptoeing backward offstage with their fingers to their lips. . . . Symptoms of a loss of self-respect by people who cannot respect what they do not know [and] do not know themselves because they spend so much of their time listening to somebody else."

Here is Brandeis University's President Abram Sachar, deploring to University of Massachusetts graduates, "a growing cult of yesmanship" in which "security becomes a craven disguise for servility. . . . To Thoreau's charge that most men lead lives of quiet desperation we answer: 'Good enough! Anything for quiet!' . . . There are many young people today who will not sign a petition for pink raspberry ice cream in the dining hall commons for fear that someday they may have to explain their color predilections to zealous congressional committees. It would be interesting to know how many would sign a piece of paper setting forth the principles of the Declaration of Independence. . . . Isn't it better to Sign Nothing, Say Nothing, Resist Nothing, Pledge Nothing, even though it may end up in the corollary, Be Nothing?"

Here is "Mr. Automation" himself, IBM's President Tom Watson Jr., who, at DePauw University, deplores the "organization man" described as being in danger of becoming "as depersonalized as a jellyfish wrapped in Cellophane." Adds Watson: "We hear of a 'silent generation,' more concerned with security than integrity . . . with conforming than performing, with imitating than creating."

What constructive answers are the orators of '57 offering? Here, too, there is a marked note of conformity, most of which could be summed up by the title of Emerson's essay back in 1841—"Self-Reliance."

But things tried and true are not necessarily obsolete in a machine age—so, some samples:

• Critic Tillich: "It is my wish and hope that many in this outgoing class are determined to preserve the power to say 'no' when the patterns prescribed by society will try to conquer them. We hope for nonconformists amongst you, for your sake, for the sake of the nation and for the sake of humanity."

• Critic Griswold: "The creative power of the individual is more sorely needed today than ever before. This alone can save us from collective sterility. ... Nor shall we recover our self-respect by chasing after it in crowds. ... It comes to us when we are alone, in quiet moments, in quiet places, when we suddenly realize that, knowing the good, we have done it; knowing the beautiful, we have served it; knowing the truth, we have spoken it."

• Critic Sachar: "A fair answer to all this mourner's bench cynicism is to be found in the ringing declaration of an ancient Hebrew sage, Hillel, who lived 30 years before Jesus and whose challenge is as much a clarion today as it was then: 'Where there are no men, Be *thou* a Man.' ... We cannot limit ourselves to the question: What must we *do* to be *safe*? We must also ask: What must we *be* to be *free*?"

• Critic Watson: "Man has made some machines that can answer questions provided the facts are previously stored in them, but he will never be able to make a machine that will *ask* questions ... the ability to *ask the right questions* is more than half the battle of finding the answer. ... America is a state of mind ... expressed by free and fearless inquiry, by the search for truth, by the respect for difference and diversity, the right to question, the right to disagree."

All this is serious and challenging talk, and we hope it strikes some serious and thoughtful answers from the Silent Generation. Its very quietness may have come about, as 27-year-old Writer Norman Podhoretz has asserted (in the *New Leader*), because it was a generation forced to will itself "from

childhood directly into adulthood," living in "a
world of severely limited possibilities balanced
precariously on the edge of an [atomic] apocalypse."
But this also raised the biggest challenge, best phrased
perhaps by the University of Colorado's President
Quigg Newton: "The preservation and the
strengthening of our system of self-government,
of law and order, of respect for the dignity of the
human being is traditionally the duty and the
obligation of each citizen. But I suggest to you that
at this time the motivation is somewhat stronger than
the abstraction of civic duty, because of the clear
involvement of self-preservation." In sum, the onetime
revolutionary slogan, "save the world," is to be sure
still idealistic but it is also selfishly necessary. O.K.,
Class of 1957, get ready to take over.[11]

It would be interesting to know how those critics might
have modified their speeches had they been able, through
some crystal ball, to see ten years ahead to the youth "revolution" of the late 1960's. But the roots of the sixties' "now
generation" extended back to the "silent generation" of the
fifties, and if the critics had looked more closely at the
teen culture of their own time they could have seen some
signs of the changes to come.

The first significant point is that there *was* a teen culture—
and that in itself was something new. Free from adult
responsibility and limited in adult contacts through high
school and, for some, through college, teen-agers tended
to spend more time together and to rely upon one another
more than in past generations. They became conscious of
themselves—and adults became conscious of them—as a
separate group within American society. And, because
they had both leisure and money to spend, they were a group
with some economic power in that they represented a large
market for clothing manufacturers, record and movie
producers, and others who were able to interpret their
tastes correctly.

The movies that evoked the strongest response from teen-
agers during the 1950's provide one clue to the psychology

[11] "*Life* Editorial: 'Arise, Ye Silent Class of '57!' " *Life,* 17 June 1957,
p.94.

Marlon Brando, surrounded by members of his motorcycle gang, in a still from the movie *The Wild One.*

of the developing youth culture. In 1953, there was *The Wild One,* with Marlon Brando as the leader of a motorcycle gang. Then, in 1955, there was *Rebel without a Cause,* starring James Dean as a Southern California high school student. In both films, the heroes projected a brooding dissatisfaction with themselves and with the society around them. In *The Wild One*, a girl asks Brando, "What are you rebelling against?" He replies, "What have you got?" Their rebellion was not intellectual. They did not really question the validity of the middle-class values they were rejecting. It was just that they could not adapt themselves to those values. They were misfits in the cool and cautious goal-oriented world of the fifties. But they were heroic misfits, figures of tragedy rather than pathos. And what is significant is that so many teen-agers—including those who could and did conform, at least outwardly, to the middle-class pattern—identified with them so deeply.

Blackboard Jungle, another film released in 1955, also struck the rebel chord with a story about big-city juvenile delinquents. But the movie's chief claim to fame was that it included a song called "Rock around the Clock" by Bill Haley and His Comets, and thus it introduced rock and roll to a mass audience. The response was immediate. And with

James Dean became a cult hero—a kind of teen-age martyr—after his death at age twenty-four in an automobile accident in 1955. He made only three films, including one based on John Steinbeck's novel *East of Eden.* More than twenty years after his death, the studio was still receiving fan mail for him.

the adoption of rock and roll, teen-agers took a step toward the development of an alternative system of values. Many young people sensed this on one level or another at the time—and so did their parents, which accounts for the violence with which many adults denounced the new music.

Rock and roll was the opposite of middle class. Unlike the cool jazz, slick pop tunes, and soft "mood music" favored by adults, rock and roll was hot, rough, and loud, with a driving beat. In origin it was lower class, a synthesis of black rhythm and blues and white country "rockabilly" styles which developed mostly in Memphis in the early 1950's. Its stars were both black—like Chuck Berry, Fats Domino, and Little Richard Penniman—and white—like Buddy Holly, Jerry Lee Lewis, and Elvis Presley. Presley, a former truck driver, projected a sultry rebelliousness similar to that of Brando and Dean. Unlike the characters they had portrayed, however, he was not a misfit, not a loser, but instead a winner on his own terms, flouting conventional tastes with arrogant indifference. For working-class kids, both black and white, rock and roll was a kind of affirmation which told them that it was all right to be what they were rather than what middle-class society said they should be. For middle-class kids it was a kind of revelation which showed them that there were other styles of life, perhaps more vital, closer to the emotions, to be found outside of the conservative, competitive world they knew. Very few young people changed their goals or behavior in any serious way as a result of that revelation. It was more a change in attitude, an increased awareness of other possibilities. Young people became more democratic—a healthy development in a society which, during the course of the 1950's, had seen a widening gap between black and white, between middle classes and lower classes.

In *On the Road*, a novel published in 1957, Jack Kerouac contrasted the warmth and simplicity that he saw in lower-class life with the coldness and control that he felt middle-class values had imposed on him:

> At lilac evening I walked with every muscle aching among the lights of 27th and Welton in the Denver colored section, wishing I were a Negro, feeling that the best the white world had offered was not enough ecstasy for me, not enough life, joy, kicks, darkness,

Elvis Presley in the 1950's. Born in Tupelo, Mississippi, in 1935, Presley influenced a whole generation of musicians, both in the United States and England, with his synthesis of country-and-western and rhythm-and-blues styles. Although his thirty-odd movies were mediocre at best, he remained a compelling concert performer up until his death, from an overdose of prescription drugs, in 1977.

music, not enough night. I stopped at a little shack
where a man sold red hot chili in paper containers;
I bought some and ate it, strolling in the dark
mysterious streets. I wished I were a Denver Mexican,
or even a poor overworked Jap, anything but what I
was so drearily, a "white man" disillusioned. All
my life I'd had white ambitions; that was why I'd
abandoned a good woman like Terry [a Mexican
migrant farm worker] in the San Joaquin Valley. I
passed the dark porches of Mexican and Negro homes;
soft voices were there, occasionally the dusky knee
of some mysterious sensual gal; and dark faces of the
men behind rose arbors. Little children sat like
sages in ancient rocking chairs. A gang of colored
women came by, and one of the young ones detached
herself from motherlike elders and came to me fast—
"Hello Joe!"—and suddenly saw I wasn't Joe, and ran
back, blushing. I wished I were Joe. I was only myself,
Sal Paradise, sad, strolling in this violet dark, this
unbearably sweet night, wishing I could exchange
worlds with the happy, true-hearted, ecstatic Negroes
of America. . . .

Down at 23rd and Welton a softball game was
going on under floodlights which also illuminated the
gas tank. A great eager crowd roared at every play.
The strange young heroes of all kinds, white, colored,
Mexican, pure Indian, were on the field, performing
with heart-breaking seriousness. Just sandlot kids in
uniform. Never in my life as an athlete had I ever
permitted myself to perform like this in front of
families and girl friends and kids of the neighborhood,
at night, under lights; always it had been college,
big-time, sober-faced; no boyish, human joy like
this. . . .[12]

Jack Kerouac, right,
with his friend Neal
Cassady, who served
as the model for
many of his fictional
heroes.

It was a romantic view of lower-class life, ignoring the
day-to-day hardships of that existence, the violence and
despair that poverty can breed. But it was a view shared
by many of Kerouac's college-age readers.

Kerouac was part of a bohemian literary movement that
he called the "beat generation." "Beat" had a number of

[12] Jack Kerouac, *On the Road* (New York: Viking Press, 1957),
pp. 180–181.

Larry Keenan, Jr.

The City Lights Book Shop in San Francisco's North Beach, owned by the poet Lawrence Ferlinghetti, was a center of the beat literary movement. In 1965 a number of the people associated with the movement gathered in front of the shop for this photograph. Included are the poets Lew Welch (seated, with tweed coat), Peter Orlovsky (seated, with long hair and beret), David Meltzer (standing at left, with woolen scarf), Michael McClure (in profile, with cross), Allen Ginsberg (with beard and glasses), Daniel Langton (next to Ginsberg, with glasses), Richard Brautigan (with white hat), and Ferlinghetti (with umbrella).

meanings that applied to the "hipster," or practitioner of the movement's philosophy. It was "beat" as in beat up or funky, "beat" as in beat down by society, "beat" as in beatific or blessed; and it was also the beat or rhythm of jazz. To the beats, middle-class morality and materialism were soul-destroying. In order to achieve individual freedom, they believed, it was necessary to drop out of conventional society and tune in to one's true nature by giving expression to basic instincts, energies, and emotions.

Drugs and free love were considered acceptable parts of that process; work, except for creative work, was regarded only as an expedient for survival. As an approach to life, the beat philosophy proved to be liberating for some, but for others it was a disastrous license for self-indulgence. (This would be true, too, for the beats' spiritual descendants, the "hippies," in the 1960's.) As an approach to literature, it inspired fiction—like that of Kerouac—and poetry—like that of Allen Ginsberg, Kenneth Rexroth, and Lawrence Ferlinghetti—which broke free of academic forms and images, finding new vitality in the natural rhythms and idioms of everyday speech.

Although the beats professed to be anti-intellectual, beat writing found its widest audience among those college students who thought of themselves as intellectuals. At that time, not many dropped out to live the beat life. A fair number did, however, adopt elements of the beat style—including the long hair, the dark, scruffy clothes, the slang expressions drawn from the street and from jazz, and the habit of gathering in coffee houses to listen to poetry and music. And, by the late 1950's, that music was most often folk music.

Folk music had some of the same appeal for college students that rock and roll had for their less privileged contemporaries. It too was drawn from black and rural white sources, and it too led its listeners to an appreciation of those other ways of life. And, like rock and roll, it offered a means of protest against the dominant forces in society. But the protest of rock and roll was mainly in the music, and in the rebellious stance of the performers. The protest of folk music was not in the music itself, or in the performance, but in the lyrics—from the implicit protest of black spirituals and work songs to the explicit protest of union organizing songs. It was thus a more conscious form of protest, more intellectual. Many established folk singers like Pete Seeger had long been associated with liberal causes, and they often adapted old songs or wrote new ones to comment on current issues. In the late 1950's, with the rapidly rising popularity of young singers like Joan Baez, such songs reached a large audience for the first time. The songs were important not only because of the messages they contained, but also because they encouraged more young people, with messages of their own, to seek expression through music.

By the end of the decade, then, many of the elements that would make up the youth culture of the 1960's were present; they would come together under the pressure of events. As form of communication there was music, which was accessible to young artists because of the importance of teen-age buying power in the radio and record businesses. There was a sympathy with black American culture which would lead many young whites to work actively in the civil rights movement of the early 1960's. And there was a spirit of restlessness, a willingness to question middle-class assumptions about order, reason, security, and progress, which for many young people would begin hardening into rebellion in the mid-1960's as the Vietnam War escalated.

Recollections of the 1950's

Television helped many young entertainers to stardom in the 1950's. In the 1970's, some of those stars were asked to comment on the version of the fifties shown on "Happy Days," a popular weekly television comedy set in the earlier decade.

As a young girl, Annette Funicello appeared daily after school on television as one of the Mouseketeers in "The Mickey Mouse Club." She recalled the fifties this way:

Annette Funicello as a Mousketeer.

> For me, those happy days were that and more! One big party. I completely rejected any possibility of nuclear war. Impossible! Not in Walt Disney's world— not in the world of the Mouseketeers! I was safe and secure, an old-fashioned girl who lived happily with old-fashioned limitations imposed by her old-fashioned Italian family. I lived at home till the day I married. My dates were subjected to the "Italian inquisition." Any boy who showed up on a motorcycle never got past Papa. . . .
> Is it better today? I don't think so. I loved my happy days. I danced and danced and I never felt deprived because I wasn't engaged in a more grown-up "endeavor." And I've never regretted it. Innocence beats being worldly wise every time!

Frankie Avalon, who became a highly popular singer while in his teens, responded:

Walt Disney Productions

Issues? Politics? We didn't deal in that. We didn't deal with the race riots, either. Why should we, when we were digging Fats Domino and Chuck Berry? That was our kind of "involvement."

Troy Donahue, a young actor in the 1950's, had somewhat different recollections:

Frankie Avalon had a number-one hit song in 1959 with his recording of "Venus."

There was an awful lot of crazy crap in the 50s that people have forgotten. Creepy, crazy crap. Like being an idol—or an idol worshiper. Connie Stevens [another performer] and I used to see those screaming, weeping kids, all reaching just to touch us, and wonder . . . why? What is it they think we have that they haven't? We saw such yearning and discontent in their eyes.

If the 50s were like "Happy Days," it's because we all played dumb. We all knew of the "red menace"; knew of the hydrogen bomb, instant death. But we didn't think about those things. Instead, we danced. I don't think most of us thought about anything in the 50s.

To some, the 50s may seem like a time of stagnation, but it was actually a transition period. Think about who the biggest teenage idol was then: James Dean—the model of teenage unrest and rebellion. He was the beginning of a bomb that burst along with the beat of rock music. And what was rock but the emergence of a new value? Man, you don't see any of that on "Happy Days," which is too bad. It's dangerous to think the past was better than the present, particularly when that isn't true.

Troy Donahue appeared in a number of movies about teen-age romance and in such popular television series as "Hawaiian Eye," "77 Sunset Strip," and "Surfside Six."

Paul Anka was considered the "boy wonder" of popular music in the 1950's. He had this to say:

If you think we laughed and danced our way through the 50s, forget it! I remember the motels who refused us accommodations because we were traveling with blacks. I remember the restaurants that wouldn't serve us, the nightly racial incidents, the bloodshed just because one man's color was different from another. That's what you don't see on "Happy Days."

Those of us who grew up in the 50s were the end of "square." We got married because it was expected, and some of us got divorced, which was not expected. But even among the "squares" some circles were appearing. The freedom of the 60s didn't just happen. Kids made idols of boys like me, Frankie Avalon, Fabian and Bobby Rydell. We became symbols of power. The seeds of unrest were there.

All the innocence and lack of responsibility of those so-called "happy days" proved false—at least for me. I'd rather not be an innocent. I think only those who prefer living like ostriches think of those times as happy days.

Tina Turner, a rhythm and blues singer, said:

Ike and Tina Turner.

Happy days? Where? When? Not in the 50s! Not for a black anyway. We were just names on jukeboxes.

I remember those days as traveling the country in an ol' beat-up car, sometimes sleeping in it, sometimes, where the feeling was charitable toward black folks, being able to sleep in a real bed with clean sheets. Why, sometimes we were even able to eat in the local diner!

When I was playing with Ike Turner, we played dives and dumps. We weren't allowed any better in those happy days. It took years before we could enter white clubs through the front door.

The happy days may have been happy for some, but those "some" were white folks. Us blacks didn't begin to know happy days until the sock-it-to-'em 60s.

Shelley Berman, who made his mark as a comedian in the 1950's, concluded:

Shelley Berman.

If you believed the audience reaction to such new comedians as [Mike] Nichols and [Elaine] May, Mort Sahl and myself, the 50s were very happy days. Audiences wanted to laugh. We comedians went wild in our expression. We were not only allowed but encouraged to say anything. And we did. Comedy became free, the way music became free.

But was it freedom or rebellion? Both? Fear underneath the naive trusting? They were strange times. While some of us weren't locking our doors at night, others were reacting to the "police action" in Korea. Still others were rebounding from McCarthyism. A few of us had unmentioned nightmares about nuclear holocaust.

Mainly, I think we desperately wanted to believe in a "perfect peace." We wanted to believe that this country was alive and well. So we laughed and danced and tooted our horns. But, quite honestly, I have always felt that our incessant need to make merry in those years was to drown out the heartbeat of fear. "Happy Days" captures the tip of the 50s iceberg. That tip was all that was visible to most of us. We saw only what we wanted to see.[13]

The Space Race

After Korea, the United States engaged in no more hot wars during the 1950's. The arms race, however, continued. Following the Russian explosion of an atomic bomb, the United States produced a much more powerful hydrogen bomb. A short time later, the Soviets exploded a hydrogen bomb too.

The Cold War became scientific, as well as political. On October 4, 1957, the Russians launched *Sputnik,* the first man-made satellite to orbit the earth. Although American scientists and the Pentagon knew of the Soviet Union's work in rocketry and satellite programs, the general public did not. Americans were shocked, and ashamed of the fact that the Russians had beaten the United States in a scientific endeavor. Americans had been working to develop rockets that could carry atomic warheads and launch satellites since the end of the war. But the program had not enjoyed wholehearted political support, and relatively little money had gone into it. The success of *Sputnik* and, a month later, of *Sputnik II* changed that.

President Eisenhower did nothing to encourage a feeling of humiliation, and he explicitly rejected the notion of a scientific race with Russia. But not everyone remained calm. Secretary of State John Foster Dulles, an avid supporter of

13 *Us,* 14 June 1977, pp. 54–57.

containment and of immediate response to any Russian move that might be perceived as a challenge, said:

> No doubt the Communist rulers gained a success. They have an opportunity to gloat, an opportunity that they have not neglected. But Sputnik, mocking the American people with its "beep-beep" [a radio signal the satellite constantly transmitted], may go down in history as [Soviet Prime Minister and Party Chairman] Khrushchev's boomerang.
>
> It jolted the American people. . . . A wave of mortification, anger, and fresh determination swept the country.[14]

The Jupiter-C space rocket was launched from Cape Canaveral in 1958.

In an address given on December 17, 1958, space administrator T. Keith Glennan remarked: "The blow to our national pride in this unexpected achievement of Soviet science was tremendous." The Russian feat, he continued, "finally shocked our people into a state of real concern about our standing in the race for technological leadership in the world."[15] Many congressmen and newspaper columnists agreed with Dulles and Glennan. Before long, congressmen were wondering if those who ran America's space program were asking for enough money.

President Eisenhower responded to *Sputnik* by establishing a scientific advisory committee to the presidency. Congress responded by raising the appropriation for the National Science Foundation from $40 million to $140 million. Further, in 1958, Congress passed the National Aeronautics and Space Act, under which the National Aeronautics and Space Administration—NASA—was created. Money began to flow toward the goal of catching up with and surpassing the Russians, for security reasons if for no other. Congress increased the total space budget from $179 million in fiscal 1957 to $1.2 billion by the end of the decade. On January 31, 1958, Americans placed a satellite, *Explorer I*, in orbit. A total of thirty-three successful launchings had

U.S. Army

---

[14] John Foster Dulles, "The Role of Negotiation," *Department of State Bulletin* 38 (3 February 1958), p. 159. Quoted in Vernon Van Dyke, *Pride and Power: The Rationale of the Space Program* (Urbana: University of Illinois Press, 1964), p. 140.

[15] Quoted in ibid.

been made by 1960. Now there was talk of putting a man—an American—on the moon.

In the meantime, the Soviets continued to make news. They sent up several more *Sputniks*—one holding two dogs, others containing dogs and other animals—all of which were recovered for study of the effects of space travel. As the 1950's closed, the Russians were on the verge of placing the first human being in orbit about the earth.

Sputnik proved of considerable aid to American industry geared to the space program, and it also had a tremendous effect on American education. In 1958, Congress passed the National Defense Education Act, which would give money to colleges and universities for scientific research and training. Programs to produce engineers, mathematicians, and physical scientists were stepped up. As the 1950's closed, NASA grants to universities and colleges neared the $100 million mark.

The effect reached the lower schools, too. Educators expressed grave concern about the quality and quantity of the mathematics and science curriculums in elementary and high schools. Programs to place more emphasis on these subjects and to spot and encourage budding young scientists and mathematicians got under way.

A Decade Ends

Nineteen-sixty car models appeared in the fall of 1959. The season witnessed the advent of the first domestically produced compacts, American automakers' response to the growing popularity of small foreign cars. Among them were Chevrolet's Corvair, Ford's Falcon, Chrysler's Valiant, and American Motors' Rambler. The Corvair listed at $1,860, about $2,000 less than the most expensive Chevrolet. Other compacts were priced competitively.

Car prices were up. And, by the end of the year, using 1947–49 as 100, the index of all food was 118.3. The price of beef, lamb, ham, poultry, and fish stood at 109.9, dairy products at 114.1, and fruits and vegetables at 125.6. The overall cost-of-living index, again taking 1947–49 as 100, rested at 124.8 for all items. The rent index was 139.8, and the utilities index was 120.1.[16]

---

[16] The World Almanac (New York: Doubleday, 1960), p. 765.

General Motors.

Chevrolet's new compact model, the Corvair.

At Christmas, 1959, Americans could look forward to January sales on Persian lamb coats, ranging from $299 to $599. Hart, Schaffner, and Marx men's suits would be priced from $64.75 to $99.75, down from $75.50 and $135.00. The popular movies during this Christmas season were *Gigi,* starring Leslie Caron and Maurice Chevalier, *Suddenly Last Summer,* with Elizabeth Taylor, and a version of Jules Verne's *Journey to the Center of the Earth.* Among the more interesting films was *On the Beach,* in which Ava Gardner, Gregory Peck, and Fred Astaire played major roles. This adaptation of a Neville Shute novel followed the final months of life of several people in Australia, where everyone awaited the arrival of southerly winds carrying deadly radioactive fallout resulting from nuclear explosions in the Northern Hemisphere, where life no longer existed. Americans at Christmas also looked forward to the usual football bowl games, now regularly televised. Wisconsin and Washington were matched in the Rose Bowl, Syracuse and Texas in the Cotton Bowl, and Mississippi and Louisiana State in the Sugar Bowl.

It had become less popular to celebrate New Year's Eve on the streets. The *New York Times* ran the story on page 1, as usual, but under a small-sized headline and at no great length. Said the *Times,* in part:

> The city and nation celebrated—and prayed—last night as the old year passed into history.
>
> As midnight marked an end and a beginning in time, millions of Americans memorialized the moment, some with a prayer for yesterday and tomorrow, many with grins for a happy past and a hopeful future.

In Times Square, the new year came in among the
reedy sounds of horns. The din was set off when an
illuminated globe dropped down the flag staff atop
the Times Tower precisely at midnight.

. . . At least 300,000 persons turned out, according
to Deputy Police Commissioner James P. Kennedy.

They spread from the square at Forty-second to
Fifty-second Street, shouting, hooting, and waving
their arms. Confetti thrown from hotel windows was
caught by the wind and lifted high in the sky, picking
up more colors from the signs. . . .[17]

The 1950's were characterized by peace, prosperity, and
conservatism. Prosperity would continue; but in other
respects, the decade to follow would be much different.

SUGGESTED READINGS

Albertson, Dean, ed. *Eisenhower As President.* Hill &
   Wang, American Century Series.
Friedan, Betty. *The Feminine Mystique.* Dell.
Huxley, Aldous. *Brave New World and Brave New World
   Revisited, 1932–1958.* Harper & Row, Colophon Books.
Mills, C. Wright. *The Power Elite.* Oxford University Press,
   Galaxy Books.
Mills, C. Wright. *White Collar: The American Middle
   Classes.* Oxford University Press, Galaxy Books.
Orwell, George. *1984.* New American Library, Signet
   Books.
Packard, Vance. *The Status Seekers.* Pocket Books.
Riesman, David. *The Lonely Crowd: A Study of the Chang-
   ing American Character.* Yale University Press.
Steinbeck, John. *Travels with Charley.* Bantam Books.
Whyte, William H., Jr. *The Organization Man.* Simon &
   Schuster, Touchstone Books.

[17] *New York Times,* 1 January 1960, pp. 1, 20.

BIBLIOGRAPHY

Chapter One

Burns, James MacGregor. *Roosevelt: The Lion and the Fox.* New York: Harcourt Brace Jovanovich, 1963.

Churchill, Winston. *The Second World War.* 6 vols. New York: Bantam Books, 1976.

Collier, Basil. *The Second World War: A Military History.* Gloucester, Mass.: Peter Smith, n.d.

Cronon, E. David, and Rosenof, Theodore D., eds. *The Second World War and the Atomic Age, 1940–1973.* Arlington Heights, Ill.: AHM, 1975.

Divine, Robert A. *The Reluctant Belligerent: American Entry into the Second World War.* New York: John Wiley & Sons, 1965.

Divine, Robert A. *Roosevelt and World War II.* Baltimore: Penguin Books, 1970.

Gunther, John. *Roosevelt in Retrospect.* New York: Harper & Row, 1950.

Havighurst, Robert J., and Morgan, H. Gerthron. *The Social History of a War-Boom Community.* New York: Longmans, Green, 1951. Reprint ed. Westport, Conn.: Greenwood Press, n.d.

Hosokawa, Bill. *Nisei: The Quiet Americans.* New York: William Morrow, 1969.

Lingeman, Richard. *Don't You Know There's a War On? The American Home Front, 1941–1945.* New York: G.P. Putnam's Sons, 1970.

Lutz, Alma, ed. *With Love, Jane: Letters from American*

Women on the War Fronts. New York: Day, 1945.

Phillips, Cabell. *The 1940s: Decade of Triumph and Trouble.* New York: Macmillan, 1975.

Polenberg, Richard, ed. *America at War: The Home Front, 1941–1945.* Englewood Cliffs, N.J.: Prentice-Hall, 1968.

Shirer, William. *The Rise and Fall of the Third Reich: A History of Nazi Germany.* New York: Simon & Schuster, 1960.

Time Capsule: History of the War Years, 1939–1945. New York: Bonanza Books, 1972.

Times in Review: 1940–1949. New York Times Decade Books, vol. 3. New York: Arno Press, n.d.

Toland, John. *The Rising Sun: The Decline and Fall of the Japanese Empire, 1936–1945.* New York: Random House, 1970.

Waitley, Douglas. *America at War: World War I and World War II.* Encino, Calif.: Glencoe, 1980.

World Almanac. New York: Doubleday, 1947.

Chapter Two

Ambrose, Stephen E. *Eisenhower and Berlin, 1945: The Decision to Halt at the Elbe.* New York: W.W. Norton, 1967.

Ambrose, Stephen E. *The Rise to Globalism: American Foreign Policy, 1938–1976.* Rev. ed. Baltimore: Penguin Books, 1976.

Bernstein, Barton J., ed. *Politics and Policies of the Truman Administration.* New York: Franklin Watts, 1970.

Cooke, Alistair. *A Generation on Trial: USA versus Alger Hiss.* New York: Alfred A. Knopf, 1950.

Divine, Robert A. *Since 1945: Politics and Diplomacy in Recent American History.* New York: John Wiley & Sons, 1975.

Freeland, Richard M. *The Truman Doctrine and the Origins of McCarthyism: Foreign Policy, Domestic Politics, and Internal Security, 1946–1948.* New York: Schocken Books, 1974.

Goulden, Joseph C. *The Best Years: 1945–1950.* New York: Atheneum, 1976.

Greenstone, J. David. *Labor in American Politics.* Chicago: University of Chicago Press, Phoenix Books, 1977.

Halle, Louis J. *The Cold War As History*. New York: Harper & Row, 1967.

Hartmann, Susan. *Truman and the Eightieth Congress*. Columbia: University of Missouri Press, 1971.

Huthmacher, J. *The Truman Years*. New York: Holt, Rinehart & Winston, 1972.

Kennan, George F. *American Diplomacy: 1900–1950*. Chicago: University of Chicago Press, Phoenix Books, 1970.

McClure, Arthur F. *The Truman Administration and the Problems of Postwar Labor, 1945–1948*. Madison, N.J.: Fairleigh Dickinson University Press, 1969.

May, Ernest R. *The Truman Administration and China, 1945–1949*. Philadelphia: J. B. Lippincott, 1975.

Miller, Merle. *Plain Speaking: An Oral Biography of Harry S. Truman*. New York: Berkley, 1974.

Schaller, Michael. *The U.S. Crusade in China, 1938–1945*. New York: Columbia University Press, 1979.

Snetsinger, John. *Truman, the Jewish Vote, and the Creation of Israel*. Stanford, Calif.: Hoover Institution Press, 1974.

Stettinius, Edward. *Roosevelt and the Russians: The Yalta Conference*. Edited by Walter Johnson. Westport, Conn.: Greenwood Press, 1949.

Stone, I. F. *The Truman Era*. New York: Random House, Vintage Books, 1973.

Times in Review: 1940–1949. New York Times Decade Books, vol. 3. New York: Arno Press, n.d.

Truman, Harry S. *Truman Speaks: On the Presidency, the Constitution, and Statecraft*. New York: Columbia University Press, 1975.

Truman, Margaret. *Harry S. Truman*. New York: William Morrow, 1973.

Tugwell, Rexford Guy. *Off Course, from Truman to Nixon*. New York: Praeger, 1971.

Vaughan, Philip. *The Truman Administration's Legacy for Black America*. Reseda, Calif.: Mojave Books, 1976.

Weinstein, Allen. *Perjury: The Hiss-Chambers Case*. New York: Alfred A. Knopf, 1978.

Wittner, Lawrence S. *Cold-War America: From Hiroshima to Watergate*. New York: Praeger, 1974.

World Almanac. New York: Doubleday, 1949.

Chapter Three

Acheson, Dean. *Present at the Creation: My Years in the State Department.* New York: W. W. Norton, 1969.

Barth, Alan. *The Loyalty of Free Men.* Hamden, Conn.: Shoe String Press, Archon Books, 1951.

Buckley, William F., Jr., ed. *American Conservative Thought in the Twentieth Century.* Indianapolis: Bobbs-Merrill, 1970.

Buckley, William F., Jr., and Bozell, L. Brent. *McCarthy and His Enemies.* New Rochelle, N.Y.: Arlington House, 1954.

Cogley, John. "McCarthyism Revisited." *The Commonweal* 62 (1951).

Cohn, Roy. *McCarthy.* New York: New American Library, 1968.

Cook, Fred J. *Nightmare Decade.* New York: Random House, 1971.

Fulbright, J. William. "Reflections: In Thrall to Fear." *The New Yorker,* 8 January 1972.

Goldman, Eric F. *The Crucial Decade and After: America 1945–1960.* New York: Random House, Vintage Books, 1960.

Hearings before a Subcommittee of the Senate Committee on Government Operations, Eighty-third Congress, Second Session. (Peress investigation and Army-McCarthy hearings.)

Hellman, Lillian. *Scoundrel Time.* Boston: Little, Brown, 1976.

Higgins, Marguerite. *War in Korea: The Report of a Woman Combat Correspondent.* New York: Doubleday, 1951.

Latham, Earl. *The Communist Controversy in Washington: From the New Deal to McCarthy.* New York: Atheneum, 1969.

Latham, Earl, ed. *The Meaning of McCarthyism.* 2nd ed. Boston: D. C. Heath, 1973.

Lattimore, Owen. *Ordeal by Slander.* 1950. Reprint ed., Westport, Conn.: Greenwood Press, n.d.

Lipset, Seymour, and Raab, Earl. *The Politics of Unreason: Right-Wing Extremism in America.* 2nd ed. Chicago: University of Chicago Press, Phoenix Books, 1978.

MacArthur, Douglas. *Reminiscences.* New York: McGraw Hill, 1964.

McCarthy, Joseph R. *America's Retreat from Victory.* Robert Welch, Inc., Western Islands Books, 1965.

McCarthy, Joseph R. *The Fight for America.* New York: Devin-Adair, 1952.

Morison, Samuel Eliot. *The Oxford History of the American People.* New York: Oxford University Press, 1965.

Overstreet, Harry and Bonaro. *The Strange Tactics of Extremism.* New York: W. W. Norton, 1964.

Potter, Charles E. *Days of Shame.* New York: Coward-McCann, 1965.

Rees, David. *Korea: The Limited War.* Baltimore: Penguin Books, 1970.

Rogin, Michael P. *The Intellectuals and McCarthy: The Radical Specter.* Cambridge: MIT Press, 1967.

Rosenstone, Robert A. *Protest from the Right.* Encino, Calif.: Glencoe, 1968.

Senate Report No. 2108, State Department Loyalty Investigation, Eighty-first Congress, Second Session. (Tydings Committee report.)

Spanier, John W. *The Truman-MacArthur Controversy and the Korean War.* Cambridge: Harvard University Press, 1959.

Times in Review: 1950-1959. New York Times Decade Books, vol. 4. New York: Arno Press, n.d.

Waitley, Douglas. *America at War: Korea and Vietnam.* Encino, Calif.: Glencoe, 1980.

Wickens, James F. *Themes in United States History.* 2nd ed. Encino, Calif.: Glencoe, 1973.

Chapter Four

Baldwin, James. *Go Tell It on the Mountain.* New York: Dial Press, 1953.

Baldwin, James. *Nobody Knows My Name.* New York: Dial Press, 1961.

Baldwin, James. *Notes of a Native Son.* New York: Dial Press, 1955.

Bates, Daisy. *The Long Shadow of Little Rock.* New York: David McKay, 1962.

Davis, John P., ed. *The American Negro Reference Book.* Englewood Cliffs, N.J.: Prentice-Hall, 1966.

Du Bois, W. E. B. *The Souls of Black Folk.* 1903. Reprint ed., New York: Fawcett Books, 1977.

Ellison, Ralph. *The Invisible Man.* New York: Random House, 1951.

Franklin, John Hope. *From Slavery to Freedom: A History of American Negroes.* 4th ed. New York: Alfred A. Knopf, 1974.

Franklin, John Hope, and Starr, Isidore, eds. *The Negro in Twentieth Century America: A Reader on the Struggle for Civil Rights.* New York: Random House, Vintage Books, 1967.

Fulks, Bryan. *Black Struggle: A History of the Negro in America.* New York: Delacorte Press, 1970.

Goulden, Joseph C. *The Best Years: 1945-1950.* New York: Atheneum, 1976.

King, Martin Luther, Jr. *Stride toward Freedom: The Montgomery Story.* New York: Harper & Row, 1958.

King, Martin Luther, Jr. *Why We Can't Wait.* New York: Harper & Row, 1964.

Lincoln, C. Eric. *The Negro Pilgrimage in America: The Coming of Age of Black America.* New York: Praeger, 1969.

Miller, Ruth, ed. *Blackamerican Literature: 1760-Present.* Encino, Calif: Glencoe, 1971.

Myrdal, Gunnar. *An American Dilemma: The Negro Problem and Modern Democracy.* New York: Harper, 1944.

Rowan, Carl T. *South of Freedom.* New York: Alfred A. Knopf, 1952.

Times in Review: 1940-1949 and *Times in Review: 1950-1959.* New York Times Decade Books, vols. 3 and 4. New York: Arno Press, n.d.

Wright, Richard. *Black Boy: A Record of Childhood and Youth.* New York: Harper, 1945.

Wright, Richard. *The Ethics of Jim Crow.* New York: Harper, 1948.

Wright, Richard. *Native Son.* New York: Harper, 1940.

Wright, Richard. *Twelve Million Black Voices: A Folk

History of the Negro in the United States. New York: Viking Press, 1941.

Chapter Five

Albertson, Dean, ed. *Eisenhower As President.* New York: Hill & Wang, American Century Series, 1963.

Chayefsky, Paddy. *The Goddess.* New York: Simon & Schuster, 1958.

Eisenhower, Dwight D. *The White House Years.* Vol. 1, *Mandate for Change, 1953–1956.* New York: New American Library, Signet Books, 1963.

Friedan, Betty. *The Feminine Mystique.* New York: W. W. Norton, 1963.

Galbraith, John Kenneth. *The Affluent Society.* Boston: Houghton Mifflin, 1958.

Goodman, Paul. *Growing Up Absurd.* New York: Random House, 1960.

Goulden, Joseph C. *The Best Years: 1945–1950.* New York: Atheneum, 1976.

Harrington, Michael. *The Other America.* Baltimore: Penguin Books, 1963.

Huxley, Aldous. *Brave New World and Brave New World Revisited, 1932–1956.* New York: Harper & Row, Colophon Books, 1969.

Keats, John. *The Insolent Chariots.* Philadelphia: J. B. Lippincott, 1958.

Kerouac, Jack. *On the Road.* New York: Viking Press, 1957.

Larsen, Lawrence H., and Branyan, Robert. *The Eisenhower Administration 1953–1961: A Documentary History.* New York: Random House, 1971.

"*Life* Editorial: 'Arise Ye Silent Class of '57!'" *Life,* 17 June 1957.

McLuhan, Marshall. *Understanding Media: The Extensions of Man.* New York: New American Library, Signet Books, 1971.

Miller, Jim, ed. *The Rolling Stone Illustrated History of Rock and Roll.* New York: Rolling Stone Press/Random House, 1976.

Mills, C. Wright. *The Power Elite.* New York: Oxford University Press, 1956.

Mills, C. Wright. *White Collar: The American Middle Classes.* New York: Oxford University Press, 1951.

Packard, Vance. *The Status Seekers.* New York: David McKay, 1959.

Peale, Norman Vincent. *The Power of Positive Thinking.* Englewood Cliffs, N.J.: Prentice-Hall, 1952.

Reich, Charles A. *The Greening of America: How the Youth Revolution Is Trying to Make America Liveable.* New York: Random House, 1970.

Riesman, David, et al. *The Lonely Crowd: A Study of the Changing American Character.* Rev. ed. New Haven: Yale University Press, 1961.

Rosenberg, Bernard, and White, David M., eds. *Mass Culture: The Popular Arts in America.* New York: Free Press, 1957.

Roszak, Theodore. *The Making of a Counter Culture.* New York: Doubleday, 1967.

Sellen, Robert, et al. *The Eisenhower Era.* New York: Holt, Rinehart & Winston, 1974.

Steinbeck, John. *Travels with Charley in Search of America.* New York: Viking Press, 1961.

Times in Review: 1950-1959. New York Times Decade Books, vol. 4. New York: Arno Press, n.d.

Van Dyke, Vernon. *Pride and Power: The Rationale of the Space Program.* Urbana: University of Illinois Press, 1964.

Whyte, William H., Jr. *The Organization Man.* New York: Simon & Schuster, 1956.

INDEX

183–84, 188–89, 191; and conscription, 184; and labor unions, 184; in wartime industry, 184–85, 187; and March on Washington movement, 184–86; and discrimination in armed forces, 185; and racial violence in North, 186; and enlistment in armed forces, 186–87; in combat zones, 186–88, 189–91; in air force, 188, 189, 190; in navy, 188–89; war decorations won by, 188–89; and 99th Pursuit Squadron, 189; and postwar expectations, 192; and GI Bill, 192; and postwar violence in South, 192–93; and Korean War, 197; and desegregation in armed forces, 197–98; and professional sports, 198–99; and civil rights movement, 200–22; conditions during 1950's, 221–22
Blood donors, 56
Bogart, Humphrey, 110
Borah, William E., 19
Brando, Marlon, 255, 256
Britain, *see* Great Britain
Brotherhood of Locomotive Engineers, and 1946 strike, 86–87
Brotherhood of Railroad Trainmen, and 1946 strike, 86–87
Brotherhood of Sleeping Car Porters, 184
Browder, Earl, 147
Brown, Oliver, 201
Brown v. *Board of Education of Topeka*, background, 200–202; excerpt from, 201; critics of, 203; results of, 204–205
Budenz, Louis F., 109
Bunche, Ralph J., 198
Burns, George, 235
Boyd, Malcolm, 246

Cadillac Eldorado, 1954 model, 230

Canada, spy ring in, 109
Caron, Leslie, 266
Cassady, Neal, 257
Central High School, Little Rock, Arkansas, racial conflict in, 206–13
Chambers, Whittaker, 113–15
Chayefsky, Paddy, 236, 245
Chevalier, Maurice, 266
Chevrolet Corvair, 1960, 266
Chiang Kai-shek, 108, 118, 124, 134
Chicago, New Year's Eve in, 1939, 14; black housing in, 179–81
China, Japanese invasion of, 17; Communist victory in, 108, 118; revisionist historians on, 123–24; and Korean War, 134–36
Christmas, 1959, 266
Chrysler Corporation, 226
Churches and religion, revival of interest in, 245–46; ecumenical movement and, 246
Churchill, Winston, 35, 103, 104, 119, 121
Civil defense, 36–37
Civil disobedience, background, 218; Martin Luther King, Jr., on, 218–21
Civil rights, and Truman administration, 93, 94; and Democratic platform, 1948, 96–97; and Congress, 1949, 101; blacks and, 184–86, 200–22
Civil Rights Act, 1957, 221
Civil Rights Commission, 221–22
Civil Rights Division, Justice Department, 221
Coast Guard auxiliary, 44
Coca, Imogene, 235
Cohn, Roy, 143–44, 150–51, 158, 159–63, 174
Cold War, beginning, 103–105; and Truman Doctrine, 105–106; and Marshall Plan, 106–107; *Amerasia* case, 108–109; spy ring in Canada,

election, 200

Reuther, Walter, 83, 85, 86, 184

Revisionist historians, and Cold War, 118–29

Riesman, David, 242–44

Right-wing organizations, 168–74

Robinson, Jackie, 198–99

Rock and roll, 256

Roosevelt, Franklin D. and Neutrality Acts, 20–21; "quarantine speech," 21; and British air and naval bases, 25; and 1940 election, 26–28; and lend-lease, 28–29; and declaration of war on Japan, 33; and election of 1944, 68–69; death, 69; at Yalta, 1945, 103–104; and wartime relations with Russia, 119; and non-discrimination in industry, 184–85; and discrimination in armed forces, 185

Rosenberg, Ethel, 117

Rosenberg, Julius, 117

Rosenberg case, 117–18

"Rosie the Riveter," 45

Rowan, Carl T., 193–97

Russia, *see* Union of Socialist Soviet Republics

Sachar, Abram, 252

Savings, during World War II, 48, 78–79

Schine, David, 159–60

Scrap drives, 55

Security Council, and Korean War, 132, 133

Seeger, Pete, 259

Segregation, in North, 178–81; in South, 181–82; in armed forces, 183–84, 188–89, 191; and March on Washington movement, 185–86; postwar in South, 191–97; ends in armed forces, 197; in professional sports, 198; ends in professional

sports, 198–99; early court decisions on, 200–201; *Brown* v. *Board of Education of Topeka,* 200–205; *Plessy* v. *Ferguson,* 201–202; results of *Brown,* 204–205; southern attitudes toward, 212–13; and colleges and universities, 213; on buses, Montgomery, Alabama, 213–18; ends on public transportation, 217–18

Seneca, Illinois, war boom town, prewar conditions, 57–58; selected for LST construction, 58; population increase, 59; wartime housing in, 59–62; expansion of community services, 62–63; human relations in, 63–64; entertainment in, 64–67; at end of war, 70–71; benefits of wartime boom, 71

Service flags, 70

Shipyard, wartime, 59

Shortages, during World War II, 53–54; postwar, 80–81

"Silent generation," 251–54

Sinatra, Frank, 57

Smith, Kate, 57

Smith, Margaret Chase, 152

Songs, World War II, 57; postwar, 255–56

Space race, Russian successes, 263, 264, 265; American response to, 263–65; effect on education, 265; American successes, 265–66

Spain, 17, 102

Sputnik, 263, 265

Stalin, Joseph, 19, 102, 104, 119–20, 121, 122

States' Rights Democrats, 97, 98

Steinbeck, John, on vending machines, 228–29; on mass culture, 239–40; on mobility, 247–48

Stevens, Robert, 160

Stevenson, Adlai, and 1952 election,